Breakthrough Language Series

CHINESE

Catherine Meek & Mao Yan

Brian Hill
General editor

Professor of Modern Languages
School of Languages, University of Brighton

palgrave

Published by
PALGRAVE MACMILLAN
Houndmills, Basingstoke, Hampshire RG21 6XS and
175 Fifth Avenue, New York, N. Y. 10010
Companies and representatives throughout the world

PALGRAVE MACMILLAN is the global academic imprint of the Palgrave Macmillan division of St. Martin's Press, LLC and of Palgrave Macmillan Ltd. Macmillan® is a registered trademark in the United States, United Kingdom and other countries. Palgrave is a registered trademark in the European Union and other countries.

ISBN 0–333–52360–1 paperback
ISBN 0–333–54693–8 cassettes
ISBN 0–333–54692–X book and cassette pack

This book is printed on paper suitable for recycling and made from fully managed and sustained forest sources.

A catalogue record for this book is available from the British Library.

10   9   8   7   6   5   4   3   2
12   11   10   09   08   07   06   05   04

Printed in China

Acknowledgements

The publishers wish to thank the following photograph sources:

Jana Bek page 120; Beijing International Hotel pages 43, 204; Alison Black pages 126, 149; Mao Yan pages 17, 39, 50, 55, 62, 65, 66, 69,119, 131, 140, 163; Catherine Meek all other photographs.

Every effort has been made to trace all copyright holders, but if any have been inadvertently ovelooked the publishers will be peased to make the necessary arrangements at the first opportunity.

Contents

Guilin

At the Great Wall

Bicycle park

HOW TO USE THIS COURSE

Following this course will help you to understand and speak the Chinese you are likely to need on holiday or business trips. The course is based on recordings made in Běijīng. You will hear Chinese people speaking in everyday situations. Step by step you will learn first to understand what they are saying and then to speak in similar situations yourself.

Before producing the course we talked to many people about why and how they learn languages. We know how important it is for learning to be enjoyable – and for it to be usable from the beginning. Because of its written form using characters to represent words, Chinese is often thought of as a difficult language to learn. In this course we concentrate on the spoken form, which in many ways is quite simple. There is after all not a lot of point in knowing the Chinese characters if you can't ask for a cup of coffee! The written form of Chinese used in this book is Pīnyīn, which is the standard form of romanization for Chinese characters (see page 39).

So the emphasis of this course is on understanding and speaking. Listen as much as possible to the native speakers on your recording to attune your ear to the new sounds and mimic their pronunciation in the exercises in each unit. By focusing on communication, *Breakthrough Chinese* will provide you with the language you need to manage on holiday or business trips in China and will also give you a firm foundation if you want to take your language study further.

General hints to help you use the course

- Have confidence in us! Real language is complex and you will find certain things in every unit which are not explained in detail. Don't worry about this. We will build up your knowledge slowly, selecting only what is most important to know at every stage.
- Try to study regularly, but in short periods. A spell of 20–30 minutes each day is usually better than 4 hours once a week.
- To help you learn to speak make sure you repeat the words and phrases on the recording with the guidance of the presenter. Say the words and phrases out loud whenever possible.
- **If you don't understand something leave it for a while. Learning a language is a bit like doing a jigsaw or a crossword puzzle; there are many ways to tackle it and it falls into place eventually.**
- Don't be afraid to write in your book and add your own notes to highlight what is most useful to you.
- Do look back over your work frequently. It also helps to get somebody to test you – they don't need to understand Chinese.
- If you can possibly learn with somebody else, you will be able to help each other and practise the language together.
- Learning Chinese may take more time than you thought. Just be patient and above all don't get angry with yourself.

Suggested study pattern

Each unit of the course consists of approximately fourteen pages in the book and around fifteen minutes of recordings. The first page of each unit will tell you what you are going to learn.

The book contains step-by-step instructions for working through the course: when to use the book on its own, when to use the recording on its own, when to use them both together, and how to use them in each case. On the recording our presenter Lǐ will guide you through the various sections. Here is an outline of the study pattern proposed.

Dialogues

Listen to the dialogues which introduce the main words and phrases to you, first without stopping, so you get a feel for the task ahead. Listen again, trying to pick out the words and phrases which appear before each dialogue in the book. Then go over each dialogue or suggested group of dialogues in conjunction with the vocabulary and the notes. You should get into the habit of playing the recordings repeatedly, listening to each of the sentences a number of times, and repeating them after the speakers. Don't leave a dialogue until you are confident that you have at least understood it. Have a go at the pronunciation exercises which appear before the exercises on the recordings.

Practise what you have learned

After each group of dialogues there are some listening and speaking exercises. To do them, you will need to work closely with the book. You will, for instance, often be asked to listen to a piece on the recording and then fill in answers or mark off boxes in the book. Or you will be asked to write an exercise and then check the answers on the recording. Use your PAUSE/STOP and REWIND or REPEAT buttons to give yourself time to think.

Your turn to speak

Throughout the *Practise what you have learned* section and again at the end of each unit there will be a chance for you to speak in a carefully structured exercise. You will hear a question or statement in Chinese, followed by a suggestion in English as to how you might reply. You should then pause the recording to give yourself time to think and respond. Switch on the recording again to hear the reply in Chinese and check to see if you were right. You will probably have to go over these spoken exercises a few times.

Key words and phrases

Study this list of the most important words and phrases from the dialogues. If possible, try to learn them by heart.

Grammar

At this stage in a unit things should begin to fall into place and you are ready for the grammar section. Most people quite enjoy finding out how the language they are learning actually works and how it is put together. In each unit we have selected just one or two grammar points which will enable you to understand the structure of the language sufficiently to adapt it to situations you may encounter in China.

Read and understand

In these sections you will have fun learning to recognize some characters you may encounter in public places on a trip to China.

Did you know?

This gives you some practical background information about life in China today. Units 2 and 3 are concerned with the Chinese language including Pīnyīn, which is the system of transliteration used throughout this course. A glimpse at these two sections in particular before you begin the course is strongly advised.

Answers

The answers to all these exercises (except those given in the recording) can be found on the last page of each unit.

At the back of the book

Using the casssettes

If your cassette recorder has a counter, set it to zero at the start of each unit and then note the number in the headphone symbol at the beginning of each dialogue. This will help you to find the right place on the tape quickly when you wind back.

Study guide

Here is a study guide for Unit 1. This is the kind of sequence you should follow throughout the book.

Dialogues 1, 2: listen straight through without the book
Dialogues 1, 2: listen, read and study one by one
Dialogues 1, 2: do pronunciation drill of key phrases on recording
Dialogues 1, 2: do the exercises in **Practise what you have learned**
Dialogues 3, 4: listen straight through without the book
Dialogues 3, 4: listen, read and study one by one
Dialogues 3, 4: do pronunciation drill of key phrases on recording
Dialogues 3, 4: do the exercises in **Practise what you have learned**
Dialogues 5, 6: listen straight through without the book
Dialogues 5, 6: listen, read and study one by one
Dialogues 5, 6: do pronunciation drill of key phrases on recording
Dialogues 5, 6: do the exercises in **Practise what you have learned**
Study the **Key words and phrases**
Study the **Grammar** section and do the exercise
Read **Did you know?**
Do the recorded exercise in **Your turn to speak**
Finally, listen to all the dialogues again straight through

TALKING ABOUT YOURSELF

What you will learn

- to exchange greetings
- to introduce someone
- to ask someone how they are
- to say how you are
- something about Chinese names

Before you begin

Before you start, read the introduction to the course on pages iv–vi.

The suggested study pattern you find there has been designed to guide you through the Unit systematically, so that you will progress from understanding the gist of the recorded dialogues to understanding them in detail, and finally to being able to produce a number of key words, phrases and sentences yourself.

Try to develop your ability to tune in to the sound of spoken Mandarin. Begin by listening to the first group of dialogues without using your book, and without worrying about the details of what is being said. This will prepare you for hearing Mandarin in China and not panicking if you can't understand every word.

Do not be put off by Mandarin's reputation as a 'difficult' language. You may even find that in many ways Mandarin is easier than other languages you know. Above all, enjoy the challenge!

Dialogues

1

Saying hello.

Receptionist
Businessman

Xiānsheng, nín hǎo!
Nín hǎo!

> **LISTEN FOR...**
> **nín hǎo**   hello (polite)

hǎo   good, well

> **xiānsheng**   mister, sir, gradually replacing the word **tóngzhì**
> meaning 'comrade', which was the popular form of address in
> socialist China
>
> **nín**   you, singular and polite form, used when talking to someone
> you don't know very well or someone older than you
> **nín hǎo**   hello, (lit. you well?), the most common greeting. Note
> that whereas in English we would say 'you *are* well', in Mandarin
> there is no verb 'to be' with adjectives.
> **xiānsheng, nín hǎo!**   can also be **nín hǎo, xiānsheng!**

2

An introduction

Hènián
Jiànjí
Zhāng Lì

Jiànjí, zhè shì wǒ fūren, Zhāng Lì.
Nǐ hǎo!
Nǐ hǎo !

> **LISTEN FOR...**
> **zhè shì**   this is
> **nǐ hǎo**   hello

shì   to be
wǒ   I, me   **fūren**   wife

> **zhè shì wǒ fūren**   This is my wife. De is usually added to **wǒ** to
> mean 'my', **wǒ de**. But with close relations **de** is often omitted.
> **Zhè shì wǒ zhàngfu.** This is my husband.
>
> **nǐ**   you, singular and familiar form. There is no need for Jiànjí
> and Zhāng Lì to use **nín** as they are the same age and are not in a
> formal situation demanding politeness.

Practise what you have learned

1

How would you greet the following people, (1) **nǐ hǎo!** or (2) **nín hǎo!**? (Answers on page 12.)

(a) a member of your family .... *nǐ hǎo!*

(b) an older colleague .... *nín hǎo!*

(c) someone you don't know very well .... *nín hǎo!*

(d) a friend .... *nǐ hǎo*

2

Listen to the conversation on the recording. Xiànbīn is greeted by the hotel receptionist; he returns his greeting and then introduces him to his wife. Fill in the blanks in the conversation. A selection of words and phrases is given to help you, but be careful – not every word is used. (Answers on page 12.)

Lǐ	Nín hǎo, _*xiānsheng*_!
Xiànbīn	Nǐ hǎo! _*zhè shì*_ wǒ fūren.
Lǐ	_*Nín*_ hǎo!
Xiǎoyūn	Nín hǎo!

	nín	
	xiānsheng	**fūren**
	nín hǎo	
nǐ	**zhè shì**	**nǐ hǎo**

3

Practise saying hello in a conversation with Xiànbīn on the recording. Lǐ will prompt you in English with your part of the conversation. Pause the recording, say your line in Chinese and release the pause button to hear the correct version.

Dialogues

3

How have you been?

> **LISTEN FOR...**
> **zuìjìn zěnmeyàng?** How have you been recently?
> **tǐng hǎo de** fine
> **yǒudiǎnr máng** a bit busy

Zhāng Píng	Nín hǎo!
Lǐ Bīn	Nǐ hǎo!
Zhāng Píng	Zuìjìn zěnmeyàng?
Lǐ Bīn	E, wǒ zuìjìn tǐng hǎo de. Nín zuìjìn zěnmeyàng a?
Zhāng Píng	Ao, wǒ zuìjìn yǒudiǎnr máng.

zuìjìn   recently
máng   busy

> **zěnmeyàng?**   (lit. how) a simple way of asking, 'How are you?', or in this case as the word 'recently' suggests, 'How have you been?'. The word for 'you', **nǐ**, can be omitted as it is obvious that Zhāng is talking to Lǐ and no one else. Mandarin is a very economical language!
>
> **wǒ zuìjìn tǐng hǎo de**   I've been fine recently (lit. I recently fine). Another reply to the same question might be, **(wǒ) hěn hǎo**, I'm very well (lit. (I) very well).
>
> **a**   often used at the end of a question. It is colloquial and optional. There is no need to learn it for active use.
>
> **wǒ zuìjìn yǒudiǎnr máng**   I have been a bit busy recently. Note that the word relating to the time, i.e. **zuìjìn** 'recently', comes straight after the subject, **wǒ** meaning 'I'. It could also go at the beginning of the sentence, but never at the end.
>
> **e, ao**   words used when hesitating, like the English 'er' or 'uh', and 'oh'.

 4   *Are you feeling well?*

LISTEN FOR...
shēntǐ hǎo ma?   Are you well?
bù tài hǎo   not too good
gǎnmào le   caught a cold

Wáng   Nín zuìjìn shēntǐ hǎo ma?
Lǐ   E, zuìjìn shēntǐ bù tài hǎo. E, zhè jǐ tiān gǎnmào le.

shēntǐ   body or health   **jǐ**   a few
tài   extremely, too   **tiān**   day

> **ma**   a word used at the end of a sentence to denote a question
>
> **nín zuìjìn shēntǐ hǎo ma?**   Have you been feeling well recently? (lit. you recently health good?) Again, note that **zuìjìn** determines the tense of the sentence.
>
> **bù**   not, no. To make a sentence negative put **bù** before the verb or adjective. **zuìjìn shēntǐ bù tài hǎo**   I have not been too well recently (lit. recently health not too good)
>
> **zhè jǐ tiān**   (lit. this few days) in the last few days.
>
> **gǎnmào**   to get a cold. **Le** indicates a completed action in the past, i.e. 'caught a cold'. Don't worry about how to use **le** at this stage, stick to learning the phrase.

Practise what you have learned

4 Match the English and Pinyin (transliterated Chinese) sentences below, all possible replies to the question, **Shēntǐ hǎo ma?** (Answers on page 12.)

(1) fine
(2) not too good
(3) a bit busy
(4) had a cold

(a) **yǒudiǎnr máng**
(b) **gǎnmào le**
(c) **tǐng hǎo de**
(d) **bù tài hǎo**

5 Listen to the conversation on the recording and work out the correct answer to the following questions. (Answers on page 12.)

(1) Xiànbin has been ....

(a) fine

(b) not too good

(2) Xiǎoyūn has been ....

(a) well

(b) unwell

6 Your turn to speak. Practise asking someone how they are and then saying how you are. Lǐ will prompt you.

Dialogues

5 *Have you eaten?*

> **LISTEN FOR...**
> **nǐ chi fàn le ma?** Have you eaten
> **wǒ chi guo le** I have already eaten

Wáng Nǐ chi fàn le ma?
Lǐ Wǒ chi guo le.

chi to eat **fàn** meal

> **nǐ chi fàn le ma?** Have you eaten? In addition to its literal meaning, this phrase is a way of greeting friends, left over from harder times in China when food was scarce. As in Dialogue 3, the word **ni** 'you' is optional.
>
> **wǒ chi guo le** I have eaten. **Wo** 'I' is optional. **Guo** after a verb indicates having done or experienced something, in this case after **chi** to indicate having already eaten. As in Dialogue 4, **le** indicates a completed action in the past; again stick to learning these phrases for now. **Guo** and **le** will come up again later on.

6 *What are you busy with?*

LISTEN FOR...
máng shénme ne?   What are you busy with?
zuò diǎnr shēngyi   doing a little business
hái xíng ba   (lit. still OK) all right

Jiànjí	Hènián, nǐ hǎo!
Hènián	Jiànjí, nǐ hǎo!
Jiànjí	Nǐ hǎo, nǐ hǎo, nǐ hǎo, nǐ hǎo...
Hènián	Kuài lái, zuò, zuò, zuò, zuò...
Jiànjí	Zěnmeyàng, máng shénme ne?
Hènián	Zuò diǎnr shēngyi bei. Nǐ zuìjìn zěnmeyàng?
Jiànjí	Hái xíng ba.

shénme what   **zuò** do   **zuò** sit

> **kuài lái, zuò, zuò, zuò, zuò...**   Quickly come, sit, sit, sit, sit... Words are often repeated for emphasis. Jiànjí is patting the chair next to him as he speaks.
>
> **ne**   a word indicating a question, like **ma** in Dialogue 5, but **ma** cannot be used with **shénme**. (See *Grammar* section of Unit 2.)
>
> **diǎnr**   a little, short for **yidiǎnr**, used with nouns; differs from **yǒudiǎnr**, which you came across in Dialogue 3, since **yǒudiǎnr** is used with verbs and adjectives.
>
> **hái xíng ba**   (lit. still OK) all right. A useful phrase to learn as it is a potential answer to all sorts of questions.

Practise what you have learned

7

Draw a line to pair each question in the left-hand column with an appropriate response in the right-hand column. There may be more than one possible response. (Answers on page 12.)

(1) **Shēntǐ hǎo ma?**	(a) **Zuò diǎnr shēngyi.**
(2) **Nǐ chī fàn le ma?**	(b) **Hái xíng ba.**
(3) **Máng shénme ne?**	(c) **Wǒ chī guo le.**
(4) **Nǐ zuìjìn zěnmeyàng?**	(d) **Bù tài hǎo.**

8

Listen to the conversation on the recording and mark off each phrase in the list below as you hear it. Which of the phrases listed does not come up in the conversation? (Answer on page 12.)

máng shénme ne	gǎnmào le	hái xíng ba
nǐ hǎo	zuìjìn zěnmeyàng	zuò diǎnr shēngyi
nín hǎo	tǐng hǎo de	yǒudiǎnr máng
bù tài hǎo	shēntǐ hǎo ma	

9

You bump into your Chinese tour guide in the hotel lobby and have a brief conversation with her. Lǐ will prompt you.

Key words and phrases

To learn

nǐ hǎo	hello
nín hǎo	hello (polite)
zěnmeyàng	how / How are you?
shēntǐ hǎo ma?	Are you well?
(wǒ) hěn hǎo	(I'm) very well
bù tài hǎo	not too good
tǐng hǎo de	fine
hái xíng ba	still OK, all right
yǒudiǎnr máng	a bit busy
gǎnmào le	caught a cold
chī fàn le ma?	Have you eaten?
chī guo le	already eaten
zuìjìn	recently
zhè jǐ tiān	these last few days
zhè shì	this is
xiānsheng	sir, mister
fūren	wife
zhàngfu	husband
máng shénme ne?	What are you busy with?
zuò diǎnr shēngyi	do a little business
yǒudiǎnr	a little (verbs and adjectives)
yìdiǎnr	a little (nouns)
shénme	what
ma, ne	question words

Grammar

Grammar can often seem disconcerting, even frightening, so the *Grammar* section of each unit is kept as simple as possible. The aim is not to tell you everything you didn't want to know about Chinese grammar, but to provide you with the basics on which you can then build. Since the emphasis of the course is on understanding and speaking language of use on a trip to China, you will often be given a model sentence to adapt for your own purpose. You are not expected to understand everything and build each sentence from scratch.

In some ways Chinese grammar is easier than that of many other languages: nouns have no grammatical gender and (with few exceptions; see Unit 15, page 194) no plural form. Verbs do not change with the subject of the sentence (conjugate). Moreover, Chinese is an economical language – often, if implied by the context, the words meaning 'I', 'you', etc. are omitted.

shēntǐ hǎo ma?   (lit. health good?), instead of **Nǐ shēntǐ hǎo ma?** (lit. you health good?) Are you well?

zuò diǎnr shēngyi   (lit. doing a little business), instead of **wǒ zuò diǎnr shēngyi** I'm doing a little business.

In addition, there is often no need for a verb to link a subject and an adjective. For example:

Wǒ zuìjìn yǒudiǎnr máng.   I (have been) a bit busy recently.

Note: A link verb *is* needed with a noun. For example:

Zhè shì wǒ fūren.   This is my wife.

Word order

An important aspect of Chinese grammar is word order, which is often different to English. There are rules of thumb which will be introduced and built on gradually through the course. However, be aware that as with all rules there are exceptions! As you become more familiar with the sound of the language, and as your knowledge increases, you may also develop a 'feel' for what sounds right where.

A   'Who', 'what'

As in other languages, the subject of the sentence comes first; it is followed by the verb or adjective. For example:

wǒ chī fàn   I eat meal

wǒ yǒudiǎnr máng   I a bit busy

shēntǐ hǎo ma?   health good?

B   'Who', 'when', 'what'

The word relating to the time something happens comes immediately before or after the subject, and before anything else. For example:

nǐ zuìjìn zěnmeyàng?   (lit. you recently how?) How have you been recently?

or,

zuìjìn nǐ zěnmeyàng?   (lit. recently you how?) How have you been recently?

Putting the time word before the subject emphasizes it. It makes sense to learn to put the time word immediately after the subject, but to bear in mind that it can alternatively come at the beginning. Most importantly, remember that it never goes at the end of the sentence.

Time and tense

Words indicating time are important in that they suggest tense, much more so than the verb, as in other languages. For example:

zěnmeyàng?   How are you?

zuìjìn zěnmeyàng?   How have you been recently?

zuìjìn indicates that the speaker is talking in the past tense. Further examples:

wǒ yǒudiǎnr máng   I'm a bit busy.

wǒ zuìjìn yǒudiǎnr máng   I have been a bit busy recently.

wǒ tǐng hǎo de   I'm fine.

wǒ zuìjìn tǐng hǎo de   I've been fine recently.

Yǒudiǎnr / yīdiǎnr   *a little*

Yǒudiǎnr is used with verbs and adjectives. For example:

wǒ yǒudiǎnr máng   I am a little busy.

Yīdiǎnr is used with nouns. For example:

zuò yīdiǎnr shēngyi   do a little business

Both can be shortened to **diǎnr**. You will come across more examples of these words in the following Units. (You may also hear **diǎn** without the **r**.)

10

(1) Unscramble the Pinyin words to make sentences which match the English ones.

    (a) **ma hǎo shēntǐ nǐ zuìjìn**
        Have you been feeling well recently?

    (b) **le nǐ fàn chī ma**
        Have you eaten?

(2) **Yǒudiǎnr / yīdiǎnr?** Fill in the gaps in the following sentences.

    (a) .... **máng**

    (b) .... **shēngyi**

(Answers on page 12.)

Read and understand

Too often Chinese is dismissed as 'difficult'; the aim of this *Read and understand* is to make the written language more accessible.

Looking at just a few characters may only provide a glimpse of the written language, but it offers a valuable insight into Chinese thought. It is often fascinating to see the thought associations made to express an idea in a Chinese character.

A word which has come up in this Unit is **hǎo**, 'good':

This character is a compound of two characters with separate meanings.

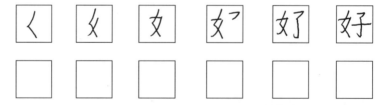

Nǚ means 'woman' and **zǐ** means 'child'. The association is that woman and child together mean good.

The boxes below show you the order in which to write the strokes which form this character. For fun have a go at copying the strokes in the boxes provided and write the character yourself. Just remember to write the strokes from top to bottom and left to right.

Incidentally, the word stroke is used because traditional Chinese calligraphy is written with brush and ink. You may have seen examples of calligraphy in shops which sell Chinese paintings, or in your local Chinese restaurant.

Calligraphy scrolls

Did you know?

Chinese names

The important thing to know about Chinese names is that the surname goes first. Máo Zédōng's family name is Máo; Dèng Xiǎopíng's family name is Dèng. This explains why Chinese people might call a westerner 'Miss Catherine', for example, assuming that 'Catherine' is a surname. You call people by their full name or by their family name. Usually only spouses, family members or close friends call each other by their given names.

Titles go after the surname: Wáng xiānsheng, Mr Wáng, and Zhāng xiǎojie, Miss Zhāng. Following the Communist takeover in 1949 people called each other comrade, Wáng tóngzhì, and Zhāng tóngzhì, but over the last decade or so this form of address has more or less faded out.

Sometimes people prefix the names of their colleagues with **xiǎo** 'little' or **lǎo** 'old'. **Xiǎo** is used for younger people, or for those with junior positions. **Lǎo** is used to show respect to senior people holding higher posts. It is not usual for foreigners to be given these titles.

Meaning is important in Chinese names. There is no gender distinction as in other cultures – however, a boy would often be given a name implying physical strength such as Dàlì, meaning 'Great Power', whereas the name Méihuā, 'Plum Blossom', would be given to a girl.

Names such as Yàn 'Scholar' and Fù 'Wealth' (the latter especially in the countryside) reflect parents' aspirations for their son or daughter. Names popular during the 1960s and 70s include Jiànguó 'Building the Country', Jiànjūn 'Building the Army', Hóngxing 'Red Star' and Shènglì 'Victory', reflecting the political climate of that era when everyone's primary responsibility was to the Revolution.

Translating foreign names into Chinese can be done phonetically, by choosing characters as near in sound as possible to the original name. However, this often seems odd to Chinese people, so a translator will usually choose characters that are reasonably close in sound to the original name, but at the same time have a meaning suitable to the owner.

Business card greetings

Business cards are everywhere! It is usual to exchange cards immediately with a handshake; if you are in China to promote your business or set up a formal link, it is a good idea to have cards with your details in English on one side and in Chinese on the other.

Your turn to speak

11

This exercise will give you an opportunity to practise using some of the most important language that you have learned in this Unit. Lǐ will guide you as usual.

And finally...

Listen to all the dialogues again straight through at least once. Make sure you are familiar with the key words and phrases before you go on to Unit 2.

Answers

Practise what you have learned

Exercise **1**	(a)1; (b)2; (c)2; (d)1
Exercise **2**	**xiānsheng, zhè shì, nín**
Exercise **4**	(1)c; (2)d; (3)a; (4)b
Exercise **5**	(1)a; (2)b
Exercise **7**	(1)b/d; (2)c; (3)a; (4)b/d
Exercise **8**	**tǐng hǎo de**

Grammar

Exercise **10** (1)(a) **Nǐ zuìjìn shēntǐ hǎo ma?** (b) **Nǐ chī fàn le ma?**

(2)(a) **yǒudiǎnr** (b) **yìdiǎnr**

TALKING ABOUT YOURSELF AND OTHERS

What you will learn

- to say your name and age
- to ask for similar information from others
- to understand and to answer
- questions about your family
- numbers 1 to 20
- some background on the language

Before you begin

This unit follows the same study pattern as Unit 1 (refer back to the sample Study Guide on p. vi, if you need to). Remember that the first stage of listening to the dialogues straight through is important even if you do not understand much of what is being said. At this point you are probably still thinking how strange the language sounds – although it must sound less strange than at the beginning of Unit 1! Get into the habit of training your listening ear: remember, you will not have a book to refer to when a Chinese person starts to talk to you in China.

On Quingdao beach

Dialogues

1

What are you called and how old are you?

> **LISTEN FOR...**
> **nǐ jiào shénme?**   What are you called?
> **jǐ suì le?**   How old are you? (to a child under 10)

Hènián	Xiǎo péngyou, nǐ jiào shénme ya?
Boy	Wǒ jiào Rén Chéng.
Hènián	Jīnnián jǐ suì le?
Boy	Jiǔ suì.

xiǎo   small, little
péngyou   friend
jīnnián   this year

suì   year of age
jiǔ   nine
jǐ   how many?

> **jiào**   to be called, used to say your full or given name
>
> **ya**   a question word like **ma**, used when speaking to children but not actually needed here with **shénme**, itself a question word. (See *Grammar* on page 22.)

2

What is the old man's name, and how old is he?

> **LISTEN FOR...**
> **nín guìxìng**   What is your name? (polite form, refers to surname)
> **wǒ xìng**   I am called (surname)
> **nín gāoshòu?**   How old are yǒu? (to an old person)

Hènián	Nín hǎo, dàye.
Old man	Ao, nǐ hǎo.
Hènián	Nín guìxìng?
Old man	Wǒ xìng Lǐ.
Hènián	Nín jīnnián gāoshòu?
Old man	Liù shí liù suì le.

liùshíliù   sixty-six.

> **dàye**   'grandpa', a courteous word used to address someone older than your father, but not your own grandfather, who is **yéye**.
>
> **nín guìxìng?**   actually means 'What is your honourable surname?' Hènián chose to be very polite because he is talking to an old man. In an informal situation or when talking to a person of your own generation, you can say simply, **Nǐ xìng shénme?** 'What is your surname?'.
>
> Don't be surprised if people ask you how old you are in conversation. In China it is not considered impolite at all!

Practise what you have learned

1

Xiǎoyūn is getting to know a family and asks each person some basic personal details. Listen to her questions and work out whether she is talking to a child or a grandparent, ticking (✓) the appropriate box below. (Answers on page 26.)

(1) (a) child ☐
    (b) grandparent ☐

(2) (a) child ☐
    (b) grandparent ☐

(3) (a) child ☐
    (b) grandparent ☐

2

This time you will hear a set of answers. After each one, choose the question below which is likely to have elicited the reply, writing the number of the recorded answer in the appropriate box. (Answers on page 26)

(a) **Nín gāoshòu?** ☐
(b) **Nǐ jiào shénme?** ☐

(c) **Jǐ suì le?** ☐
(d) **Nín guìxìng?** ☐

3

Your turn to speak. How would you ask the following questions? If you wish, write down your question below before saying it out loud, then check it against Xiǎoyūn's on the recording.

(1) an old man how old he is...

(2) a boy how old he is..

(3) a person for their full name ....

(4) a person politely for their surname ....

Grandad: 'in-house child care'

Dialogues

3

How many people are there in your family?

Hènián	Dàye, nín jiā yǒu jǐ kǒu rén ne?
Old man	Sān kǒu.
Hènián	En, tāmen shì…?
Old man	Ao, yǒu lǎobànr, hái yǒu wǒ de xiǎo nǚ'ér, jiā shang wǒ, sān kǒu rén.

jiā	family	**hái**	in addition
yǒu	to have, there is / are	**wǒ de**	my / mine
rén	person / people	**jiā shang**	add on, plus
sān	three	**xiǎo nǚ'ér**	little / youngest daughter

nín jiā yǒu   your family has

kǒu   (lit. mouth). In Mandarin there must be a word separating a number or quantity and a noun. This word often tells you something about the noun; **kǒu** 'mouth', for example, is used with people. **Jǐ kǒu rén?** (lit. how many mouths people?). Words with this function will keep cropping up, so you will become more accustomed to their use. For now, stick to learning the phrase, and note that, as in the reply **sān kǒu** 'three mouths', the original noun can be omitted after it has once been stated.

ne   a question word is not needed with **jǐ**, which is a question word itself. However, in colloquial language Chinese people tend to throw them in everywhere. (See *Grammar* on page 22.)

en   em, a hesitation word before speaking.

tāmen shì…?   they are…? 'He' or 'she' is **ta**, and **-men** is added to form the plural. Similarly, **-men** is added to **wǒ, wǒmen**, to change it from 'I' to 'we', and to **nǐ, nǐmen**, to mean 'you' plural. **Péngyoumen** is 'friends'.

lǎobànr   a word for the husband or wife of a marriage long-standing, 'the missus'. Other members of the family are **fùqin** father, **mǔqin** mother and **érzi** son

wǒ de, my. De is added to personal pronouns to indicate possession. **Nǐ de/nín de/nǐmen de** 'yours', **tā de/tāmen de** 'his'/'hers'/'theirs', **wǒmen de** 'ours'. Usually when talking about members of their family people don't use **wo de**, etc. In Unit 1, Dialogue 2, you came across, **Zhè shì wǒ fūren**. This is my wife.

4

How old are you? Are you married?

> **LISTEN FOR...**
> **nǐ duōdà le?** How old are you? (used for children over 10 and adults of your own generation)
> **nǐ jiéhūn le ma?** Are you married?
> **hái méiyǒu jiéhūn** not yet married

Lǐ	Nǐ jīnnián duōdà le?
Wáng	Èr shí wǔ.
Lǐ	Nǐ jiéhūn le ma?
Wáng	Hái méiyǒu jiéhūn.

èr shí wǔ twenty-five   **jiéhūn** to get married

> **hái méiyǒu** not yet (but the possibility remains). **Méiyǒu** can be shortened to **méi**.

A Qingdao wedding

Practise what you have learned

4

(1) Listen to the conversation on the recording. An official is asking a woman some questions. What does he ask and in what order? Choose from the options below and write the letter of your answer in the appropriate box. (Answers on page 26.)

First he wants to know... ☐

Second he wants to know... ☐

Third he wants to know... ☐

(a) whether she is married
(b) how she is feeling
(c) her full name
(d) her surname
(e) her age
(f) what she is busy with

(2) Only one of the following answers is given by the woman. Which one? (Answer on page 26.)

(a) **Bù tài hǎo.**
(b) **Wǒ xìng Wáng.**
(c) **Wǒ jiào Zhāng Hóng.**

(d) **Hái méiyǒu jiéhūn.**
(e) **Zuò diǎnr shēngyì.**
(f) **Wǒ liù shí liù suì.**

5

Match the Pīnyīn words for members of the family with the English meanings. (Answers on page 26.)

(1) **fùqin**
(2) **mǔqin**
(3) **yéye**
(4) **érzi**
(5) **nǚ'èr**

(a) son
(b) daughter
(c) father
(d) mother
(e) grandfather

6

Your turn to speak. Ask a new friend a few questions about herself and her family. You will need:

Nǐ duōdà le?
Nǐ jiéhūn le ma?

Nǐ jiā yǒu jǐ kǒu rén?
Tāmen shì...?

Dialogues

5

Where do you come from?

> **LISTEN FOR...**
> **nǐ shì nǎr (de) rén?** Where do you come from?
> (lit. you are where person?)
> **wǒ shì Qīngdǎo rén** I come from Qīngdǎo
> (lit. I am Qīngdǎo person)
> **piàoliang** beautiful

Wáng Wěi	Nǐ shì nǎr de rén?
Dōng Ruì	Wǒ shì Qīngdǎo rén. Qīngdǎo nǐ qù guo ma?
Wáng Wěi	Qīngdǎo wǒ qù guo. Qīngdǎo hěn piàoliang.
Dōng Ruì	Shì ma? Nǐ shì nǎr rén ne?
Wáng Wěi	Wǒ jiù shì Běijīng rén.

nàr	where	**hěn**	very
qù	to go	**shì ma?**	really?

> **Qīngdǎo** a coastal city in northern China
>
> **nǐ shì nǎr de rén?** Where are you from? (lit. you are which place's person?) The **de** changes **nǎr** to an adjective, but it is not necessary here. (It will come up again later.) Wáng could have simply asked, **Nǐ shì nǎr rén?** Learn this simpler phrase.
>
> **qù guo** ever been. **Guo** means to have had the experience of doing something and goes after the verb it refers to. **Qīngdǎo nǐ qù guo ma? / nǐ qù guo Qīngdǎo ma?** Have you ever been to Qīngdǎo? **Qīngdǎo** is put at the beginning for emphasis.
>
> **Běijīng** capital of China (lit. northern capital), formerly referred to as Peking
>
> **wǒ jiù shì Běijīng rén.** (lit. I just am Běijīng person.) I am from Běijīng. The dialogue was recorded in Běijīng, and this Běijīnger used **jiù** 'just' for emphasis.

6

Numbers 1 to 20

Boy Yī, èr, sān, sì, wǔ, liù, qī, bā, jiǔ, shí, shí yī, shí èr, shí sān, shí sì, shí wǔ, shí liù, shí qī, shí bā, shí jiǔ, èr shí.

> **yī** one, **èr** two, **sān** three, **sì** four, **wǔ** five, **liù** six, **qī** seven, **bā** eight, **jiǔ** nine, **shí** ten
>
> **shí yī** eleven, **shí èr** twelve, **shí sān** thirteen, **shí sì** fourteen, **shí wǔ** fifteen, **shí liù** sixteen, **shí qī** seventeen, **shí bā** eighteen, **shí jiǔ** nineteen, **èr shí** twenty
>
> The numbers 1 to 10 are important. Once you have mastered them, larger numbers are easy. The 'teens' are ten plus the appropriate number, for example, **shí wǔ** 'fifteen'. When you get to twenty, you say the number of tens, then ten; so **èr shí** is 'twenty'.

Practise what you have learned

7 Listen to the recording and cross out the numbers on the grid below as Xiànbin calls them out. Which number are you left with? Lǐ will give the answer on the recording.

1	3	5
7		9
	2	4
6	8	10

8 How do you say the following numbers? A selection of Pinyin answers is given below. First link them with the numerals, but be careful as you will not need all of them. Then say each number out loud, and check your answer on the recording.

10
25
40
9
66
12
3

jiǔ	**shí sì**	**èr shí wǔ**
sì shí	**shí**	**liù shí liù**
èr shí	**shí èr**	**sān**

9 Your turn to speak. You have been invited to a banquet. Take part in a short conversation with the person sitting next to you, consisting of a greeting, saying where you come from and whether you have been to Běijīng before. Lǐ will prompt. You will need the word **Lúndūn** 'London'.

Mao's mausoleum, Tian'anmen Square

Key words and phrases

To learn

nǐ jiào shénme?	What are you called?
wǒ jiào	I am called
nín guìxìng?	What is your name? (polite form, refers to surname)
wǒ xìng	I am called (surname)
jǐ suì le?	How old are you? (to a child under 10)
nín gāoshòu?	How old are you? (to an old person)
nǐ duōdà le?	How old are you (children over 10 and adults of your own generation)
nín jiā yǒu jǐ kǒu rén?	How many people are there in your family?
tāmen	they
nǚ'ér	daughter
érzi	son
mǔqin	mother
fùqin	father
péngyou(men)	friend(s)
hái	in addition
jiā shang	add on, plus
jiéhūn le	married
hái méiyǒu jiéhūn	not yet married
nǎr	where
nǐ shì nǎr rén?	Where do you come from?
wǒ shì…rén	I am from…
hěn piàoliang	very beautiful
nǐ qù guo … ma?	Have you ever been to …?
méiyǒu qù guo	I haven't been before
shì ma?	really?
jīnnián	this year

yī one, **èr** two, **sān** three, **sì** four, **wǔ** five, **liù** six, **qī** seven, **bā** eight, **jiǔ** nine, **shí** ten

shí yī eleven, **shí èr** twelve, **shí sān** thirteen, **shí sì** fourteen, **shí wǔ** fifteen, **shí liù** sixteen, **shí qī** seventeen, **shí bā** eighteen, **shí jiǔ** nineteen, **èr shí** twenty

To understand

lǎobànr	'the missus'
dàye	'grandpa'

Grammar

Asking questions

A   The easiest way to form a question is to make a statement and add **ma** at the end. For example:

Nǐ qù guo Qīngdǎo.   You have been to Qīngdǎo.
Nǐ qù guo Qīngdǎo ma?   Have you ever been to Qīngdǎo?

Nǐ jiā yǒu sān kǒu rén.   There are three people in your family.
Nǐ jiā yǒu sān kǒu rén ma?   Are there three people in your family?

You will come across alternatives to **ma**, such as **ne**, **ba**, **a** and **ya**. These have subtle differences of meaning, but if you stick with using **ma** you won't go far wrong. Recognizing the others as question indicators is enough.

B   Questions containing the following question words don't need **ma** or any of the above alternatives, since the question words themselves indicate a question is being asked:

shénme what?	**zěnmeyàng** how?
jǐ how many?	**nǎr** where?

For example:
Nǐ jiào shénme?   What are you called?
Jǐ suì le?   How old are you?
Nǐ zěnmeyàng?   How are you?
Nǐ shì nǎr rén?   Where are you from?

Answering questions

A   An easy way to answer questions containing question words is to use the word order of the sentence and replace the question word with the answer. For example:

Nǐ jǐ suì le?   How old are you?
Wǒ bā suì le.   I am 8 years old.

Nǐ jiào shénme?   What are you called?
Wǒ jiào Rén Chéng.   I am called Rén Chéng.

Nǐ shì nǎr rén?   Where do you come from?
Wǒ shì Qīngdǎo rén.   I come from Qīngdǎo.

Notice the word order of these sentences. The question word does not go at the beginning of the sentence.

B   When responding to questions in which there is no question word, to answer 'yes' repeat the verb / adjective, and to answer 'no', say **bù** plus the verb / adjective ('yes' and 'no' do not translate directly into Mandarin). For example:

Nǐ chī ma?   Are you eating?
Chī.   Yes.   **Bù chī.**   No.

Nǐ máng ma?   Are you busy?
Máng.   Yes.   **Bù máng.**   No.

The exception is when the verb is **yǒu**, 'to have'. **Yǒu** is negated with **méi**, not **bù**. For example:

Nǐ yǒu nǚ'ér ma?   Do you have a daughter?
Yǒu.   Yes.   **Méi yǒu.**   No.

Personal pronouns

wǒ	I	**wǒ de**	my
nǐ / nín	you	**nǐ / nín de**	your
tā	he / she / it	**tā de**	his / her / its
wǒmen	we	**wǒmen de**	our
nǐmen	you (plural)	**nǐmen de**	your
tāmen	they	**tāmen de**	their

Note: As the person changes the verb remains the same. For example:

wǒ yǒu	I have
nǐ yǒu	you have
tā yǒu	he / she / it has
wǒmen yǒu	we have
nǐmen yǒu	you have
tāmen yǒu	they have

10

Change the subject of the following sentences to 'he' / 'she'. (Answers on page 26.)

(1) **Nǐ jiào shénme?**   What are you called?

_____ _____ **shénme?**   What is he / she called?

(2) **Nǐ jǐ suì le?**   How old are you?

_____ **jǐ suì le?**   How old is he / she?

(3) **Nǐ jiéhūn le ma?**   Are you married?

_____ _____ **le ma?**   Is he / she married?

(4) **Nǐ shì nǎr rén?**   Where do you come from?

_____ **shì nǎr rén?**   Where does he / she come from?

11

Select from the box below to fill the gaps in the following sentences so that they match their English meanings. (Answers on page 26.)

(1) _____ _____ **Lúndūn rén.**   We are from London.

(2) _____ _____ **guo Běijīng.**   They have been to Běijīng before.

(3) _____ _____ **fàn le ma?**   Have you eaten? (plural)

qù	tāmen
wǒmen	nǐmen
chī	shì

Read and understand

To give you further insight into Chinese characters, some are listed below. These are all characters in their own right, and combine with other characters to form new words, as the examples here show.

kǒu
mouth

口

rén
person

人

dà
big

大

rén kǒu
population

人口

rén mín
the people

人民

dà rén
adult

大人

yuè
moon; month

月

rì
sun; day

日

zhōng
middle

中

yuè piào
monthly ticket

月票

rì bào
daily newspaper

日报

Zhōng Dōng
Middle East

中东

Mao's wisdom

Did you know?

The Chinese language (1)

There are eight major Chinese dialects. Of these the official language of the People's Republic is **pǔtōnghuà** ('common speech'), usually known in English as Mandarin, spoken by about 70 per cent of the population. Cantonese is spoken in the far south including Hong Kong, and by the majority of Chinese people who emigrated to the West. Speakers of Mandarin and Cantonese find each other unintelligible, and may have to write down what they wish to communicate to one another.

Chinese characters

Chinese writing began about 3,500 years ago as pictographs, images representing features of nature and human life.

The character for 'mountain' is a string of hills 山

'Stream' is depicted as flowing water 溪

'Rain' is represented by drops of water falling from heaven 雨

Later, combinations of pictographs were made to communicate ideas. 'Sun' and 'moon' combine to create the ideograph for 'bright', 'sun' and 'tree' together represent 'east', and two trees together mean 'forest'.

As civilization advanced, pictographs and ideographs were no longer adequate to cope with the language of daily life or abstract notions. A new system introduced phonetic symbols reflecting the pronunciation of the word. Today about 90 per cent of characters are made up of a phonetic element and a 'radical', an element reflecting the sense. There are about 200 radicals. Characters with related meanings usually contain the same radical. For example, 'mud', 'lake', 'river' and 'oil' all contain the radical for 'water'. You can see it on the very left of the characters as follows:

mud 泥　　　　　　river

lake 湖　　　　　　oil

The characters for 'blue', 'emotion', 'pure' and 'request' all contain the same phonetic element, **qīng**, and are all pronounced 'qing', although with different tones. The radical is different in each case, making them visually distinct.

blue / green / black 青　　　pure, clear 清

emotion, feeling 情　　　request, to ask 请

There are about 50,000 Chinese characters, and roughly 5,000 are in common use.

12

Your turn to speak

You have an inquisitive neighbour at a banquet. Take the opportunity to practise talking about yourself, using the vocabulary you have learned so far.

Answers

Practise what you have learned

Exercise **1** (1)(a); (2)(b); (3)(b)

Exercise **2** (a)(2); (b)(1); (c)(4); (d)(3)

Exercise **4** (1)(c), (e), (a); (2)(c)

Exercise **5** (1)(c); (2)(d); (3)(e); (4)(a); (5)(b)

Grammar

Exercise **10** (1) **Tā jiào** (2) **Tā** (3) **Tā jiéhūn** (4) **Tā**

Exercise **11** (1) **Wǒmen shì** (2) **Tāmen qù** (3) **Nǐmen chī**

ORDERING DRINKS

What you will learn

- to ask if there are seats available
- to ask about and understand what drinks are on offer
- to order drinks
- to ask for the bill (= check)
- to understand Chinese currency and how much something costs
- numbers 20 to 100
- more background on the language

Before you begin

The study pattern for this unit is similar to those you followed in Units 1 and 2. Try, as far as possible, to work aloud – you are much more likely to be able to say the correct word when you need it if you have practised it beforehand. Remember to take your time over the unit.

Street snacks – Xian

Dialogues

1

Are there any seats?

> **LISTEN FOR...**
> **yǒu wèizhi ma?** Are there any seats?
> **wǒmen yǒu liù wèi** there are six of us

Man	Xiǎojie, yǒu wèizhi ma?
Waitress	Nǐmen jǐ wèi a?
Man	En... wǒmen yǒu liù wèi dàrén, yī... yī wèi xiǎoháir.
Waitress	Hǎo lei, gēn wǒ dào zhè bianr lái ba.
Man	Hǎo ba.

xiǎojie miss
dàren adult
xiǎoháir child or children

dào to reach, to
lái to come

---

wèi refers to people. As mentioned in Unit 2, Dialogue 3, in Chinese there must be a word separating a number and a noun and throughout this Unit you will come across further examples. **Yī wèi xiǎoháir**, 'one child'. **Wèi** has the same function here as **kǒu** in **sān kǒu rén**, which you came across in Unit 2. (See *Grammar* on page 37 for further explanation of this important point.)

nǐmen jǐ wèi? How many of you are there?

wǒmen yǒu... (lit. we have...) meaning in this case 'There are...of us'

hǎo lei often used by people in shops and restaurants to show their readiness to serve you or their willingness to go along with what has been suggested. **Hǎo** would have been enough. There is no direct translation and no need to learn it for active use.

zhè bianr this side. **Gēn wǒ dào zhè bianr lái ba** (lit. with me to this side come) 'Come to this side with me'. Note that in complex sentences the verb goes at the end of the sentence, after everything else – except question elements like **ma**, or as in the Dialogue **ba**.

ba you will notice this element cropping up again and again. Generally it indicates a suggestion or an agreement, or is used to confirm a supposition. Don't worry about using it yourself now. You will get a feel for how to use it as you move through the course.

hǎo ba OK, all right.

On Li River, Guilin

2 *Ordering a beer in the bar.*

LISTEN FOR...
nín yào shénme yǐnliào? (lit. you want what drink?)
What would you like to drink?
wǒ yào I want
yī bēi píjiǔ a glass of beer

Waitress	Xiānsheng, qǐng wèn nín yào shénme yǐnliào?
Man	Wǒ yào yī bēi píjiǔ.
Waitress	Qǐng wèn, nín hái yào diǎnr biéde shénme dōngxi ma?
Man	Ao, bù yào le.
Waitress	Qǐng shāo děng.

wèn to ask   **biéde** other
bēi glass, cup   **dōngxi** thing/s

---

qǐng please. It always goes at the beginning of a sentence. **qǐng wèn**, may I ask. Similarly, this phrase always goes at the beginning of a question.

nín hái yào diǎnr biéde shénme dōngxi ma? (lit. you still want a little other what things?) Would you like something else? **shénme** is optional.

bù yào le nothing more. **Le** indicates a change in situation, i.e. I did want something, I ordered it, and I want nothing more. As a beginner you are not expected to use **le**, but do learn to recognize it, as it will come up again.

qǐng shāo děng (lit. please a moment wait) Please wait a moment

---

Practise what you have learned

1

(a) The sentences below are the jumbled up conversation which takes place between a waitress and a customer on his arrival at a restaurant. He and his companions are shown to a table by the waitress, who then finds out what drinks they want. Listen to their conversation on the recording and put the sentences below in the right order, numbering them 1 to 7 in the boxes provided.

Wǒmen yào liǎng bēi píjiǔ. ☐

Gēn wǒ dào zhè bianr lái ba. ☐ 3

Qǐng wèn nǐmen yào shénme yǐnliào? ☐

Nǐmen jǐ wèi a? ☐ 1

Qǐng wèn nǐmen hái yào diǎnr biéde dōngxi ma? □

Wǒmen yǒu liǎng wèi dàrén, yī wèi xiǎoháir. 乙

Bù yào le. 丁

(b) Now identify which Pinyin sentence corresponds to which English translation below.

(1) How many of you are there?
(2) Two adults and one child.
(3) Come with me to this side.
(4) May I ask, what would you like to drink?
(5) We want two beers.
(6) Do you want anything else?
(7) Nothing more.

(Answers on page 40.)

2

You go to a restaurant with two friends, and order drinks for all three of you.

Looking at the pictures for clues, write an appropriate response to each of the waitress's questions in the space provided. Three jumbled sentences are given below to help you. (Answers on page 40.)

(1) *Waitress* **Nǐmen jǐ wèi?**

....

(2) *Waitress* **Qǐng wèn, nǐmen yào shénme yǐnliào?**

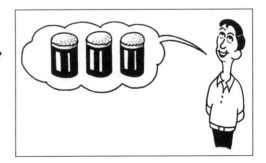

....

(3) *Waitress* **Qǐng wèn, nǐmen hái yào diǎnr biéde dōngxi ma?**

---

le yào bù
                    wèi wǒmen sān yǒu
        bēi wǒmen sān píjiǔ yào

 3   This exercise is on the recording only. Have a go at ordering drinks in a bar.

Dialogues

 3

Ordering tea and coffee

> **LISTEN FOR…**
> **yì bēi kāfēi**   a cup of coffee
> **yì bēi chá**   a cup of tea

Waitress	Qǐng wèn, nǐmen yào shénme yǐnliào?
Liú Hóng	Wǒmen yào yì bēi kāfēi hé yì bēi chá.
Waitress	Qǐng wèn, kāfēi lǐ jiā nǎi ma?
Liú Hóng	Yào jiā nǎi de.
Waitress	Hǎo, qǐng shāo hòu.

lǐ   inside   **nǎi**   milk
jiā   to add

> **hé**   and. Only used to link two nouns and not two sentences.
>
> **kāfēi lǐ jiā nǎi ma?**   (lit. coffee inside add milk?) Would you like milk in your coffee? The word **lǐ**, 'inside', goes after the noun it refers to, for example, **chá lǐ**, 'in the tea'.
>
> **yào jiā nǎi de**   Yes, I want milk added. In this case **de** emphasises the affirmation, but it's not necessary. Learn this phrase without it. Liú Hóng might have said, **bù yào**, 'No, I don't'.
>
> **qǐng shāo hòu**   Please wait a moment. Slightly more formal than **qǐng shāo děng** in Dialogue 2.

4 *What alcoholic drinks do you have here?*

LISTEN FOR...

nín zhèr yǒu shénme jiǔ? (lit. you here have what alcoholic drinks?) What alcoholic drinks do you have here?
pútaojiǔ wine
gěi wǒ lái bring me

Waitress	Xiānsheng, qǐng wèn nín yào shénme yǐnliào?
Wáng	Nín zhèr yǒu shénme jiǔ?
Waitress	Wǒmen zhèr yǒu pútaojiǔ, *whiskey*, báilándì, hái yǒu *rum* jiǔ.
Wáng	Nà gěi wǒ lái yī bēi báilándì ba.
Waitress	Hǎo de, qǐng shāo děng.

zhèr	here	**báilándì**	brandy
pútaojiǔ	wine	**gěi**	for

nín zhèr (lit. you here) loosely 'your place', used to indicate the place (in this case the bar) without being specific. Similarly, **wǒmen zhèr** can mean 'our place'.

whiskey, usually wēishìjì; *rum*, usually lángmǔ

jiǔ denotes an alcoholic drink

lái means 'to come', or 'to make come' and is used to order meals and drinks, and to ask for things in shops. **Gěi wǒ lái...** (lit. for me make to come...) Bring me... Simply saying **lái...** is enough.

nà...ba in that case, indicates that you have made up your mind when faced with a choice. **Nà gěi wǒ lái yī bēi báilándì ba**. In that case bring me a glass of brandy.

hǎo de OK. **De** adds formality.

Practise what you have learned

4 What would you like to drink? **Nín yào shénme yǐnliào?** Fill in the blanks with the appropriate words and match up each sentence with its English equivalent. (Answers on page 40.)

(1) **Wǒ** (want) ____ ...
(2) **Wǒ yào** (coffee) ____ .
(3) **Wǒ yào kāfēi** (and) ____ **chá.**
(4) **Wǒ de kāfēi** (in) ____ **yào jiā nǎi.**
(5) **Nǐmen** (here) ____ **yǒu shénme yǐnliào?**
(6) ____ (in that case) **gěi wǒmen lái liǎng bēi pútaojiǔ** ____ .

(a)	I want milk in my coffee.	(d)	What drinks do you have here?
(b)	In that case, bring us two glasses of wine.	(e)	I want coffee.
(c)	I want...	(f)	I want coffee and tea.

5

What do you think these people are drinking? Selecting from the box below, write the name of the drink on the dotted line in Pīnyīn beneath the pictures. (Answers on page 40.)

(1)...

(2)...

(3)...

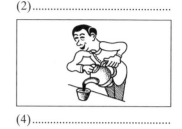

(4)...

chá   kāfēi
píjiu   pútaojiǔ

6

Wáng Dōng and his two colleagues are ordering drinks. Listen to what they say on the recording, and when you have worked out which drinks they are having, connect each person with his or her drink. Wáng Dōng and his colleagues are pictured in the order in which they speak. (Answers on page 40.)

New phrase: **nín hē diǎnr shénme?** (lit. you drink a little something?) Do you want something to drink? An alternative to **nín yào shénme yǐnliào?**, which you are likely to come across in China

Wáng

a glass of beer

first colleague

a glass of wine

a cup of coffee

second colleague

a brandy

7

Now you ask for each of the drinks pictured in Exercise 6. Each time the waitress asks what you would like, speak in the pause and then listen to the correct version.

Dialogues

5

The numbers after 20 (tens 30 to 100)

Boy Sān shí, sì shí, wǔ shí, liù shí, qī shí, bā shí, jiǔ shí, yī bǎi

> **sān shí** thirty,   **sì shí** forty,   **wǔ shí** fifty,   **liù shí** sixty,   **qī shí** seventy,   **bā shí** eighty,   **jiǔ shí** ninety,   **yī bǎi** one hundred
>
> Numbers are easy to form in Mandarin. Twenty is 'two ten', thirty is 'three ten', and so on. Twenty-one is **èr shí yī**, 'two ten one'. Sixty-five is **liù shí wǔ**, 'six ten five', and so on.

6

Asking for the bill (= check)

> **LISTEN FOR...**
> **qǐng jié yīxià zhàng**   Can we just pay the bill?
> (lit. please pay briefly the bill)
> **kuài**   a unit of currency, colloquial word for Yuán.
> **xièxie**   thanks

Wáng Píng Xiǎojie, qǐng jié yīxià zhàng.
Waitress Hǎo de, yīgòng shì yī bǎi liù shí sì kuài qī, gěi wǒ yī bǎi liù shì sì ba.
Wáng Píng Hǎo, hǎo, zhè shì èr bǎi.
Waitress Hǎo lei, wǒ zhǎo nǐ sān shí liù kuài qián.
Wáng Píng Hǎo, hǎo, hǎo, xièxie, xièxie, xièxie, xièxie.
Waitress Nín yào fāpiào ma?
Wáng Píng E... kāi yī zhāng ba.
Waitress Hǎo lei, shāo děng yīxià.

yīgòng	altogether	**zhǎo**	to give change
bǎi	hundred	**fāpiào**	a receipt
gěi	give		

> **yīxià**   briefly, makes the request more polite, and has the effect of 'just' in the English sentence, 'Could we just pay the bill, please?' It is also used with a verb to mean 'have a quick ... of something', e.g. **kàn yīxià** (have a quick look), **tīng yīxià** (listen for a while). This word crops up a lot and you will develop a feel for the way it's used.
>
> **kuài**   colloquial word for Yuán, a unit of Chinese currency. **Kuài**, **máo**, **fēn** are denominations of money, like pound, ten pence, penny; **máo** and **fēn** are often omitted when they are the last unit, as demonstrated in the text. In full the bill amounts to **yī bǎi liù shì sì kuài qī máo** (¥164.70), but the word **máo** is left off. This is as in the English ten pounds twenty, or sixty dollars fifty, where the 'pence' / 'cents' is understood but not spoken. Note that **kuài** or **yuán** is never omitted. **Qián** 'money' is optional in a statement, but is commonly used. Note also that .70 Yuán is **qī** (**máo**) and not **qī shí**; .75 Yuán would be **qī máo wǔ**. (See *Read and understand*.)
>
> **gěi wǒ yī bǎi liù shí sì ba**   give me one hundred and sixty-four. The waitress is disregarding the small change. **Ba** here indicates a suggestion, as in Dialogue 1.
>
> **hǎo hǎo hǎo, xièxie xièxie xièxie xièxie**   good, thanks. Chinese

people are fond of repeating words – remember **zuò zuò zuò** in Dialogue 6, Unit 1. Here the speaker is being polite and grateful.

nín yào fāpiào ma? Do you want a receipt?

zhāng (lit. a sheet, as in a sheet of paper) in this case referring to the receipt, **yì zhāng fāpiào**, 'a / one receipt'. Remember there must be a word separating a number and a noun but it's not always translated. (Have a look at the *Grammar* section for a further explanation of these words.)

kāi yì zhāng ba write one out. In this sentence **yì zhāng** refers to the receipt. Because the word **fāpiào** 'receipt' occurred earlier in the conversation, there is no need to repeat it. (Again, refer to the *Grammar* section which explains this point with further examples.) The speaker could also have said simply, **wǒ yào yì zhāng fāpiào**, I want a receipt.

shāo děng yíxià one of the various ways of saying 'just a moment'. As this is a phrase you are unlikely to use much, don't learn to say all the versions – stick to **qǐng shāo děng** which appeared in Dialogue 2.

Practise what you have learned

8

How would you write these numbers in Pinyin and how would you say them aloud? Write them out first. Then have a go at saying them, and then check your answers with Xiǎoyún on the recording. (Answers on page 40.)

20 ....

55 ....

98 ....

170 ....

164 ....

9

How much are they? Listen to the recording first and then write out each price in the space below, using the format ¥164.70. (Answers on page 40.)

(1) ————————————————

(2) ————————————————

(3) ————————————————

(4) ————————————————

(5) ————————————————

Key words and phrases

To learn

xiǎojie	miss
xièxie	thanks
qǐng	please
qǐng wèn	may I ask
yǒu wèizhi ma?	Are there any seats?
jǐ wèi?	how many (people)?
yào	to want
nín zhèr yǒu shénme jiǔ?	What (alcoholic) drinks do you have here?
nǐ yào shénme yǐnliào	What drinks do you want?
bēi	glass, cup
píjiǔ	beer
pútaojiǔ	wine
báilándì	brandy
kāfēi	coffee
chá	tea
bù yào le	no more
zhèr	here
nà…ba	in that case
gěi wǒ lái	bring me
jiā	add
nǎi	milk
jié yixià zhàng	to pay the bill
yi zhāng fāpiào	a receipt
yigòng	altogether

sān shí thirty, **sì shí** forty, **wǔ shí** fifty, **liù shí** sixty, **qi shí** seventy, **bā shí** eighty, **jiǔ shí** ninety, **yi bǎi** one hundred

To understand

gēn wǒ dào zhè bianr lái	come with me to this side
qǐng shāo hòu	please wait a moment
shāo děng yixià	please wait a moment
qǐng shāo děng	please wait a moment
nǐ hái yào diǎnr biéde dōngxi?	Do you want anything else?
zhǎo	to give change

Spirit of China

Grammar

'Measure words' / classifiers

In Mandarin, there must be a word separating a number and a noun for the phrase to make sense. For example:

yi bēi píjiǔ   a glass of beer
yi bēi chá   a cup of tea

(It is incorrect to say **yī píjiǔ** or **yī chá**.)

This word is often called a 'measure word' but it also acts as a classifier, that is, it often implies something about the noun to which it refers.

There is a range of measure words to select from, and sometimes it is obvious which to use, as in **yi bēi chá**. However, not all measure words have an exact English translation, and their use must therefore simply be learned. Here are some of those you have come across so far:

yi zhāng fāpiào   a receipt
Zhāng means 'sheet' as in a sheet of paper and is used with various nouns for items made of paper, for example, a piece of paper, a ticket, a receipt. Note that while **zhāng** must appear in the Mandarin phrase **yi zhāng fāpiào**, it is not necessary to translate it.

liǎng wèi dàrén   two adults
Wèi is used when indicating numbers of people in a social situation, for example in a restaurant. It sounds formal. **Wèi** is not translatable into English.

sān kǒu rén   three people
When talking about members of the family, use **kǒu**, literally 'mouth' (think of mouths to feed).

Sān kǒu rén can be shortened to **sān kǒu**, **liǎng wèi dàrén** can be shortened to **liǎng wèi**, and **yi zhāng fāpiào** can be shortened to **yi zhāng**. The 'measure word' then takes on the meaning of the noun which is omitted. Thus **liǎng wèi** is translatable as 'two people' (or in this case 'two adults'), **sān kǒu** means 'three people', and **yi zhāng** means 'a receipt'. (Note that the noun can only be omitted when it has been mentioned earlier in a conversation and can therefore be understood from the context.)

10

Fill in the blanks in the following questions. (Answers on page 40.)

(1) **Wǒmen yào liǎng** _____ **kāfēi.**
   We want two cups of coffee.

(2) **Gěi wǒ kāi liǎng** _____ **fāpiào.**
   Give me two receipts.

(3) **Wǒmen yǒu sān** _____ **rén.**
   There are three people in our family.

(4) **Wǒmen yǒu sān** _____ **dàrén.**
   There are three adults – at a restaurant.)

(5) **Wǒ yào yī** _____ **píjiǔ.**
   I want a glass of beer.

Read and understand

Qián 钱 *money*

Chinese currency comes in units of Yuán 元, jiǎo 角, and fēn 分. Ten **fēn** equal one **jiǎo**, and ten **jiǎo** make one Yuán. **Fēn** are worth very little relative to Western currency. In speech, **jiǎo** are often referred to as **máo** and Yuán often called **kuài** – this is comparable to the way people in the UK might say 'quid' for 'pound'. **Fēn**, **jiǎo** and smaller denominations of Yuán come in notes and coins; larger denominations of Yuán come in notes only.

1 jiǎo

5 jiǎo

2 Yuán

1 Yuán

10 Yuán

50 Yuán

100 Yuán

5 jiǎo

5 fēn

1 jiǎo

1 Yuán

Did you know?

The Chinese language (2)

Pīnyīn

Pīnyīn ('spelling by sound') is a system for transliterating Mandarin into the Western alphabet – it is used throughout this book. Introduced in 1958, it replaced Wade–Giles and other systems of romanization. Thus for example, Peking became Běijīng, Canton became Guǎngzhōu, and Mao Tse-tung became Máo Zédōng.

Street signs in major Chinese cities are often in both Pīnyīn and characters. Advertising billboards and the front covers of magazines also use Pīnyīn. However, it would not usually be possible to communicate with, for example, a person on the street by writing in Pīnyīn. The average Chinese person is not fluent in Pīnyīn, although it is used to teach children in elementary schools correct Chinese pronunciation.

For Westerners beginning Chinese, it is obviously less daunting to use Pīnyīn than to embark on learning characters, and much less time-consuming. Indeed, for beginners who are learning the language for the purpose of touring in China or to communicate with their counterparts on a business trip, and who need to concentrate on listening and speaking, it is not essential to learn characters. However, someone wishing to study the language much beyond the limits of this book would probably need to learn characters simultaneously.

Each Chinese character is represented by one Pīnyīn syllable, so syllables are usually written separately:

lù chá   green tea   **Zhōng guó**   middle country

However, if two or more syllables are seen to represent one idea, they can be written together:

lùchá   green tea   **Zhōngguó**   China

Both of the above are correct. Do not get bogged down by the fact that sometimes Pīnyīn syllables are written together, and sometimes not. Do remember that each syllable represents a character, and each character an idea. In this book, you will see from the vocabulary lists and the notes which syllables go together to express a single idea, and are considered comparable to an English word.

A bus stop

Your turn to speak

11

You go to a restaurant with friends and order drinks. Before you listen to the recording, you may find it useful to look again at the words and phrases you have come across in this Unit. You'll need **yǒu wèizhi ma?** and **wǒmen yào...** As usual Lǐ will guide you.

Answers

Practise what you have learned

Exercise 1	(a) 5, 3, 4, 1, 6, 2, 7
	(b) 5 matches up with 5, 3 with 3, 4 with 4, 1 with 1, 6 with 6, 2 with 2, 7 with 7
Exercise 2	(1) **wǒmen yǒu sān wèi** (2) **wǒmen yào sān bēi píjiǔ** (3) **bù yào le**
Exercise 4	(1) **yào**, (2) **kāfēi**, (3) **hé**, (4) **lǐ**, (5) **zhèr**, (6) **nà...ba**; 1 = c, 2 = e, 3 = f, 4 = a, 5 = d, 6 = b
Exercise 5	(1) **yī bēi kāfēi** (2) **yī bēi píjiǔ** (3) **yī bēi pútaojiǔ** (4) **yī bēi chá**
Exercise 6	Wáng orders a glass of beer, his first colleague orders a cup of coffee and his second colleague orders a glass of wine.
Exercise 8	(1) **èrshí** (2) **wǔshíwǔ** (3) **jiǔshíbā** (4) **yībǎiqīshí** (5) **yībǎiliùshísì**
Exercise 9	(1) ¥1.20 (2) ¥1.32 (3) ¥63 (4) ¥2.40 (5) ¥123.75

Grammar

Exercise 10	(1) **bēi**, (2) **zhāng**, (3) **kǒu**, (4) **wèi**, (5) **bēi**

What you will learn

- to find out if there are any hotel rooms free
- to say how many days you want to stay
- to book (= reserve) a room
- to check out the room's / hotel's facilities
- to find out on which floor something is located
- more on the language

Before you begin

The dialogues in this Unit all take place in the foyer of the International Hotel in the centre of Beijing, one of many large Western-style hotels which have been built as part of China's economic development.

Dialogues

1

Is there a room available in the hotel?

> **LISTEN FOR...**
> **kōng fángjiān**   empty room
> **duìbuqǐ**   sorry, excuse me

Man | Nǐ hǎo, xiǎojie
Receptionist | Nín hǎo, xiānsheng
Man | Qǐng wèn, nǐmen zhèr hái yǒu kōng fángjiān ma?
Receptionist | Duìbuqǐ, méi yǒu le.
Man | Ao...

> **nǐmen zhèr hái yǒu...?**   (lit. you here still have...?) Do you have...? **méi yǒu le**   there aren't any more. **Le** indicates a change of situation; compare **bù yào le** which occurred in Dialogue 2 of the last Unit. There were some rooms available, but now there are not.

New word: **fàndiàn**   hotel

2

Checking into a hotel

> **LISTEN FOR...**
> **Wǒ néng zài zhèr zhù ma?**   Can I stay here?
> **lǚyóu**   tourism, to tour
> **wǒ yào zhù sān tiān**   I want to stay three days

Receptionist | Zǎoshang hǎo, xiānsheng. Wǒ kěyǐ wèi nín zuò yìxiē shénme ma?
Man | Nín hǎo, xiǎojie. Wǒ néng zài zhèr zhù ma?
Receptionist | Kěyǐ. Qǐng wèn, nín shì lái lǚyóu ma?
Man | Bù, wǒ shì lái zuò shēngyì de.
Receptionist | En, nàme qǐng wèn nín zài zhè lǐ yào zhù jǐ tiān ne?
Man | Ao, wǒ xiǎng wǒ dàyuē yào zhù sān tiān ba.
Receptionist | En, hǎo de, nà qǐng nín tián yíxià rùzhùdēngjìdān, hǎo ma?
Man | Hǎo de, xièxie.

kěyǐ   can (permission)   **zhè lǐ**   here
néng   can (to be able)   **xiǎng**   to think, to think of
yìxiē   some   **dàyuē**   approximately
zhù   to stay, to live   **tián**   to fill in
nàme   in that case, so   **rùzhùdēngjìdān**   registration form

zǎoshàng hǎo good morning

wǒ kěyǐ wèi nín zuò yīxiē shénme ma? (lit. I can for you do some what?) What can I do for you? Phrases such as **wèi nín**, 'for you', go before the verb. Compare **gēn wǒ**, 'with me', as in **gēn wǒ dào zhè bianr lái ba**, 'come with me to this side', in Unit 3, Dialogue 1.

zài zhèr (lit. at here). **Zài** is used before a noun indicating place, just as 'in', 'on' or 'at' is used in English. Note its position in the sentence, before the verb. (See *Grammar* on page 51.)

wǒ néng zài zhèr zhù ma? (lit. I can at here stay?) Can I stay here? You have come across two ways of asking whether there are rooms available. Another useful phrase is simply, **Wǒ yào dìng yī ge fángjiān**. I want to book (reserve) a room.

nín shì lái lǚyóu ma? (lit. you are come to tour?) Have you come as a tourist? The answer might have been, **Wǒ shì lái lǚyóu de**. I have come to travel / as a tourist.

wǒ shì lái zuò shēngyì de (lit. I am come to do business.) I have come on business. Questions and answers of this type emphasise the time, locale, manner or reason for a completed action. The pattern is **Wǒ shì...de**. Compare **Wǒ shì lái chī fàn de**. (lit. I am come to eat).

tián Although the Chinese words for 'day' and 'to fill in' are composed of the same sounds, and are therefore spelled the same in Pinyin, the Chinese characters and the tones are different. *Did you know?* on page 53 tells you more about tones.

ba accompanies suggestions, and is used to confirm a supposition, for example **hǎo ba?** all right? or **hǎo ba**, all right.

Beijing International Hotel, Starlight Revolving Restaurant

Practise what you have learned

1 You will hear a receptionist ask someone wishing to check into a hotel three questions. After each question there is a pause for you to give the most appropriate response from the list below. The correct answer will follow on the recording each time.

Wǒ shì lái zuò shēngyì de.
Wǒ yào zhù sān tiān.
Wǒ néng zài zhèr zhù ma?

2 First match each picture to its Pīnyīn description.

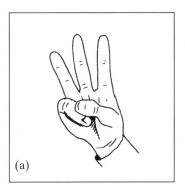

(a)

(b)

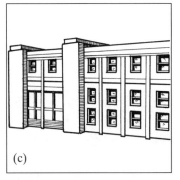

(c)

(d)

(1) **kōng fángjiān**   (3) **rùzhùdēngjìdān**
(2) **fàndiàn**   (4) **sān tiān**

Then, listen to Xiǎoyún read out the words on the recording and write them down in the same order.

....

....

(Answers on page 54.)

3 Your turn to speak. Practise booking a room in a hotel. Lǐ will prompt you. You will need: **Wǒ yào dìng yī ge fángjiān**.

Dialogues

3

What facilities does the room have?

Receptionist	Nín dìng de shì yī ge shuāngrénfáng, shì ba?
Zhào Xiān	Duì de, qǐng wèn wǒ zhè ge fángjiān lǐ yǒu diànshì ma?
Receptionist	Yǒu.
Zhào Xiān	Yǒu diànhuà ma?
Receptionist	Yǒu de.
Zhào Xiān	Yǒu wèishēngjiān ma?
Receptionist	Dāngrán yǒu.
Zhào Xiān	Tài hǎo le!

dìng   to book, reserve
fángjiān   room
duì   correct

wèishēngjiān   bathroom
dāngrán   of course

ge   the most common of the 'measure words'. (Measure words were explained in the *Grammar* section of Unit 3.) Ge is used with a variety of words – you will come across many examples throughout the course – and does not have a specific translation into English. **Zhè** 'this' + noun needs a measure word; in this respect **zhè** functions exactly like a number. **Zhè ge fángjiān**, this room. Note the pronunciation of **zhè**. In Běijīng, where the recording was made, locals often pronounce it **zhèi**.

nín dìng de shì yī ge shuāngrénfáng   (lit. your booked [room] is a double room). The one you booked is a double room. Putting **de** after a verb makes the verb function like an adjective: **nín dìng de** (lit. your booked [room]) 'the one you booked'. There is no word for room after **dìng de**, since it is understood from the context. The full sentence would have been, **Nín dìng de fángjiān shì yī ge shuāngrénfáng**. Have a look at the *Grammar* section for further examples and instructions on how to use **de** in this way.

shuāngrénfáng   double room. Single rooms are few, and you pay per room not per person. Single occupancy of a double room is of course acceptable. The word for single room is **dānrénfáng**.

shì ba?   isn't it?

duì de   yes. **Duì** means 'correct'; adding **de** makes it slightly more formal and emphasises the affirmation.

wǒ zhè ge fángjiān lǐ yǒu diànshì ma?   (lit. I this room in have TV?) Is there a TV in my room? **Lǐ** 'in' goes after the noun, just as in the phrase **kāfēi lǐ**, 'in the coffee', in Unit 3. Note the position of the phrase 'in the room', between the subject and the verb. 'Where' always goes before 'what'.

yǒu de   yes (lit. there is). The same use of **de** as in **duì de**.

tài hǎo le! very good! **Tài...le** sandwiching an adjective means 'extremely', 'too', 'very'. There are further examples in the *Grammar* section on page 51.

This dialogue takes place in one of China's newest and most modern hotels, so Zhào Xiān can expect her room to be of a high standard. Rooms in all China's major hotels are equipped with private bathroom, air conditioning, colour TV, radio and telephone.

4 *What restaurants does the hotel have and where are they?*

LISTEN FOR...
Cānting zài nǎr? Where is the restaurant?
(lit. restaurant at where?)
xī cānting Western restaurant
kāfēitīng coffee shop
zhōng cānting Chinese restaurant

Hènián	Qǐng wèn, cānting zài nǎr?
Manager	Nǐ wèn de shì shénme cānting?
Hènián	Xī cān....
Manager	Xī cānting hé kāfēitīng dōu zài yī lóu.
Hènián	Hái yǒu zhōng cānting ma?
Manager	Yǒu zhōng cānting. Zhōng cānting zài èr lóu hé sān lóu.

wèn	to ask	**lóu**	storey, floor
dōu	all		

---
cānting zài nàr? Where is the restaurant? The simplest way to ask where something is. Note that the noun goes first. **Tā zài nǎr?** Where is he?

nín wèn de shì shénme cānting? (lit. your questioned [restaurant] is what restaurant?) What kind of restaurant are you asking about? As in **dìng de** in Dialogue 3, **de** makes the verb, here **wèn** 'to ask', into an adjective. To avoid repetition the **cānting** 'restaurant' described by **wèn de** is omitted. (The full sentence would have been: **Nín wèn de cānting shì shénme cānting?**)

zhōng literally means 'middle', but often means 'China' or 'Chinese'. Chinese people once considered China to be at the centre of the world, so China is called the 'middle kingdom', **Zhōngguó**. The Chinese language is **Zhōngwén**.

zài yī lóu (lit. on the first floor). In China, the ground floor is referred to as the 'first floor', as in the USA. **Zài èr lóu**, 'on the second floor' (confusing if you are British because in the UK this would be the first floor!)

Practise what you have learned

4

Match each picture with the correct word. (Answers on page 54.)

(a)

(b)

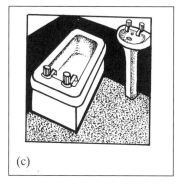
(c)

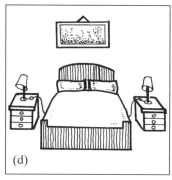
(d)

(1) **diànhuà**   (3) **diànshì**
(2) **shuāngrénfáng**   (4) **wèishēngjiān**

5

Match the Pinyin sentences with their English translations. (Answers page 54.)

(1) **Wǒ zhè ge fángjiān lǐ yǒu diànshì ma?**
(2) **Xī cānting zài nǎr?**
(3) **Hái yǒu zhōng cānting ma?**
(4) **Kāfēiting hé xi cānting dōu zài yi lóu.**

(a) Where is the Western restaurant?
(b) The coffee shop and the Western restaurant are both on the ground floor.
(c) Do I have a TV in this room?
(d) Is there also a Chinese restaurant?

6

Practise asking where the various facilities are and understanding on which floor they are located.

Dialogues

5

Where can I send a fax?

> **LISTEN FOR...**
> **fā chuánzhēn**   to send a fax
> **shāngwù zhōngxīn**   business centre
> **dǎ guójì chángtú**   to make an international long distance call
> **fùyìn**   to photocopy

Businessman	Qǐng wèn, wǒ zài nǎr néng fā chuánzhēn ne?
Manager	Fā chuánzhēn, kěyǐ qù shāngwù zhōngxīn. Shāngwù zhōngxīn zài yī céng.
Businessman	Nàr hái yǒu shénme fúwù shèshī ne?
Manager	Nàr hái kěyǐ dǎ guójì chángtú, hái kěyǐ fùyìn.

fúwù shèshī   service facility
nàr   there

> **ne**   at the end of a sentence makes it into a question, as does **ma**.
> It is not strictly necessary here because **zài nǎr**, 'at where', is a
> question phrase. However, the businessman chose to add **ne** for
> emphasis. **Ne** is the only question element which can properly be
> used in conjunction with such questions words as **nǎr** 'where', and
> **shénme** 'what'. (Look back at the *Grammar* section in Unit 2 for a
> reminder if you need to.)
>
> **kěyǐ qù**   (lit. one can go). The structure **kěyǐ** plus verb, 'one
> can...' or 'can one...?' is simple and useful for finding out /
> stating information. It comes up again in the Dialogue when the
> manager says **kěyǐ dǎ guójì chángtú**, 'one can make international
> long distance calls'.
>
> **céng**   another word for floor, equivalent to **lóu**.
>
> **nàr hái yǒu shénme fúwù shèshī ne?**   (lit. there in addition there
> are what service facilities?) What other facilities are there over
> there? The place, **nàr**, 'there', goes at the beginning of the
> sentence.

6

More about the hotel's facilities

> **LISTEN FOR...**
> **jiànshēnfáng**   gym
> **yóuyǒngchí**   swimming pool
> **wàihuì duìhuànchù**   bureau de change

Businessman	Qǐng wèn, nǐmen zhèr hái yǒu shénme qítā de fúwù shèshī?
Manager	Wǒmen zhèr yǒu jiànshēnfáng, dànzǐfáng, yóuyǒngchí, hái yǒu bǎolíngqiú.
Businessman	Yǒu wàihuì duìhuànchù ma?
Manager	Yǒu. Wàihuì duìhuànchù zài yī lóu.

qítā   other   **bǎolíngqiú**   bowling alley
dànzǐfáng   billiards room

> **nǐ zhèr hái yǒu shénme qítā de fúwù shèshī?**   What other
> facilities do you have here? **de** is optional.

Practise what you have learned

7 Xiànbīn will say five sentences. Match each one to its English translation below, writing the number of the recorded sentence in the appropriate box. (Answers on page 54.)

(a) One can go to the business centre. ☐

(b) What other facilities do you have here? ☐

(c) Where can I make an international long distance call? ☐

(d) Where can I book a room? ☐

(e) One can also send a fax there. ☐

Listen to the sentences again, repeating them after Xiànbīn to practise your pronunciation. You may also wish to learn these sentences as they can be used as the basis for structuring questions in many different situations.

8 Your tour leader explains to you where the hotel's business and leisure facilities are to be found. Listen to her introduction, and then show on which floor the various facilities are located by ticking (✓) the relevant boxes. (Answers on page 54.)

Facility	1st floor	2nd floor	3rd floor
business centre			
fax			
international telephone calling			
Western restaurant			
bureau de change			
swimming pool			
gym			

9 Your turn to speak. Check your understanding of your tour leader's introduction to the hotel's facilities.

Key words and phrases

To learn

kōng	empty
fángjiān	room
shuāngrénfáng	double room
dānrénfáng	single room
dìng yī ge fángjiān	to book a room
wǒ de fángjiān lǐ	in my room
diànshì	TV
diànhuà	telephone
duìbuqǐ	sorry, excuse me
méi yǒu le	no more
zǎoshang hǎo	good morning
zài	in, on, at
zhù	to stay, to live
lǚyóu	to tour; tourism
néng	can (to be able)
kěyǐ	can (permission)
kěyǐ + verb	one can…
ge	measure word
zài zhè lǐ	at this place
wèn	to ask
lóu	floor
fā chuánzhēn	to send a fax
shāngwù zhōngxin	business centre
dà guójì chángtú	to make an international long distance call
fùyìn	photocopy
wàihuì duìhuànchù	bureau de change
cāntīng	restaurant
zhōng / xī cāntīng	Chinese / Western restaurant

To understand

Wǒ kěyǐ wèi nín zuò yìxiē shénme?	What can I do for you?
tián rùzhùdēngjìdān	fill in hotel registration form
shì…de	a way of adding emphasis (see notes to Dialogue 2).

Grammar

Word order

'Who', 'where', 'what'

As a rule of thumb, phrases referring to place 'where' go between the subject 'who', and the verb 'what':

Nǐmen zhèr yǒu shénme yǐnliào?
(lit. You here have what drinks?)

Wǒ zhè ge fángjiān lǐ yǒu diànshì ma?
(lit. I in this room have a TV?)

(Note: **lǐ** always goes after the noun to which it refers.)

When the place in question is specific, or is preceded by 'in', 'on', 'at', then **zài** must be used before the place word:

Wǒ zài nǎr néng fā chuánzhēn?
(lit. I where (*at which place*) can send a fax?)

Nǐ zài shāngwù zhōngxīn néng fā chuánzhēn.
(lit. You at the business centre can send a fax.)

or simply:

Zài shāngwù zhōngxīn.
At the business centre.

If there is no 'who' (subject), then 'where' comes first:

Nàr kěyǐ dǎ guójì chángtú.
(lit. There can make an international long distance call.)

Exclamation

An adjective sandwiched between **tài** and **le** gains emphasis. For example:

hǎo good	**xiǎo** small
Tài hǎo le!	**Tài xiǎo le!**
Wonderful!	Tiny!
dà big	**duì** correct
Tài dà le!	**Tài duì le!**
Massive!	Absolutely correct!

Adjectives from verbs

De after a verb and before a noun, makes a verb into an adjective. For example:

nǐ dìng de fángjiān
(lit. your 'booked' room)
the room you booked

nǐ wèn de cāntīng
(lit. your 'asked about' restaurant)
the restaurant you asked about

When using this structure, there is no need to state the noun after **de** if it is implied by the context. For example:

Nǐ dìng de (fángjiān) shì yī ge shuāngrénjiān.
The room you booked is a double room.

Nǐ wèn de (cāntīng) shì shénme cāntīng?
Which restaurant are you asking about?

At this stage this structure is one to recognize and understand rather than to learn.

10 Unscramble the Pinyin words to make sentences which match the English ones: (Answers on page 54.)

(1) **zài ma wǒ zhù néng zhèr**
Can I stay here?

(2) **lǐ tiān wǒ zài yào zhù sān zhè**
I want to stay here three days.

(3) **ge lǐ diànhuà wǒ fángjiān zhè yǒu**
I have a telephone in this room.

(4) **lǐ nǎi tā kāfēi jiā yào de**
He wants milk in his coffee.

(5) **fā zài chuánzhēn zhōngxīn wǒ shāngwù néng**
I can send a fax at the business centre.

(6) **lóu zhōng zài cāntīng èr**
The Chinese restaurant is on the second floor.

Read and understand

Signs

Recognizing the following characters may help you when looking for signs in public places.

Entrance	**rù kǒu**	入口
Exit	**chū kǒu**	出口
Toilet	**cèsuǒ**	厕所
Ladies' toilet	**nǔcèsuǒ**	女厕所
Men's toilet	**náncèsuǒ**	男厕所

Did you know?

The Chinese language (3)

Tones

Despite its thousands of characters, Chinese has only around 400 syllables; the use of tones increases the number of sounds available. In Mandarin there are four distinct tones:

first tone	level	ˉ
second tone	rising	´
third tone	falling rising	ˇ
fourth tone	abrupt downward	`

Almost every syllable can be spoken four different ways, so in conversation the difference in intonation is the deciding factor in determining the meaning of words. For example **wěn** (to kiss) and **wèn** (to ask) are only differentiated by tone!

Here are some more examples. Some are words you have already come across, others may come up in future units. Listen to Z read these words on the recording to hear the difference in tone.

yī	**yí**	**yǐ**	**yì**
(one)	(aunt)	(chair)	(hundred million)
bā	**bá**	**bǎ**	**bà**
(eight)	(pull up)	(hold)	(father)
mā	**má**	**mǎ**	**mà**
(mother)	(hemp)	(horse)	(scold)
yāo	**yáo**	**yǎo**	**yào**
(waist)	(shake)	(bite)	(medicine)

Some rules to bear in mind:

(i) It is difficult to say two third tones one after the other without interrupting the flow of speech. So, when there are two third tones together, for example, **nǐ hǎo**, the first one is spoken as a second tone, **ní hǎo**. (It is marked as a third tone in the text to avoid giving the impression it is always spoken as a second tone.)

(ii) If three third tones occur together, **wǒ yě hǎo**, then the first two are spoken as second tones, **wó yé hǎo**.

(iii) **Bù** is fourth tone but becomes second before another fourth.

(iv) **Yī** is first tone as a number, but when it precedes other syllables it is fourth tone before a first, second, or third tone, and second tone before a fourth tone.

(v) Some syllables are toneless: the second half of a duplicated word, **xièxie** (thanks); particles like **le** and **de**.

The importance of tones cannot be overestimated, and it is essential to be aware of them. However, don't get burdened by them. The emphasis in this course is on listening and repeating, and up to now you have been learning tones as an integral part of the language, perhaps without realizing it.

Your turn to speak

11 Practise booking a hotel room.

Answers

Exercise **2**	(1)(d); (2)(c); (3)(b); (4)(a); **kōng fángjiān, sān tiān, fàndiàn, rùzhùdēngjìdān**
Exercise **4**	(1)(b); (2)(d); (3)(a); (4)(c)
Exercise **5**	(1)(c); (2)(a); (3)(d); (4)(b)
Exercise **7**	(a)2; (b)4; (c)1; (d)5; (e)3
Exercise **8**	The Western restaurant and swimming pool are on the second floor. The gym is on the third floor. Everything else is on the first floor.

Grammar

Exercise **10**	1. **Wǒ néng zài zhèr zhù ma?** 2. **Wǒ zài zhè lǐ yào zhù sān tiān.** 3. **Wǒ zhè ge fángjiān lǐ yǒu diànhuà.** 4. **Tā de kāfēi lǐ yào jiā nǎi.** 5. **Wǒ zài shāngwù zhōngxīn néng fā chuánzhēn.** 6. **Zhōng cāntīng zài èr lóu.**

Hotel in Guangzhan

What you will learn

- to ask for and understand directions
- to ask whether somewhere is nearby
- about taking a bus
- to say you are lost
- something about the people of China

Before you begin

Since it is unlikely that a Chinese person will approach you in the street and ask you the way, this unit concentrates on understanding directions; pronunciation and speaking exercises feature the questions you need to have on the tip of your tongue to ensure that wandering down an interesting street does not mean you lose your way never to find your hotel again!

'The capital welcomes you' – Beijing transport map

Dialogues

1

Asking the way to Xīdān.

> **LISTEN FOR...**
>
> **dào...zěnme zǒu?** How do I get to...? (lit. to reach...how to go?)
> **běi** north
> **xī** west

Zhāng Lì	Xiānsheng, qǐng wèn dào Xīdān zěnme zǒu?
Xiānsheng	Xiàng xī zǒu. Ránhòu, yù dào hónglǜdēng, xiàng běi, zhíjiē zǒu, jiù dào le.
Zhāng Lì	Ao, xièxie nín.
Xiānsheng	Hǎo, bù kèqi.

zěnme	how	**yù**	to come across, to run into
zǒu	to go, walk	**hónglǜdēng**	traffic lights
xiàng	towards	**běi**	north
ránhòu	then	**zhíjiē**	straight on

> **Xīdān** a shopping area in central Beijing
>
> **xiàng xī zǒu** (lit. towards west go) Go west. Note that the verb **zǒu** is positioned at the end of the sentence. (Refer to the *Grammar* section for more information on word order.)
>
> **yù dào** having reached. This structure will come up again later in the course. Just understand the phrase for now.
>
> **jiù dào le** it's just there / you've arrived. This phrase will crop up again and again.
>
> **bù kèqi** not at all. If you thank someone they will usually say, 'not at all'. You will come across several ways of saying it, but **bù kèqi** is the most popular.

2

Is there a post office nearby?

> **LISTEN FOR...**
>
> **zhè fùjìn yǒu...** is there a...nearby? (lit. this vicinity has...?)
> **yóujú** post office
> **yòu** right

Zhāng Lì	Xiǎojie, qǐng wèn zhè fùjìn yǒu yóujú ma?
Passer-by	Yǒu a, bù yuǎn, wǎng qián zǒu, xiàng yòu guǎi, zǒu wǔ fēnzhōng dào shí fēnzhōng, jiù dào le.
Zhāng Lì	Ao, xièxie nín.
Passer-by	Bù xiè.

fùjìn	vicinity; nearby	**guǎi**	to turn
yuǎn	far	**yòu**	right
wǎng	towards	**dào**	to
qián	ahead, forward	**fēnzhōng**	minute

zhè fùjìn yǒu yóujú ma? (lit. this vicinity has a post office?) Is there a post office around here?

bù yuǎn not far.

wǎng towards, exactly the same as **xiàng** in Dialogue 1. Also pronounced **wàng**.

wǎng qián zou (lit. towards ahead go) go straight ahead. Note again that the verb, **zǒu** 'to go', goes at the end of the sentence.

xiàng yòu guǎi (lit. towards right turn) turn right. 'Turn left' is **xiàng zuǒ guǎi**. **Zuǒ** is 'left'.

fēnzhōng minute, only used when talking about the length of time it takes to do something. **Zǒu wǔ fēnzhōng dào shí fēnzhōng**, to walk for five to ten minutes.

bù xiè (lit. not to thank) not at all, an alternative to **bù kèqi**.

Practise what you have learned

1

The English sentences below correspond to ten numbered sentences in Mandarin on the recording. Write the number of each recorded sentence in the appropriate box. (Answers on page 68.)

Go straight ahead, turn right. ☐

It's just there. ☐

Go west. ☐

Walk for five to ten minutes. ☐

Yes. Not far. ☐

May I ask, how do I get to Xidan? ☐

Having reached the traffic lights, go north. ☐

May I ask, is there a post office nearby? ☐

Go directly north. ☐

How do I go to the post office? ☐

2

On the recording you will hear five short dialogues. In each case Xiànbin is trying to find the post office. Listen to the directions he is given and answer the questions below. (The question numbers relate to dialogue numbers.) (Answers on page 68.)

(1) (a) What is Xiànbin's question?

Qǐng wèn, zhè fùjìn yǒu yóujú ma? ☐

Qǐng wèn, dào yóujú zěnme zǒu? ☐

(b) Should he walk…

west? ☐ north? ☐

(2) Should he turn…

right? ☐ left? ☐

(3) After turning left, how long will it take him?

five to ten minutes. ☐

five to eight minutes. ☐

(4) (a) What is Z's question?

Qǐng wèn, zhè fùjìn yǒu yóujú ma? ☐

Qǐng wèn, dào yóujú zěnme zǒu? ☐

(b) Is there a post office nearby?

Yes, not far. ☐　　　　No. ☐

(5) When he comes across a set of traffic lights should he go...

west? ☐　　　　　　north? ☐

3 Your turn to speak. Have a go at asking a passer-by the way to different places. Lǐ will prompt you.

Dialogues

3

Where is the post office?

LISTEN FOR...
dōng　east

Zhāng Lì	Xiānsheng, qǐng wèn zhè fùjìn yǒu yóujú ma?
Passer-by	Lí zhèr bù yuǎn jiù yǒu.
Zhāng Lì	Zěnme zǒu?
Passer-by	Wǎng dōng zǒu, yì zhàn dì, jiù dào le.
Zhāng Lì	Ao, xièxie nín.
Passer-by	Bù yòng xiè, bù yòng xiè. Hǎo, zàijiàn a!

dōng　east　　　　**dì**　distance, land　　　　**zhàn**　bus stop, station

---

lí　from, used when talking about distance from a place. **Lí zhèr yǒu shí fēnzhōng**, ten minutes from here. **Lí** goes before the place.

lí zhèr bù yuǎn jiù yǒu　(lit. from here not far just there is) There is one not far from here. **Jiù**, 'just', emphasizes that there is one, also that it is not too far, it's a manageable distance away. **Jiù** crops up a lot, so you will get a feel for how it is used.

yì zhàn dì　(lit. one bus stop distance) one stop away. People often count the number of bus stops to measure distance, even if they are not travelling by bus.

bù yòng xiè　another way of saying 'not at all'. Note that the speaker repeats the phrase. As in previous examples of repetition, this is for emphasis.

zàijiàn　goodbye

4

How do I get to Fùxìngmén?

LISTEN FOR...
nán south

Zhāng Lì	Xiānsheng, qǐng wèn dào Fùxìngmén zěnme zǒu?
Man	Ao ... jiù shì shuō, xiān wǎng nán, ránhòu zài wǎng xī guǎi, yǒu yī ge lìjiāoqiáo, jiù dào Fùxìngmén le.
Zhāng Lì	Xièxie nín.
Man	Méi shì, béng kè.

zài again

nán south

lìjiāoqiáo flyover

Fùxìngmén an area in central Beijing.

jiù shì shuō (lit. just is say) that is to say.

xiān..., ránhòu zài... first..., then...

méi shì it doesn't matter, not at all.

béng kè not at all, a Beijing colloquial expression. Don't worry about learning all these phrases for 'not at all'; to recognize them is enough. Stick with **bù kèqi**, the most common, which you came across in Dialogue 1.

You now know all four points of the compass. Whereas in English the compass points are usually ordered 'north, south, east, west', the Chinese say, **dōng**, **xī**, **nán**, **běi**, 'east, west, south, north'. 'East' goes first because China is in the east. Sometimes **zhōng** 'middle' is also included.

On the buses

Shanghai flyover

Practise what you have learned

4

Listen to the three short conversations between a tourist and a passer-by. What directions are given in each case? Select your answers from the list below and fill in the blanks in the sentences. (Answers on page 68.)

(1) **Xiān** (first)..., **ránhòu zài** (then)...
(2) **Xiān...**, **ránhòu ..., jiù dào le.**
(3) **Xiān...**, **...**, **...**, **ránhòu ..., jiù dào le.**

yù dào hónglǜdēng	yì zhàn dì
wǎng zuǒ guǎi	wǎng dōng zǒu
xiàng dōng zǒu	yù dào hónglǜdēng
xiàng xi guǎi	xiàng qián zǒu

5

Listen to Xiànbin giving directions. Can you work out by looking at the map below which of the following questions he is answering? (Answer on page 68.)

Dào yóujú zěnme zǒu?
Dào fàndiàn zěnme zǒu?
Zhè fùjìn yǒu yóujú ma?

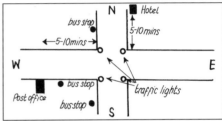

6

Your turn to speak. A Chinese person has advised you how to get back to your hotel using the map above. Make sure you have understood by repeating the way back to her, following the English prompts. Look at the map to help you imagine the way you are going.

Dialogues

5

How do I get to Běitàipíngzhuāng?

> **LISTEN FOR...**
> **nǐ děi** you must
> **zuò èr shí èr lù** take the number 22 (bus)

Wáng Jiànjí	Qǐng wèn, xiǎojie, Běitàipíngzhuāng zěnme zǒu a?
Passer-by	Běitàipíngzhuāng, zhèr shì Xīdān... Xīdān, nǐ děi wǎng qián zuò yìdiǎnr, zuò èr shí èr lù huò sì shí qī lù, dào nèige zhōngdiǎn zhàn jiùshì le.
Wáng Jiànjí	Ao, hǎo, xièxie.
Passer-by	Méi guānxi.

zuò to sit	**lù** road
yìdiǎnr a little	

Běitàipíngzhuāng   another area of Běijīng

nǐ děi wǎng qián zuò yìdiǎnr   (lit. you towards ahead sit a little) You must go a little way by bus. When it appears in conjunction with a bus number, **zuò** 'to sit' is translated in English as 'take'. **Zuò** is also used with other means of transport, including plane, ship, taxi, train.

lù   road, used together with a bus number, means route; here it is route 22. In English we would say the number 22 (bus). **Zuò èr shí èr lù**. Take the number 22 bus. (Numbers on buses, trains and signs are not written in Chinese characters.)

huò   short for **huòzhě**, 'or'. Used in a statement. In a question of choice, use **háishi**, for example, **Nǐ qù zhōng cāntīng háishi xī cāntīng?** Are you going to the Chinese or Western restaurant?

nèige   also pronounced **nàge**, 'that'.

zhōngdiǎn zhàn   last stop, terminus.

jiùshì le   (lit. just is) 'nothing else but': in this case equivalent to 'you're there' (and nowhere else) or 'that's it' (and nothing else).

méi guānxi   another common way of saying 'not at all', 'it doesn't matter', also used in response to an apology.

6

I'm lost

> **LISTEN FOR...**
> **Wǒ mí lù le**   I'm lost

Wáng Jiànjí   Duìbuqǐ xiǎojie, wǒ mí lù le. Qǐng wèn, Běijīng Fàndiàn zěnme zǒu a?
Passer-by   Chū le shìchǎng de kǒu, guò mǎlù, zuò yī lù, sì lù, dào Dōngdān xià chē, jiù kěyǐ dào Běijīng Fàndiàn le.
Wáng Jiànjí   Hǎo, xièxie.
Passer-by   Méi guānxi.

chū to go out, to exit		**mǎlù** road	
shìchǎng market		**xià** to get off	
kǒu entrance, exit		**chē** bus, vehicle	
guò to cross			

> **shìchǎng de kǒu**   the exit of the market
>
> **chū le**   once out. The **le** indicates a complete action.
> **chū le shìchǎng de kǒu**, once you have exited the market.
>
> **zuò yī lù, sì lù**   take the number 1 / number 4 (bus)
>
> **Dōngdān**   an area of Běijīng
>
> **jiù kěyǐ dào Běijīng Fàndiàn le.**   Then [you] can get to the Běijīng Hotel.

Practise what you have learned

7

You will hear a series of phrases spoken by Xiànbin. Match each one to the most appropriate English phrase below, writing the number of the recorded sentence in the box. (Answers on page 68.)

(a) Get off the bus ☐

(b) I'm lost ☐

(c) Here is Dōngdān ☐

(d) Take the number 22 ☐

(e) Cross the road ☐

8

Fill in the blanks using the words in the box below. The English sentences will help you. (Answers page 68.)

(1) We are lost.
Women... le.

(2) Here is Dōngdān.
...shì Dōngdān.

(3) You must go a little way by bus.
...wǎng qián....yìdiǎnr.

(4) First cross the road.
Xiān...

(5) Then take the number 1 or the number 4 bus.
....yī lù...sì lù.

(6) Get off the bus at the Běijīng Hotel.
...Běijīng Fàndiàn...

zuò		dào
xià chē	nǐ děi	
	mí lù	zhèr
guò mǎlù		zuò
ránhòu		huò

9

You are lost and need to get back to the Běijīng Hotel. You stop a man in the street and ask the way. Do this exercise twice. The first time, respond as usual to Lǐ's English prompts. The second time, note down in English the directions the passer-by gives you. Finally, check your answers on page 68 to make sure you have understood.

Beijing hotel

Key words and phrases

To learn

dào...zěnme zǒu?	how do I get to...?
zǒu	to go, to walk
xiàng / wǎng	towards
xiàng / wǎng xī zǒu	to go west
xiān..., ránhòu zài...	first..., then...
hónglǜdēng	traffic lights
jiù dào le	it's just there
fùjìn	nearby, vicinity
zuǒ	left
yòu	right
wǔ dào shí fēnzhōng	five to ten minutes
lí zhèr bù yuǎn	not far from here
wǒ mí lù le	I'm lost
fàndiàn	restaurant, hotel
kǒu	entrance / exit
zuò 22 lù	to take the number 22 (bus)
guò mǎlù	to cross the road
děi	must
xià chē	to get off the bus
dōng	east
xī	west
nán	south
běi	north
bù kèqi	not at all

To understand

bù xiè	not at all
béng kè	not at all
méi guānxi	it doesn't matter, not at all
méi shì	it doesn't matter, not at all

Grammar

Word order using directions

In Chinese the word order of a sentence is often different from that of its English equivalent. Whereas in English in questions asking the way the word indicating place goes at the end, 'How do I get to Xīdān?', in Chinese it comes at the beginning, preceded by the direction word or **dào**, 'to reach'. The verb, often **zǒu** 'go', goes at the end. For example:

a) **dào**
   Dào Xīdān zěnme zǒu?   (lit. To reach Xīdān how to go?) How do I get to Xīdān?

b) **wǎng / xiàng**
   Wǎng dōng zǒu.   (lit. towards east go) Go east.
   Xiàng zuǒ guǎi.   (lit. to left turn) Turn left.

c) **zhíjiē**
   Zhíjiē zǒu.   (lit. straight on go) Go straight ahead.
   Wǎng nán zhíjiē zǒu.   (lit. towards south straight on go) Go directly south.
   or,   **Zhíjiē xiàng nán zǒu.**   (lit. directly towards south go) Go directly south.

Wǎng/xiàng   **Wǎng** and **xiàng** are interchangeable; they both mean 'towards'. Note, however, that when giving directions one or other must be used. (It is incorrect to say **dōng zǒu.**)

Lí   **Lí** meaning 'away from' also goes at the beginning of the sentence, before the word indicating place. For example:

Lí zhèr bù yuǎn.   (lit. Away from here not far) Not far from here.

When the distance between two places is being compared, **lí** is positioned between the two places: A **lí** B (lit. A away from B). For example:

Wǒ jiā lí zhèr bù hěn yuǎn.   (lit. My home away from here not very far) My home is not very far away from here.
Yóujú lí Xīdān bù yuǎn.   (lit. Post office away from Xīdān not far.) The post office is not far from Xīdān.

No wǒ   Note again that in Chinese there is often no need to say **wǒ** 'I', or **nǐ** 'you'. They are simply understood. For example:

(Wǒ) Dào nǐ jiā zěnme zǒu?   (lit. To reach your home how to go?) How do I get to your home?
(Nǐ) Zhíjiē zǒu.   (lit. (You) straight on go) (You) go straight on.

Zǒu/qù   **Zǒu** is used for travel within a specified area like a city and indicates that your destination is within manageable distance on foot, by car or by bus. **Zǒu** cannot be used, for example, when you are in Shànghǎi to ask 'How do I get to Běijīng?' In this case **qù**, 'to go', is used, following a similar sentence pattern as **zǒu**. For example:

Qù Běijīng zěnme qù?   (lit. To go to Běijīng how to go?) How do I get to Běijīng?

10 Put the words in the right order to match the English sentences. (Answers on page 68.)

(1) How do I get to his home?
dào zěnme jiā tā zǒu

(2) Turn left, go east.
zuǒ xiàng dōng wǎng zǒu guǎi

(3) Go directly north.
zhíjiē xiàng zǒu běi

(4) His home is not far from mine.
wǒ jiā tā lí jiā yuǎn bù

(5) How do I go to England?
Yīngguó qù zěnme qù

Getting around Beijing

Read and understand

Maps, street signs and the compass

Chinese people tend to give directions in terms of 'east', 'west', 'north', and 'south', rather than 'left' and 'right'. City districts are often labelled according to their location and sometimes street names tell you your location in relation to a monument or main street, letting you know whether you are on the northern, southern, western or eastern side or part of it:

Dōng Cháng'ān Dàjiē   (lit. East Cháng'ān Avenue) Cháng'ān Avenue East

Cháng'ān is Běijing's main artery, running east–west through the centre of the city.

If you learn the following words, you may be able to work out where you are in a Chinese city, using either a map or signposts – usually in Pinyin as well as in characters.

DŌNG	
XĪ	+ name of street + (usually goes just before or just after the direction)
NÁN	
BĚI	

jiē   street

dàjiē   avenue

lù   road

hútòng   lane

Wangfujing Avenue

Did you know?

China's people

The People's Republic of China (PRC) is the third largest country in the world, after the USSR and Canada, and with over one billion people has the largest population, four times greater than the USA. China's people represent one-fifth of the world's total, and there are also millions of Chinese in other countries in Asia.

The population, however, is not evenly distributed throughout China's twenty-three provinces, four municipalities (Běijīng, Shànghǎi, Tiānjīn and Chóngqìng) and five Autonomous Regions. Owing to striking contrasts in relief and climate – over half the country is covered in mountains and only 12 per cent of the land is arable – 90 per cent of the population inhabits little more than 15 per cent of the total area. Even this productive land, mainly the area stretching inwards from the eastern coastline, is vulnerable to drought and flood.

Only about one-fifth of the population resides in cities and towns; the most populous are Chóngqìng with around 30 million, Shànghǎi with 14 million, and Běijīng with 12 million. The remaining 80 per cent lives in the countryside. This huge population – still growing and unevenly distributed – is therefore a major challenge to China's economic growth.

Birth control

Programmes to control the birth rate were first instituted in the 1950s, but abandoned during the 1960s by Máo Zédōng who believed a large population could only strengthen China. By 1973, however, it was recognized that a reduction in population growth was vital for the successful modernization of China. Whereas in the 1950s planning had concentrated on family planning for 'completed families' which already had perhaps two or three children, the focus now turned to couples wishing to start a family. Campaigns for 'later, spaced and fewer' births were supported by a newly created nationwide committee for family planning, and free contraception available to all. In 1979, the 'single child policy' was introduced, backed up by incentives for compliance, and penalties for non-compliance.

Social and cultural factors have influenced the success of the policy. In the cities, where there is an overall shortage of housing, birth control measures have been more effectively adhered to than in the countryside. The traditional desire of peasants for sons to carry on the family name, and a requirement for large families to work on the family farm, have made implementation of the policy almost impossible. Attempts by peasant families to get round the policy include female infanticide which has created a new problem, namely an imbalance in the ratio of boys to girls, which in turn is expected to create social difficulties as these children come of age.

China's population is imbalanced in other ways: two-thirds are under 30, and half below 20. In addition, there is a growing stratum of old people, life expectancy having increased as a result of improved economic conditions, and this increases pressure on already limited resources, especially in cities.

Ethnicity

Hàn Chinese make up around 94 per cent of the total population; the remaining 6 per cent is composed of 50 or so minority nationalities, including Tibetans and Mongols, who reside mainly, but not exclusively, in border regions.

Your turn to speak

11

First ask the way to the post office following Lǐ's prompts. Then listen to the directions you are given and choose the list below which most accurately reflects what you have heard. (Answers below.)

A
go west
one stop
come to traffic lights
turn right
go two to three minutes
take 22 bus to hotel
cross road

B
go straight ahead
go west
turn left
go five to ten minutes
come to traffic lights
go straight ahead a little bit
take number 22 bus
get off at hotel

Make sure you understand all the directions before moving on to the next Unit.

Answers

Exercise **1**	10, 3, 8, 2, 5, 1, 9, 4, 7, 6
Exercise **2**	(1)(a) **Qǐng wèn, dào yóujú zěnme zǒu?** (b) west (2) right (3) five to eight minutes (4)(a) **Qǐng wèn, zhè fùjìn yǒu yóujú ma?** (b) Yes, not far. (5) West
Exercise **4**	(1) **Xiān wǎng dōng zǒu, ránhòu zài xiàng xī guǎi.** (2) **Xiān xiàng dōng zǒu, ránhòu yù dào hónglǜdēng, jiù dào le.** (3) **Xiān xiàng qián zǒu, yī zhàn dì, yù dào hónglǜdēng, ránhòu wǎng zuǒ guǎi, jiù dào le.**
Exercise **5**	**Dào yóujú zěnme zǒu?**
Exercise **7**	(a)3, (b)2, (c)5, (d)4, (e)1
Exercise **8**	(1) **Wǒmen mí lù le.** (2) **Zhèr shì Dōngdān.** (3) **Nǐ děi wǎng qián zuò yīdiǎnr.** (4) **Xiān guò mǎlù.** (5) **Ránhòu zuò yī lù huò sì lù.** (6) **Dào Běijīng Fàndiàn xià chē.**
Exercise **9**	The Běijīng Hotel is far from here. You must go on a little. Take the number 22 or the 47 bus. At Dōngdān get off the bus, then cross the road. The Běijīng Hotel is just there.

Grammar

Exercise **10**	(1) **Dào tā jiā zěnme zǒu?** (2) **Xiàng / Wǎng zuǒ guǎi, wǎng / xiàng dōng zǒu.** (3) **Xiàng běi zhíjiē zǒu.** or, **Zhíjiē xiàng běi zǒu.** (4) **Tā jiā lí wǒ jiā bù yuǎn.** (5) **Qù Yīngguó zěnme qù?**

Your turn to speak

Exercise **11**	List A is correct.

UNDERSTANDING AND ASKING ABOUT TIME

What you will learn

- to ask and to say the time
- to ask when someone's birthday is
- to say the date and year

- the days of the week
- to say how long (in time)
- about Chinese Spring Festival

Before you begin

You will find the new words and structures in this Unit much easier to cope with if you have a firm grasp on numbers. Revise these by looking at the *Key words and phrases* sections of Units 2 and 3. Learning a language is more effective if you gradually build up knowledge, so make sure you are building on solid, not shaky, foundations.

Airport departures

Dialogue

1

What time is it?

> **LISTEN FOR...**
> **xiànzài shì jǐ diǎn?**   What time is it now?
> (lit. now is how many o'clock?)
> **chà yī kè shí diǎn**   Quarter to ten.
> (lit. short of one quarter ten o'clock)
> **qī diǎn shí fēn**   Ten past seven. (lit. seven o'clock ten minutes)
> **shí yī diǎn bàn**   Half past eleven (lit. eleven o'clock half)

Wáng Jiàn	Qǐng wèn, xiànzài shì jǐ diǎn?
Lǐ	Chà yī kè shí diǎn.
Hènián	Xiànzài shì wǔ diǎn.
Teacher	Xiànzài de shíjiān shì qī diǎn shí fēn.
Yáng	Xiànzài zhènghǎo shì jiǔ diǎn yī kè.
Qián	Xiànzài shì bā diǎn èr shí.
Zhāng	Xiànzài shì shí yī diǎn bàn.
Wèi	Xiànzài shì shí diǎn sān kè.
Chéng	Xiànzài shì chà wǔ fēn shí èr diǎn.

xiànzài	now	**shíjiān**	time
diǎn	o'clock	**fēn**	minute
chà	short of	**zhènghǎo**	exactly
kè	quarter	**bàn**	half

> **xiànzài de shíjiān**   the time now. **De** links a noun with a word which describes it. The main noun comes after **de. Péngyou de fángjiān**. The friend's room.
>
> **qī diǎn shí fēn**   (lit. seven o'clock ten minutes). Ten past seven.
>
> **zhènghǎo shì jiǔ diǎn yī kè**   (lit. exactly it is nine o'clock one quarter.) It's exactly a quarter past nine.
>
> **shí diǎn sān kè**   (lit. ten o'clock three quarters). Ten forty-five.

So, there are three ways to start a sentence stating the time:

Xiànzài shì...   Now it is...
Xiànzài de shíjiān ...   The time now...
Zhènghǎo shì ...   It is exactly...

Another way of asking the time is:
Jǐ diǎn le?   (lit. How many o'clock?) What time is it?

Before going on to the exercises, have a look at the *Grammar* section on page 78 which gives more detail about telling the time.

Practise what you have learned

1

| chà yī kè sì diǎn | jiǔ diǎn yī kè | shí diǎn sān kè | chà wǔ fēn shí èr diǎn |

 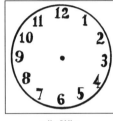 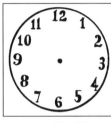 

| bā diǎn èr shí | wǔ diǎn | shí yī diǎn bàn | qī diǎn shí fēn |

Draw hands on these clocks so that they show the times written below them in Pinyin. (Answers on page 82.)

2

Match each Pinyin phrase with the corresponding time in figures. (Answers on page 82.)

(1)	**chà yī kè jiǔ diǎn**	(a) 3.20
(2)	**wǔ diǎn wǔ fēn**	(b) 8.45
(3)	**shí diǎn yī kè**	(c) 3.45
(4)	**qī diǎn yī kè**	(d) 11.55
(5)	**sān diǎn èr shí**	(e) 8.30
(6)	**bā diǎn bàn**	(f) 7.15
(7)	**sān diǎn sān kè**	(g) 5.05
(8)	**chà wǔ fēn shí èr diǎn**	(h) 10.15

3

You will hear six different clock times. After each one tick off (✓) the corresponding time in the box below. Which times did you not hear? (Answers on page 82.)

New word **liǎng** two. Unless you are counting, **èr** 'two' changes to **liǎng**: **liǎng wèi** 'two people' (at restaurant), **liǎng kǒu rén** 'two family members', **liǎng bēi píjiǔ** 'two glasses of beer', **liǎng diǎn** 'two o'clock'.

9.00	7.45	2.05	
	2.45	5.15	1.30
1.55	11.30	8.15	
	12.00		

4 Your turn to speak. Practise telling the time following Lǐ's prompts. A list of times is given below to help you, but not in the order you will need them.

jiǔ diǎn shí fēn
qī diǎn sān kè
liǎng diǎn bàn
chà wǔ fēn liù diǎn

wǔ diǎn
jiǔ diǎn èr shí
chà yī kè sì diǎn
shí yī diǎn yī kè

Dialogues

2

When is your birthday?

LISTEN FOR...

nǐ de shēngri shì nǎ tiān?   When is your birthday?
wǒ de shēngri shì...   My birthday is...
yuè   month
nián   year

Wáng   Nǐ de shēngri shì nǎ tiān a?
Boy   Wǒ de shēngri shì wǔ yuè wǔ rì.
Wáng   Nǎ yī nián ne?
Boy   En ... yī jiǔ bā sān nián.
Wáng   Nǐ shǔ shénme de?
Boy   Wǒ shǔ zhū de.

shēngri   birthday   **zhū**   pig
tiān   day

---

rì   date, a more usual word is **hào**.

nǎ   which. In Běijīng, where the recording was made, the locals pronounce it **něi**.

nǐ de shēngri shì nǎ tiān a?   (lit. your birthday is which day?) Notice how the reply copies the form of the question. **Nǐ de** is replaced by **wǒ de**, and the words for 'which day', **nǎ tiān**, are replaced by the date.

wǔ yuè   May (lit. five month). The months are easy to form: **yī yuè**, 'one month', is January; **èr yuè**, 'two month', February; **sān yuè**, 'three month', March; and so on.

wǔ yuè wǔ rì   as mentioned above, a more usual way of saying this would be **wǔ yuè wǔ hào**, '5th of May'. To express a year, simply say each number of the year individually and add **nián**. So the '5th of May 1983' is **yī jiǔ bā sān nián wǔ yuè wǔ hào**. The '21st June 1954' is **yī jiǔ wǔ sì nián liù yuè èr shí yī hào**. Note that the year comes first, then the month, then the date. The words 'year' **nián**, 'month' **yuè**, 'date' **hào**, which separate the numbers, cannot be omitted.

nǎ yī nián ne?   which year? **Nǎ nián**, 'which year', would have been enough, but adding **yī** makes the question more pointed, 'which particular year?'

> **shǔ** to be born in the year of (one of the twelve animals of the Chinese horoscope).
>
> **Nǐ shǔ shénme de?** which horoscope year were you born in?
>
> **Wǒ shǔ zhū de.** I was born in the year of the pig. **De** in the question means 'which one?' and in the answer 'the one'. This point is explained fully in the *Grammar* section.

3

The days of the week

> **LISTEN FOR...**
>
> **xīngqī yī** Monday, **xīngqī èr** Tuesday, **xīngqī sān** Wednesday, **xīngqī sì** Thursday, **xīngqī wǔ** Friday, **xīngqī liù** Saturday, **xīngqī tiān** Sunday
>
> **shàngwǔ** morning, **zhōngwǔ** midday, **xiàwǔ** afternoon

Wáng Qǐng wèn, dào Xī'ān yī zhōu yǒu jǐ cì hángbān?

Ticket assistant Qǐng děng yīxià, wǒ gěi nín chá. Měi xīngqī yī liǎng bān, xīngqī èr ... xīngqī èr sì bān, xīngqī sān méi yǒu, xīngqī sì yī bān, xīngqī wǔ yī bān, xīngqī liù liǎng bān, xīngqī tiān yī bān.

Wáng Néng gàosu wǒ xīngqī èr hángbān de shíjiān ma?

Ticket assistant Xīngqī èr shàngwǔ liǎng bān: qī diǎn yī kè, hái yǒu zhōng ... zhōngwǔ shí èr diǎn èr shí wǔ. Xiàwǔ sì diǎn sì shí hái yǒu sì diǎn wǔ shí.

yī zhōu a week, per week, every week		**chá** to check
hángbān scheduled flight		**měi** every
gěi for		**gàosu** to tell

> **Xī'ān** capital of Shǎanxi province. One of the ancient capitals of China, famous for the terracotta warriors excavated there.
>
> **cì** refers to **hángbān**, 'flight'. Another 'measure word' as explained in Unit 3. There needs to be a word separating a quantity – in this case **jǐ** 'how many' – from a noun.
>
> **dào Xī'ān yǒu jǐ cì hángbān?** How many scheduled flights per week are there to Xī'ān? **Dào Xī'ān** 'to Xī'ān', goes at the beginning of the sentence; compare the question **Dào Xīdān zěnme zǒu?** in Unit 5.
>
> **(wǒ) gěi nín chá** I'll check for you.
>
> **xīngqī yī** Monday. The days of the week are easy to form. Simply add the number corresponding to the day to **xīngqī**; Monday corresponds to 'one', and the other days from Tuesday to Saturday follow. Sunday is **xīngqī tiān**.
>
> **liǎng bān** two flights; **hángbān** is abbreviated to **bān**.
>
> **néng gàosu wǒ xīngqī èr hángbān de shíjiān ma?** (lit. can you tell me Tuesday's flight times?) As well as linking two nouns (as in Dialogue 1), **de** links complex phrases to nouns. The main noun comes after **de**.
>
> **xīngqī èr shàngwǔ liǎng bān** There are two flights on Tuesday morning.

New words: **jīntiān** today, **míngtiān** tomorrow, **zuótiān** yesterday

Practise what you have learned

5

Grandad 1.6.1915 ☐ Grandma 25.5.1918 ☐ Mother 14.9.1940 ☐ Father 14.2.1939 ☐

Son 19.7.1964 ☐ Daughter-in-law 4.4.1966 ☐ Baby son 2.10.1990 ☐

Which of the dates below correspond to which picture? Write the appropriate letter in the space provided under each picture. (Answers on page 82.) *New word:* **líng** zero.

(a) **yī jiǔ liù liù nián sì yuè sì hào**
(b) **yī jiǔ yī bā nián wǔ yuè èr shí wǔ hào**
(c) **yī jiǔ jiǔ líng nián shí yuè èr hào**
(d) **yī jiǔ sì líng nián jiǔ yuè shí sì hào**
(e) **yī jiǔ yī wǔ nián liù yuè yī hào**
(f) **yī jiǔ liù sì nián qī yuè shí jiǔ hào**
(g) **yī jiǔ sān jiǔ nián èr yuè shí sì hào**

 6 On the recording you will hear a ticket clerk going through the timetable of scheduled flights to Xi'ān. On the notebook below, take down the times of flights available. (Answers on page 82.)

	shàngwǔ (morning)	zhōngwǔ (midday)	xiàwǔ (afternoon)		shàngwǔ (morning)	zhōngwǔ (midday)	xiàwǔ (afternoon)
Xīngqī yī				Xīngqī wǔ			
Xīngqī èr				Xīngqī liù			
Xīngqī sān				Xīngqī tiān			
Xīngqī sì							

7 Practise saying more dates, and have a go at asking someone when their birthday is.

Dialogue

4 *How long is the journey?*

> **LISTEN FOR...**
> **hángchéng dàyuē duōcháng shíjiān?** Approximately how long is the journey? (lit. journey approximately how long time?)
> **xiǎoshí** hour
> **fēnzhōng** minute

Wáng	Nàme wǒ jiù zuò xīngqī èr de fēijī ba.
Ticket assistant	Shàngwǔ háishi xiàwǔ?
Wáng	Shàngwǔ.
Ticket assistant	Ao, shàngwǔ qī diǎn yī kè de?
Wáng	Ao, wǒ jiù zuò qī diǎn yī kè de hángbān.
Ticket assistant	Jǐ ge rén ne?
Wáng	Yī ge rén.
Ticket assistant	Qǐng děng yīxià.
Wáng	Qǐng wèn, hángchéng dàyuē duōcháng shíjiān?
Ticket assistant	Yī xiǎoshí wǔ shí fēnzhōng.

fēijī aeroplane, flight
duōcháng how long? (length of time)

> **nàme...ba** in that case..., the same as **nà...ba** in Unit 3. **Nàme wǒ jiù zuò xīngqī èr de fēijī ba.** (lit. In that case I just sit on Tuesday's flight.) I'll travel on Tuesday's flight. **Jiù** often occurs when a sentence introduces a consequence or conclusion. Remember **zuò**, 'sit', is used to indicate travel by a mode of transport (refer to Unit 5). **De** links two nouns: **xīngqī èr** (Tuesday) and **fēijī** (flight).
>
> **háishi** or. Used in a question that poses a choice, without **ma**. Differs from **huò** 'or', introduced in Unit 5, which is used in a statement.
>
> **shàngwǔ qī diǎn yī kè de [fēijī]** the one at a quarter past seven in the morning. (There is more in the *Grammar* section on page 78 to help you learn how to use **de** in this way.) The **de** gives the preceding phrase the force of an adjective describing the noun **fēijī**. The word flight does not need to be stated as it is obvious from the context; in contrast, in English it is necessary to insert a phrase, either 'the flight at' or 'the one at'.
>
> **hángchéng** journey, usually used to refer to a flight or boat trip.
> **Lùchéng** 'journey' is the more usual word for a train journey.

> yi xiǎoshí wǔ shí fēnzhōng   an hour and fifty minutes. **Diǎn** and
> **fēn** are only used for telling the time. To express length of time,
> **xiǎoshí** 'hour' and **fēnzhōng** 'minute' are used.

Useful phrases: **wǎndiǎn le**   to be delayed. **Wǒ de fēiji wǎndiǎn le.**   My plane is
delayed.
tuīchí liǎng ge xiǎoshí qǐfēi   (lit. postponed two hours take-off)
take-off postponed by 2 hours.

Practise what you have learned

8

Match each Pinyin sentence with its corresponding English sentence.
(Answers on page 82.)

(1) Two hours and forty minutes.
(2) Take-off is postponed by one hour.
(3) My plane is also delayed.
(4) Morning or afternoon.
(5) Approximately how long is the journey?
(6) The one at 7.15 in the morning?
(7) In that case I'll go on Tuesday's flight.

(a) **Shàngwǔ háishi xiàwǔ?**
(b) **Tuīchí yī xiǎoshí qǐfēi.**
(c) **Nàme wǒ jiù zuò xīngqī èr de fēiji ba.**
(d) **Wǒ de fēiji yě wǎndiǎn le.**
(e) **Liǎng xiǎoshí sì shí fēnzhōng.**
(f) **Hángchéng dàyuē duōcháng shíjiān?**
(g) **Shàngwǔ qī diǎn yī kè de?**

9

Snow is causing delays at the airport. On the recording listen to
passengers discussing the situation and indicate below how long each
has been delayed. (Answers on page 82.)

Passenger 1: His plane has been postponed for ___ hours, ___ minutes.

Passenger 2: His plane has been postponed for ___ hours, ___ minutes.

Passenger 3: Her plane has been postponed for ___ hours, ___ minutes.

10

It is your turn to speak. Practise finding out about times of flights and
lengths of journeys.

Key words and phrases

To learn

xiànzài shì jǐ diǎn?	What time is it now?
jǐ diǎn le?	What time is it?
shíjiān	time
diǎn	o'clock
fēn	minute
xiǎoshí	hour
fēnzhōng	minute (length of time)
zhènghǎo	exactly
chà yī kè	quarter to
bàn	half past
yī kè	quarter past
shēngri	birthday
nǐ de shēngri shì nǎ tiān?	when is your birthday?
nián	year
yuè	month
tiān	day
hào	date
shǔ	to be born in (horoscope year)
nǐ shǔ shénme de?	In which horoscope year were you born?
wǒ shǔ...de	I was born in the year of...
zhū	pig
qǐfēi	take-off, to take off
jīntiān	today
míngtiān	tomorrow
zuótiān	yesterday
tuīchí	to postpone
wǎndiǎn le	to be delayed
hángbān	scheduled flight
dào...yǒu jǐ cì hángbān?	How many scheduled flights are there to...?
hángchéng	journey (flight / boat)
lùchéng	journey
...dàyuē duōcháng shíjiān?	Approximately how long (time) is the...?
xīngqī	week

xīngqī yī Monday, **xīngqī èr** Tuesday, **xīngqī sān** Wednesday, **xīngqī sì** Thursday, **xīngqī wǔ** Friday, **xīngqī liù** Saturday, **xīngqī tiān** Sunday, **yī zhōu** a week, per week, every week

shàngwǔ morning, **xiàwǔ** afternoon, **zhōngwǔ** midday

yī yuè January, **èr yuè** February, **sān yuè** March, **sì yuè** April, **wǔ yuè** May, **liù yuè** June, **qī yuè** July, **bā yuè** August, **jiǔ yuè** September, **shí yuè** October, **shí yī yuè** November, **shí èr yuè** December

To understand

chá	check

Grammar

Telling the time

In Chinese, as in English, there are various ways of expressing the time:

(i) The simplest way is to say first the number corresponding to the hour, then **diǎn**, 'o'clock', then the number corresponding to minutes past, then **fēn** 'minute(s)'. Using this method the times shown on the above four clocks are:

  1.15   **yī diǎn shí wǔ fēn**   'one fifteen'
12.50   **shí èr diǎn wǔ shí fēn**   'twelve fifty'
11.30   **shí yī diǎn sān shí fēn**   'eleven thirty'
  9.45   **jiǔ diǎn sì shí wǔ fēn**   'nine forty-five'

Fēn 'minute' is optional for multiples of five or ten minutes above twenty. For example:

shí yī diǎn sān shí (fēn)

(ii) Alternatively you can use **kè** 'quarter', **bàn** 'half', **chà** 'short of', **sān kè** 'three quarters'. So the times on the four clocks can also be expressed as follows:

  1.15   **yī diǎn yī kè**   (lit. one o'clock one quarter) quarter past one
12.50   **chà shí fēn yī diǎn**   (lit. short of ten minutes one o'clock) ten to one
11.30   **shí yī diǎn bàn**   (lit. eleven o'clock half) half past eleven
  9.45   **chà yī kè shí diǎn**   (lit. short of a quarter ten o'clock) quarter to ten
       or, **jiǔ diǎn sān kè**   (lit. nine o'clock three quarters) quarter to ten

Remember that **chà** and the number of minutes go before the hour, for example:

10.45 **chà yī kè shí yī diǎn**   (lit. short of one quarter eleven o'clock)

Dates

(i) When saying a date in Mandarin, the year comes first, then the month, then the date and day. For example:

yī jiǔ jiǔ qī nián yī yuè shí qī hào (or **rì**) **xīngqī èr**   (lit. 1997 year 1 month 17 day Tuesday) Tuesday 17th January 1997

Nián 'year', **yuè** 'month' and **rì** (or **hào**) 'date' cannot be omitted. For the year, simply say the individual numbers in succession, and add **nián**. For example:

yī jiǔ jiǔ qī nián   1997

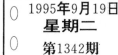

19 September 1995

De Which one? The one...

(1) **Shàngwǔ qī diǎn yī kè de (fēijī)?**
The one at 7.15 am?

(2) **Wǒ jiù zuò xīngqī èr de (fēijī).**
I'll just take the Tuesday flight.

In the above sentences, **de** links a noun with a word or phrase describing it. The main noun goes after **de**. However, the noun can be omitted, if it is understood from the context.

In a question using **de** in this way, the emphasis is on 'which one?' In an answer or statement, the emphasis is on 'the one which'. For example:

Jǐ diǎn de fēijī?   The flight at which time?
Shàngwǔ qī diǎn yī kè de (fēijī).   The one at 7.15 in the morning.

11

Select one of the lists, (a) or (b), to fill in the the blanks. (Answers on page 82.)

(1) My birthday is 28 April 1972.
Wǒ de shēngri shì 1972 ___ 4 ___ 28 ___ .
(a) **nián, hào, yuè**   (b) **nián, yuè, hào**

(2) His birthday is 28 April 1972.
Tā de shēngri shì yī jiǔ qī èr ___ sì ___ èr shí bā ___ .
(a) **nián, ge yuè, tiān**   (b) **nián, yuè, hào**

(3) His flight is at 9.30, the journey lasts approximately six hours twenty minutes.
Tā de fēijī shì jiǔ ___ bàn de, hángchéng dàyuē liù ___ èr shí ___ .
(a) **diǎn, ge diǎn, fēn**   (b) **diǎn, xiǎoshí, fēnzhōng**

(4) His flight is the one at 1.45.
Tā de hángbān shì ___ yī kè ___ diǎn de.
(a) **chà, liǎng**   (b) **diǎn, liǎng**

(5) The morning flight at 8.30 or the afternoon one at 3.45?
___ bā diǎn bàn ___ , háishi ___ sān diǎn sān kè ___ ?
(a) **shàngwǔ, de, xiàwǔ, de**   (b) **shàngwǔ, ge, zhōngwǔ, de**

(6) Now it is 2.30.
Xiànzài shì ___ .
(a) **liǎng diǎn bàn**   (b) **liǎng diǎn sān shí fēn**

(7) Two hours, ten minutes.
Liǎng ___ shí ___ .
(a) **diǎn, fēn**   (b) **xiǎoshí, fēnzhōng**

(8) It is now 2.10.
Xiànzài shì liǎng ___ shí ___ .
(a) **diǎn, fēn**   (b) **xiǎoshí, fēnzhōng**

Read and understand

Astrology

According to legend, one Chinese New Year before 500 BC, Buddha invited all the animals in creation to come to him. Twelve animals did go, and to thank them Buddha offered each a year which for ever would carry the animal's name, and express its symbolic character and specific psychological traits, marking the personality and behaviour of people born during that year.

Tiger hǔ 虎

8.2.1902/28.1.1903
26.1.1914/13.2.1915
13.2.1926/1.2.1927
31.1.1938/18.2.1939
17.2.1950/5.2.1951
5.2.1962/24.1.1963
23.1.1974/10.2.1975
9.2.1986/28.11.1987

Rabbit tù 兔

29.1.1903/15.2.1904
14.2.1915/2.2.1916
2.2.1927/22.1.1928
19.2.1939/7.2.1940
6.2.1951/26.1.1952
25.1.1963/12.2.1964
11.2.1975/30.1.1976
29.1.1987/16.2.1988

Dragon lóng 龙

16.2.1904/3.2.1905
3.2.1916/22.1.1917
23.1.1928/9.2.1929
8.2.1940/26.1.1941
27.1.1952/13.2.1953
13.2.1964/1.2.1965
31.1.1976/17.2.1977
17.2.1988/5.2.1989

Snake shé 蛇

4.2.1905/24.1.1906
23.1.1917/10.2.1918
10.2.1929/29.1.1930
27.1.1941/14.2.1942
14.2.1953/2.2.1954
2.2.1965/20.1.1966
18.2.1977/6.2.1978
6.2.1989/26.1.1990

Horse mǎ 马

25.1.1906/12.2.1907
11.2.1918/31.1.1919
30.1.1930/16.2.1931
15.2.1942/4.2.1943
3.2.1954/23.1.1955
21.1.1966/8.2.1967
7.2.1978/27.1.1979
27.1.1990/14.2.1991

Goat yáng 羊

13.2.1907/1.2.1908
1.2.1919/19.2.1920
17.2.1931/5.2.1932
5.2.1943/24.1.1944
24.1.1955/11.2.1956
9.2.1967/28.1.1968
28.1.1979/15.2.1980
15.2.1991/3.2.1992

Monkey hóu 猴

2.2.1908/21.1.1909
20.2.1920/7.2.1921
6.2.9132/25.1.1933
25.1.1944/12.2.1945
12.2.1956/30.1.1957
29.1.1968/16.2.1969
16.2.1980/4.2.1981
4.2.1992/22.1.1993

Rooster jī 鸡

22.1.1909/9.2.1910
8.2.1921/27.1.1922
26.1.1933/13.2.1934
13.2.1945/1.2.1946
31.1.1957/15.2.1958
17.2.1969/5.2.1970
5.2.1981/24.1.1982
23.1.1993/9.2.1994

Dog gǒu 狗

19.2.1910/29.1.1911
28.1.1922/15.2.1923
14.2.1934/3.2.1935
2.2.1946/21.1.1947
16.2.1958/7.2.1959
6.2.1970/26.1.1971
25.1.1982/12.2.1983
10.2.1994/30.1.1995

Pig zhū 猪

30.1.1911/17.2.1912
16.2.1923/4.2.1924
4.2.1935/23.1.1936
22.1.1947/9.2.1948
8.2.1959/27.1.1960
27.1.1971/14.2.1972
13.2.1983/1.2.1984
31.1.1995/18.2.1996

Rat shǔ 鼠

18.2.1912/5.2.1913
5.2.1924/24.1.1925
24.1.36/10.2.1937
10.2.1948/28.1.1949
28.1.1960/14.2.1961
15.2.1972/2.2.1973
2.2.1984/19.2.1985
19.2.1996/7.2.1997

Ox niú 牛

6.2.1913/25.1.1914
25.1.1925/12.2.1926
11.2.1937/30.1.38
29.1.1949/16.2.1950
15.2.1961/4.2.1962
3.2.1973/22.1.1974
20.2.1985/8.2.1986
8.2.1997/27.1.1998

Dates specify first and last day of the year of the sign.

Did you know?

Spring festival

The main Chinese holiday is the three-day Spring Festival, known as Chinese New Year in the West. It starts on the first day of the lunar calendar, usually in late January or early February. Traditionally the Spring Festival was one of three occasions for businesses to balance their books. Debtors unable to pay by this time often went into hiding from their creditors until New Year's Day, when unrecovered debts would have to be held over until the Dragon Boat Festival in early May. Today it is a time for family reunions and visits to friends, and respite from the hard work of the rest of the year. A desire for happiness and prosperity is reflected in the customs surrounding the festival. Many couples choose this time for their wedding.

Great importance is attached to eating and drinking, with food prepared in advance – traditionally no knife or other sharp object could be used during the first few days of the New Year in case it cut off the good luck. The large quantity of food prepared symbolizes abundance and wealth for the household; food is also often given as a present, implying that the giver does not lack the necessities of life and wishes to share abundance. In south China favourite dishes are **nián gāo**, sweet steamed glutinous rice pudding, and **zòng zì**, a pyramid of glutinous rice wrapped in leaves. In the North, steamed wheat bread, **mán tou**, and small meat dumplings, **jiǎo zi**, are popular. Sweets, coins, peanuts, dates and chestnuts are added to the fillings of some of the dumplings; to get one of these is considered good luck. Coins mean one will never lack money, peanuts stand for long life, and dates and chestnuts signify the imminent arrival of a son.

Preparations begin at least a week ahead, although children are already setting off firecrackers – to scare off evil spirits and ghosts -two weeks in advance. In keeping with the traditional belief that misfortune is swept away with dust, homes are thoroughly cleaned, and decorated with paper lanterns and New Year pictures signifying abundance, wealth and happiness. The fish is one symbol, the words for 'fish' and 'abundance' both being **yú**; peaches symbolize long life. Long strips of red paper – couplets – are pasted up either side of doorways wishing good luck in the year to come.

On New Year's Eve families stay at home, exchange small gifts – sweets, toys, perhaps money – and feast together, often settling down later to watch comedy or other entertainment on TV. The first day of the year is devoted to feasting and visiting friends, usually wearing new clothes.

People greet each other saying, **guò nián hǎo** (lit. passing year good) 'happy New Year' or **gōng xǐ fā cái** 'happiness and prosperity'.

A country wedding

Your turn to speak

12

Look over the *Key words and phrases* again before you do this
exercise. Then, listening to the recording and following Lǐ's prompts,
have a go at booking a ticket to Xī'ān.

Answers

Practise what you have learned	Exercise **1**	3.45, 9.15, 10.45, 11.55, 8.20, 5.00, 11.30, 7.10
	Exercise **2**	(1)(b); (2)(g); (3)(h); (4)(f); (5)(a); (6)(e); (7)(c); (8)(d)
	Exercise **3**	You did not hear 12.00, 1.30, 1.55, 8.15
	Exercise **5**	Grandad (e), grandma (b), mother (d), father (g), son (f), daughter-in-law (a), baby son (c)
	Exercise **6**	**xīngqī yī, shàngwǔ** 8.30; **xīngqī èr, shàngwǔ** 10.00, **xià wǔ** 3.15; **xīngqī sān**, none; **xīngqī sì, shàngwǔ** 7.55, **xià wǔ** 4.45, 6.20; **xīngqī wǔ, zhōngwǔ** 12.25; **xīngqī liù, zhōngwǔ** 12.25; **xīngqī tiān**, none
	Exercise **8**	(1)(e); (2)(b); (3)(d); (4)(a); (5)(f); (6)(g); (7)(c)
	Exercise **9**	Passenger 1: two hours and twenty minutes Passenger 2: one hour Passenger 3: three hours and ten minutes

Grammar	Exercise **11**	(1)(b); (2)(b); (3)(b); (4)(a); (5)(a); (6)(a) and (b) are both correct; (7)(b); (8)(a)

SHOPPING (1)

What you will learn

- to understand and to answer a shop assistant's questions
- to ask for what you want in a shop
- to ask the price of an item
- to request something cheaper
- to send an airmail letter
- weights and measures
- something about Chinese medicine

Before you begin

In this Unit you will learn phrases needed for shopping. Some of the key ones are similar to those you encountered in Unit 3 for ordering drinks, and you may find it helpful to refer back. There is also more practice in dealing with Chinese currency, again building on what you learned in Unit 3.

Indoor market

Dialogues

1

Buying cigarettes

> **LISTEN FOR...**
> **mǎi**   to buy

Seller	Xiānsheng, nín mǎi diǎnr shénme?
Wáng	En... mǎi hé yān.
Seller	Mǎi shénme yān?
Wáng	En, wànbǎolù.
Seller	Wànbǎolu bā kuài wǔ.
Wáng	En, zài lái yī hé huǒchái.
Seller	Huǒchái yī máo. Yīgòng bā kuài liù.

hé	packet	**Wànbǎolù**	Marlboro
yān	cigarette	**huǒchái**	matches

nín mǎi diǎnr shénme?   (lit. you buy a little what?) What would you like to buy?

en   a hesitation word

mǎi hé yān   (lit. buy a packet of cigarettes). This is the most basic way of expressing what you want: say the verb **mǎi** 'buy', then the thing you want to buy

mǎi shénme yān?   (lit. buy what cigarettes?). In other words, 'What type of cigarettes do you want to buy?'

Wànbǎolù bā kuài wǔ   (lit. Marlboro eight yuán five máo). Refer back to Dialogue 6, Unit 3, if you need to remind yourself about Chinese money.

zài lái yī hé huǒchái   In addition, bring me a box of matches. **Lái** 'come', means 'bring' in this context, just as in Dialogue 4 of Unit 3, when Wáng said, **Gěi wǒ lái yī bēi báilándì ba.** Bring me a glass of brandy. As when he asked for cigarettes, Wáng might alternatively have said **Zài mǎi yī hé huǒchái.**

2

Buying tea

> **LISTEN FOR...**
> **wǒ xiǎng mǎi**   I would like to buy
> **nín zhèr dōu yǒu shénme chá?**   What teas do you have here?
> **gěi wǒ lái...**   Bring me...

Shop assistant	Nín hǎo, nín xūyào xiē shénme?
Wáng	Wǒ xiǎng mǎi diǎnr cháyè, nín zhèr dōu yǒu shénme chá ya?
Shop assistant	Wǒmen zhèlǐ yǒu hóng chá, huā chá, lǜ chá, nín xǐhuan nǎ zhǒng?
Wáng	Yào... gěi wǒ lái yī liǎng hóng chá, liǎng hé huā chá, sān dàir lǜ chá ba.
Shop assistant	Hǎo de, qǐng shāo děng.

xūyào	to need	huā chá	jasmine tea
cháyè	tea leaves	xǐhuan	to like
lù chá	green tea	dàir	bag
hóng chá	black tea		

xiē some, short for **yīxiē**.

nín xūyào xiē shénme? (lit. you need some what?) What do you need?

cháyè tea leaves. **Chá** and **cháyè** are interchangeable in the context where the tea itself is indicated. But if you want a *drink* of tea, only **chá** is correct.

nín zhèr dōu yǒu shénme chá ya? **dōu** 'all' can be used in two ways: (i) Here, **dōu** refers to the *object* of the question, the tea, and emphasizes the expectation of a list of teas in reply. Similarly, **Nǐ dōu xiǎng chī shénme?** You would like to eat what? The **dōu** relates to **shénme** and emphasizes that a list of several things the person would like to eat is expected. (ii) You will also come across sentences where **dōu** refers to the *subject*, for example, **Wǒmen dōu hē píjiǔ.** We are all drinking beer. This time the emphasis is on everyone having a beer.

ya a question indicator, optional with **shénme** (as explained in the *Grammar* section of Unit 2).

nǎ zhǒng which kind, which type?

liǎng about 50 grams, one-tenth of a **jīn** (about half a kilogram). Weights and measures are explained in *Read and understand* in Unit 8. **Liǎng** is not to be confused with the other **liǎng** meaning 'two'. You have learned that when talking about a quantity 'two' is **liǎng**. The exception is when you are talking about two-tenths of a **jīn**, two **liǎng**, in which case you say **èr liǎng** and not **liǎng liǎng**, to avoid confusion.

yào... gěi wǒ lái yī liǎng hóngchá, liǎng hé huāchá, sān dàir lùchá ba Bring me a *liǎng* of black tea, two packets of jasmine tea, three bags of green tea. After **yào** 'want' Wáng changed his mind about what he was going to say. He then used **gěi wǒ lái**, 'bring me'. This phrase was also used in Unit 3, dialogue 4. As you can see tea is sold in a variety of packaging – note that there must be a measure word, whether *liǎng*, box, or bag, separating the number and the noun 'tea'.

Tea plantation

Practise what you have learned

1 Match each Pīnyīn sentence with its English translation. Try to work out the meaning of the sentences before you look back to the dialogues for help. (Answers on page 96.)

(a) **Nín xūyào xiē shénme?**
(b) **Nín mǎi diǎnr shénme?**

(c) **Yī liǎng hóng chá.**

(d) **Mǎi hé yān.**
(e) **Nín xǐhuan nǎ zhǒng?**
(f) **Sān dàir lǜ chá.**
(g) **Nín zhèr yǒu shénme chá?**
(h) **Mǎi shénme yān?**

(i) **Zài lái yī hé huǒchái.**
(j) **Wǒ xiǎng mǎi diǎnr cháyè.**
(k) **Liǎng hé huā chá.**

(1) One *liǎng* of black tea.
(2) In addition bring me a box of matches.
(3) Which cigarettes do you want to buy?
(4) What teas do you have here?
(5) Two packets of jasmine tea.
(6) I would like to buy some tea.
(7) Three bags of green tea.
(8) Do you want to buy something?
(9) Do you need something?
(10) I want a packet of cigarettes.
(11) Which type do you like?

2 Complete five question and answer dialogues between Lǐ and the shop assistant. Note that the assistant has four questions and Lǐ has one. The first two take place at the tobacco kiosk and the remainder at the counter selling tea. (Answers on page 96.)

(1) **Nín mǎi diǎnr shénme?**
(2) **Mǎi shénme yān?**
(3) **Nín xūyào xiē shénme?**
(4) **Nín xǐhuan nǎ zhǒng?**
(5) **Wǒmen zhèr yǒu hóng chá, huā chá, lǜ chá.**

(a) **Mǎi hé yān.**

(b) **Wǒ xiǎng mǎi diǎnr cháyè.**

(c) **Lái yī liǎng hóng chá.**

(d) **Nín zhèr dōu yǒu shénme cháyè?**

(e) **Wànbǎolù.**

3 It is now your turn to practise responding to a shop assistant's questions and saying what you want to buy. You'll need the phrases for buying a packet of cigarettes and some jasmine tea: **yī hé yān** and **yī liǎng huā chá**.

Dialogues

3

Too expensive! I want to buy a cheaper one.

LISTEN FOR...
tài guì le   too expensive
Wǒ xiǎng mǎi piányi yìdiǎnr de   I want to buy a slightly cheaper
one.

Shop assistant	Zhè hé cháyè shì sì shí wǔ yuán.
Zhāng Lì	Sì shí wǔ yuán tài guì le. Wǒ xiǎng mǎi piányi yìdiǎnr de.
Shop assistant	Zhè hé cháyè shì sān shí wǔ yuán.
Zhāng Lì	Nà jiù yào zhè hé.

guì   expensive
piányi   cheap

> **tài guì le**   too expensive. As explained in the *Grammar* section of
> Unit 4, **tài** and **le** sandwiching an adjective emphasize it – they
> mean 'too', or 'very'. **Tài hǎo le**, 'very good', 'excellent'.
>
> **piányi yìdiǎnr de**   a slightly cheaper one. In full **de** would connect
> the adjectival phrase **piányi yìdiǎnr** with the noun **cháyè**, but
> because **cháyè** can be understood from the context, it is omitted.
> So it can be translated as 'the one', as explained in Unit 6. Refer
> back to the *Grammar* section of Unit 6 for a reminder on this
> point.
>
> **zhè hé cháyè sān shí wǔ yuán**   this packet of tea is thirty-five
> Yuán.
>
> **nà jiù yào zhè hé**   (lit. in that case just want this packet) I'll take
> this packet.

4

Sending an airmail letter

LISTEN FOR...
hángkōng xìn dào...   airmail to...
Měiguó   America, the USA (lit. beautiful country)
guàhào xìn   registered mail
píng xìn   ordinary mail

Hènián	Hángkōng xìn dào Měiguó.
Post office assistant	En, nín yào shì guàhào háishi yào píng xìn ne?
Hènián	Píng xìn jiù kěyǐ le.
Post office assistant	Píng xìn shì liǎng kuài qián.
Hènián	Hǎo de.

xìn letter
qián money

> **Měiguó** America. **Guó** means 'country'. In Unit 4 you came across **Zhōngguó** 'China'. Some other countries are **Yīngguó** 'the UK' **Fǎguó** 'France', **Déguó** 'Germany'.
>
> **nín yào shì guàhào háishi yào píng xìn?** Do you want registered or ordinary mail? To be grammatically correct this sentence should be **Nín yào de shì...**, 'The mail you want...', i.e. the same type of sentence you came across in Unit 4 (refer to the *Grammar* section of that Unit).
>
> **píng xìn jiù kěyǐ le** ordinary mail is OK / will do. **Jiù kěyǐ le** is a useful phrase to have at the ready since it can be used in all sorts of situations, often to round off a conversation.
>
> **liǎng kuài qián** two Yuán. Remember, **qián** 'money' is optional in a statement, but is commonly used.

Some useful   **yì zhāng yóupiào** a stamp, **yì zhāng míngxìnpiàn** a postcard,
words: **jì xìn** to send a letter

Practise what you have learned

 4

On the recording you will hear a conversation between a shop assistant and Zhāng Lì, who wants to buy some tea. There is plenty of choice and prices vary. Listen to the conversation first, then write down in English the answers to the following questions. (Answers on page 96.)

(1) What teas does the shop stock? ....

(2) What kind of tea does Zhāng Lì want? ....

(3) How much is the first packet of tea? ....

(4) What does she say when she hears the price of the second, cheaper tea? ....

(5) How much is the tea that she buys? ....

5

From the box below, select the most appropriate words to fill in the blanks in the sentences. The English translation is given to help you. (Answers on page 96.)

(1) _____ **dào Měiguó.** Airmail to America.

(2) **Píng xìn háishi** _____? Ordinary or registered mail?

(3) **Tài** _____ **le!** Too expensive!

(4) **Zhè hé chá** _____. This packet of tea is cheap.

(5) **Wǒ xiǎng mǎi** _____.
I want to buy a cheaper one.

(6) _____ **zhè hé.** In that case I'll take this packet.

> **nà jiù yào**
>
> **piányi**
>
> **qián**
>
> **guì**
>
> **guàhào xìn**
>
> **píng xìn**
>
> **piányi yìdiǎnr de**
>
> **hángkōng xìn**

6

Practise buying tea and asking for something cheaper to improve your bartering skills.

Useful phrases are:

tài guì le! too expensive!
wǒ xiǎng mǎi piányi yìdiǎnr de. I want to buy a slightly cheaper one.

Dialogues

5

Buying vegetables in the market

> **LISTEN FOR...**
> **duōshao qián** (lit. how much money) How much does it cost?
> **yī jīn** a *jīn*, half a kilogram

Vegetable seller	Nín yào diǎnr shénme?
Man	Yào diǎnr hélándòu. Zhè hélándòu duōshao qián yī jīn ne?
Seller	Bā kuài.
Man	Bā kuài ya.
Seller	Lái duōshao, nín?
Man	Lái bàn jīn ba.

hélándòu mange-touts, snowpeas

duōshao how many, how much. This is a question word, and therefore **ma** is not needed at the end of the sentence. Refer to the *Grammar* section of Unit 2.

zhè hélándòu duōshao qián yī jìn? How much for a *jīn* of mange-touts? As usual, the noun of interest occurs at the beginning of the question.

lái duōshao? (lit. bring how many / how much). The seller means, 'How much do you want?'

bàn jīn half a *jīn*.

Lái bàn jīn ba. Bring me half a *jīn*. Again, **lái** can be translated as 'I want', or 'give me', as explained in Unit 3, Dialogue 4.

6

More shopping at the market

> **LISTEN FOR...**
> **zěnme mài?** Another way of asking how much things cost. (lit. how sell?) How much are you selling [it] for?

Seller	Nín zhè yángcōng chà liǎng qián yī jīn.
Man	Ai, liǎng qián yī jīn, jiù zhè yàng ba. Duōshao qián zhè ge?
Seller	Zhè ge shì jiǔ máo bā de.
Man	Jiǔ máo bā a. Zhè ge shēngjiāng zěnme mài?
Seller	Shēngjiāng liǎng kuài wǔ yī jīn.
Man	Liǎng kuài wǔ yī jīn a, gěi lái ge èr liǎng ba.
Seller	Zhè duō diǎnr xíng ba, nín?
Man	Duō diǎnr, xíng, xíng, xíng, xíng.

yángcōng	onion	**duō**	more
shēngjiāng	fresh ginger		

qián about 5 grams, one-tenth of a **liǎng** (see *Read and Understand*, Unit 8.) **Nín zhè yángcōng chà liǎng qián yī jīn** (lit. your these onions short of two **qián** a **jīn**) These onions weigh two *qián* less than a *jīn*.

jiù zhè yàng ba so be it. Learn this phrase – it is a useful one and will keep on cropping up.

duōshao qián zhè ge? How much is this? The speaker was referring to the onions which had been weighed for him. **Zhè ge**, 'this' (plus measure word), is useful. If you don't know the word for something you wish to buy, you can point to it and ask this question.

zhè ge shì jiǔ máo bā de This one is nine *máo* eight *fēn*. This use of **de**, 'the one', was introduced in Unit 6. The noun omitted after **de** is **yángcōng**, 'onions'.

gěi lái ge èr liǎng ba Bring me two *liǎng*. **Wǒ** is omitted after **gěi** 'for', since it is obvious and understood that the man wants the ginger for himself. **Ge** is not needed here.

zhè duō diǎnr (lit. this more a little) This is a little bit over.

xíng ba, nín? Is it all right? The seller keeps referring to the man as **nín**, which is a way of being politely familiar.

Turn now to the *Key words and phrases* for more shopping vocabulary.

Practise what you have learned

7

To improve your communication with others it is useful to learn alternative ways of expressing the same thing. Each of the questions in the left-hand column is interchangeable with one in the right. Can you match them up? (Answers on page 96.)

(1) **Nǐ mǎi diǎnr shénme?**
(2) **Nín yào diǎnr shénme?**
(3) **Duōshao qián?**
(4) **Mǎi shénme yān?**
(5) **Nín hái yào diǎnr shénme?**
(6) **Lái duōshao?**

(a) **Nín zài lái diǎnr shénme?**
(b) **Nín mǎi diǎnr shénme?**
(c) **Yào duōshao?**
(d) **Zěnme mài?**
(e) **Nǐ xǐhuan nǎ zhǒng yān?**
(f) **Nǐ xūyào xiē shénme?**

8

Xiànbīn is price conscious and always asks how much things cost. Listen to his conversations with various shop assistants on the recording. Then fill in the price of each of the items on his list. A selection of prices to choose from is given below to help you. You will need to recognize the words for units of currency, **kuài**, **máo** and **fēn**, as well as those for weights, **jīn** and **liǎng**. (Answers on page 96.)

SHOPPING LIST		
quantity	item	price
....	Marlboro cigarettes	....
....	matches	....
....	green tea	....
....	onions	....
....	ginger	....
....	apples	....

Next, listen again to ascertain how much he buys of each item. Now fill in the quantity column on the list. A selection of quantities is also given below. (Answers on page 96.)

1 packet 1 box 2 *liǎng* 1 *liǎng* 1 bag half a *jīn* 2	¥10 ¥8.50 ¥3 ¥2.50 ¥4 ¥10 ¥0.10 ¥1 ¥8

9

Practise saying how much of an item you want, and asking how much it costs. Lǐ will prompt you. You will need:
duōshao qián?
zěnme mài?
lái...

Key words and phrases

To learn

mǎi	to buy
mài	to sell
hé	box, packet
dàir	bag
yān	cigarettes
huǒchái	matches
cháyè	tea leaves
yǒu shénme chá?	What tea do you have?
hóng chá	black tea
lǜ chá	green tea
huā chá	jasmine tea
xǐhuan	to like
guì	expensive
tài guì le	too expensive
piányi	cheap
piányi yìdiǎnr	a bit cheaper
hángkōng xìn	air mail
guàhào xìn	registered mail
píng xìn	ordinary mail
duōshao	how much
duōshao qián?	how much (money)?
zěnme mài?	How much are you selling it for?
yángcōng	onion
shēngjiāng	fresh ginger
duō	more
dōu	all
jiù zhè yàng ba	so be it
Měiguó	America
Fǎguó	France
Yīngguó	the UK
Déguó	Germany

To understand

nín mǎi diǎnr shénme?	What would you like to buy?
mǎi shénme yān?	Which cigarettes do you want to buy?
nǐ xūyào xiē shénme?	What do you need?
nín xǐhuan nǎ zhǒng?	Which type do you like?

More shopping vocabulary:

Vegetables

cōng spring onion, scallion
qīngjiāo green pepper
tǔdòu potato
xīhóngshì tomato
báicài Chinese leaves, Chinese cabbage
húluóbo carrot

Fruit

píngguǒ apple
lí pear
táo peach
júzi orange
xiāngjiāo banana
pútáo grapes
xiguā water melon

Grammar

Asking the price

If you do not know the Chinese for the goods you wish to buy, and they are on display, the simplest way of finding out how much they cost is to point and say,
zhè ge duōshao qián? (lit. this how much?) How much is this?
or, **duōshao qián?** How much?

Alternatively, state the name of the things you want to buy and follow up with **duōshao qián?** or **zěnme mài?**

Prices of things sold by weight and bought in large quantities, like onions, are generally asked about and quoted per *jīn* (500 grams). For example:
duōshao qián yī jīn? How much for a *jīn*?
sì kuài yī jīn Four Yuán a *jīn*

For goods usually sold in smaller quantities, like ginger, prices tend to be quoted per *liǎng* (50 grams):
duōshao qián yī liǎng?

For goods sold in some sort of package, ask,
duōshao qián yī hé? How much for a box?
duōshao qián yī dàir? How much for a bag?
etc.

Duōshao qián? 'How much (money)?' can go before or after the quantity. For example,

Yángcōng duōshao qián yī jīn?
or, **Yángcōng yī jīn duōshao qián?**
How much is a *jīn* of onions?

Yān duōshao qián yī hé?
or, **Yī hé yān duōshao qián?**
How much is a packet of cigarettes?

Zhè zhǒng cháyè duōshao qián yī liǎng?
or, **Zhè zhǒng cháyè yī liǎng duōshao qián?**
How much is it for a *liǎng* of this kind of tea?

An alternative way of asking how much things cost is using **zěnme mài?** (lit. how sell). For example:
Shēngjiāng zěnme mài? How much is the fresh ginger?
Yángcōng zěnme mài? How much are the onions?
Zhè ge zěnme mài? How much are you selling this for?

Questions and Answers

As explained in *Grammar* sections of Units 2 and 3, a simple way of forming answers is to use the basis of the question. For example:

Mǎi diǎnr shénme? (lit. buy some what?) What do you want?
Mǎi diǎnr cháyè. (lit. buy some tea) Some tea.

Nǐ mǎi shénme? What are you buying?
Mǎi hé yān. Buying a packet of cigarettes.

Lái duōshao? How much do you want?
Lái yī jīn. A *jīn*.

In each of the examples, the question word is replaced in the answer by the relevant noun.

10 Fill in the blanks with the options (a) or (b) below. (Answers on page 96.)

(1) **Yángcōng _____ yī jīn?**
How much for a *jīn* of onions?
(a) **duōshao qián**   (b) **duōshao**

(2) **Huǒchái duōshao qián yī _____?**
How much for a box of matches?
(a) **hé**   (b) **jīn**

(3) **Cháyè _____ duōshao qián?**
How much for a box of tea?
(a) **yī hé**   (b) **hé**

(4) **Lái _____ nín?**
How much do you want?
(a) **duōshao**   (b) **duōshao qián**

(5) **Zhè zhōng cháyè duōshao qián yī _____?**
How much for a *liǎng* of this type of tea?
(a) **jīn**   (b) **liǎng**

Read and understand

Gestures are as important in China as they are anywhere. Learn how to count using hand signals, and you will run no risk of getting 10 (**shí**) oranges from the fruit-seller in the market when you wanted 4 (**sì**)!

  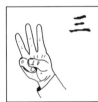 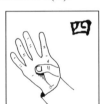

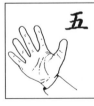  

Did you know?

Health

'Prevention before cure' sums up the Chinese approach to health. Emphasis is on a balanced diet, as described in *Did you know?* Unit 10, and daily exercise – walk around any park at about 6 a.m. and you will find it full of people of all ages doing exercises or practising **tài jí quán** (t'ai chi ch'üan).

Medicine

Chinese medicine is essentially holistic: balance of mind, body and spirit is necessary for complete health. Imbalance within this system means there will be sickness. The focus of healing, therefore, is to restore balance to the system, and not simply to treat any one symptom in isolation.

Taking into account the whole picture means looking at external, internal and miscellaneous causes of disharmony. External causes are environmental – man is part of nature and is therefore affected by seasonal and climatic changes. Internal causes are emotional; there can be no separation of feelings from the body. For example, people who are sad are considered prone to lung disease: depressed people do not breathe enough, which is why they sigh a lot, and it follows that problems will arise in the lungs and respiratory system. Vice versa, it is thought that people with lung disease often suffer from melancholy. Taking a brisk walk will make the walker breathe more deeply and temporarily counteract depression. Miscellaneous causes are neither external nor internal. Examples include unhealthy eating, or a serious injury – the latter, through blockages in blood circulation, may result in cell damage and give rise to linked diseases.

The 'Four Examinations'

On a visit to a Chinese doctor a person undergoes the 'Four Examinations'. These are concerned with 'looking', including a reading of the tongue, according to a highly developed system which sees significance in the colour, shape and coating of it; 'listening and smelling', checking for indications of excess or deficiency; 'asking', about behaviour and sleep patterns, family history, diet, emotional state; and 'touching', focusing on the pulse, from which the doctor can tell the condition of the various internal organs.

Acupuncture

A basic principle in Chinese beliefs about the body is that there are a number of 'meridians', channels connecting major organs through which energy, **qì**, flows. Blockages in these channels, preventing the free flow of energy, cause illness. Acupuncture uses needles, and acupressure the fingers, to press on strategic points along the meridians and to create a surge of energy flow, which will in turn break through such blockages. There are around 2,000 such points, but only about 150 are commonly used.

11

Your turn to speak

Before attempting this exercise, make sure you are familiar with the *Key words and phrases* of this Unit. Then have a go at buying a few things. See how you get on understanding and responding to the assistant's questions. Lǐ will prompt you.

Guilin market

Answers

Practise what you have learned	**Exercise 1** (1)(c); (2)(i); (3)(h); (4)(g); (5)(k); (6)(j); (7)(f); (8)(b); (9)(a); (10)(d); (11)(e)
	Exercise 2 1(a); (2)(e); (3)(b); (4)(c); (5)(d)
	Exercise 4 (1) Black tea, green tea, jasmine (2) Jasmine (3) 24 Yuán (4) Too expensive! (5) 12 Yuán.
	Exercise 5 (1) **hángkōng xìn** (2) **guàhào xìn** (3) **guì** (4) **piányi** (5) **piányi yìdiǎnr de** (6) **nà jiù yào.**
	Exercise 7 (1)(f); (2)(b); (3)(d); (4)(e); (5)(a); (6)(c)
	Exercise 8 1 packet Marlboro, ¥8.50; 1 box matches, ¥0.10; 1 bag green tea, ¥10; 2 onions, ¥3 a *jin*; 2 *liǎng* of ginger, ¥2.50 a *jin*; half a *jin* of apples, ¥8 a *jin*.
Grammar	**Exercise 10** (1)(a); (2)(a); (3)(a); (4)(a); (5)(b)

SHOPPING (2)

What you will learn

- to buy medicine for a cold
- to ask if you can pay by credit card
- to buy an item of clothing and

change it for a different size
- to exchange travellers cheques
- to buy souvenirs
- about shopping in China

Before you begin

Now that you are half way through the course you should be getting a feel for how to express yourself in Chinese. Often, it is quite straightforward to form sentences because of the economical use of words – there are no link verbs with adjectives for example. Word order, however, may be quite different to English. The *Grammar* section in this Unit draws together the principles of word order, illustrated by example sentences. It is worth spending some time on this section.

Painting fans

Dialogues

1

Chinese or Western medicine?

> **LISTEN FOR...**
> **yào**   medicine
> **Zhōng yào hǎo háishi xī yào hǎo?**   Is Chinese medicine good or
> Western medicine good?

Wáng	Yǒu zhì gǎnmào de yào ma?
Shop Assistant	Yǒu. Yào zhōng yào, yào xī yào?
Wáng	Zhōng yào hǎo háishi xī yào hǎo a?
Shop Assistant	Zhōng yào hǎo.
Wáng	Nà, yǒu shénme zhōng yào ne?
Shop Assistant	Zhōng yào yǒu nàge gǎnmào ruǎn jiāonáng.
Wáng	Duōshao qián?
Shop Assistant	Sān kuài jiǔ yī hé.
Wáng	Wǒ mǎi yī hé ba.
Shop Assistant	Yī hé shì shí lì.
Wáng	Yào zěnme chī?
Shop Assistant	Yī tián liǎng cì, měi cì chī liǎng lì.

zhì	to cure, to treat	**ruǎn jiāonáng**	capsule
gǎnmào	cold	**lì**	tablet
yào	medicine	**cì**	time
xī yào	Western medicine		

> **yǒu zhì gǎnmào de yào ma?**   (lit. have any to treat a cold medicine).
> Do you have any medicine to treat a cold? The **de** links **zhì gǎnmào**,
> the words which describe the noun, with **yào**, the noun.
>
> **Zhōng yào**   Chinese medicine. Remember **zhōng** (lit. middle)
> often means China or Chinese. Both Chinese and Western
> medicine are widely available in China.
>
> **Yào zhōng yào, yào xī yào?**   (lit. want Chinese medicine, want
> Western medicine?)
>
> **Zhōng yào hǎo háishi xī yào hǎo?**   Is Chinese medicine good or
> Western medicine good? A simple way of asking for a
> recommendation. A useful sentence to learn as you can modify it
> with words appropriate to various situations, such as shopping or
> eating a meal out. **Lù chá hǎo háishi huā chá hǎo?** Is the green
> tea or the jasmine tea good?
>
> **háishi**   or. As explained in Unit 6, Dialogue 5, **háishi** is used in a
> question that poses a choice. (**Huò** or **huòzhě** is used in a statement.)
>
> **yǒu shénme zhōng yào ne?**   What Chinese medicine have you got?
>
> **zhōng yào yǒu nàge gǎnmào ruǎn jiāonáng**   (lit. Chinese
> medicine we have those cold capsules). Putting **Zhōng yào** at the
> beginning like this emphasizes it. The phrase can be translated
> loosely as 'in the Chinese medicine line we have...'
>
> **yī hé shì shí lì.**   One box is ten tablets.
>
> **yào zěnme chī?**   (lit. medicine how eat?) How do I take the
> medicine?
>
> **yī tián liǎng cì, měi cì liǎng lì.**   (lit. every day two times, every
> time two tablets). Two tablets twice a day.

Some common sǎngzi téng sore throat. **Wǒ sǎngzi téng**. I have a sore throat.
ailments: tóuténg headache. **Wǒ tóu téng**. I have a headache.
       wèi téng stomach ache. **Wǒ wèi téng**. I have a stomach ache.

 2 *Do you take credit cards?*

> **LISTEN FOR...**
> **wǒ kěyǐ yòng xìnyòngkǎ fù kuǎn ma?** (lit. I OK use credit card to
> pay money?) Can I pay by credit card?

Zhāng Lì Wǒ kěyǐ yòng xìnyòngkǎ fù kuǎn ma?
Shop assistant Kěyǐ.

yòng to use **fù** to pay
xìnyòngkǎ credit card

> **kuǎn** a formal word for money, less commonly used than **qián**.

Practise what you have learned

1 Selecting from the words in the box below fill in the blanks in the
following sentences. The English sentences are given as a guide.
(Answers on page 112.)

(1) **Yǒu _____ yào ma?**
Do you have medicine to treat a cold?

(2) **Yào _____, yào _____?**
Do you want Chinese or Western medicine?

(3) **Yǒu nàge gǎnmào _____.**
We have those cold capsules.

(4) **Yì hé shì shí _____.**
There are 10 tablets in a box.

(5) **Yào zěnme _____?**
How do I take the medicine?

(6) **Yì tiān liǎng _____, měi _____ chī liǎng lì.**
Two tablets twice a day.

(7) **Wǒ kěyǐ yòng _____ fù kuǎn ma?**
Can I pay by credit card?

```
                    xìnyòngkǎ
                                        cì
        lì
                        zhōng yào
    xī yào
                                    ruǎn jiāonáng
        zhì gǎnmào de
                            chī
        cì
```

 2

Listen to the conversation between the pharmacist and a customer, and indicate whether the statements below are true, 'T' or false, 'F'. (Answers on page 112.)

(1) The customer wants some medicine for a cold. ☐

(2) She likes Western medicine. ☐

(3) She likes Chinese medicine. ☐

(4) She buys a box of tablets. ☐

(5) Two tablets twice a day. ☐

(6) She can pay by credit card. ☐

 3

Your turn to speak. Go into a pharmacy and have a go at buying medicine, following the prompts. You will need the following phrases, but not necessarily in the same order.

Nà jiù yào yī hé ba.
Duōshao qián yī hé?
Yǒu zhì gǎnmào de yào ma?
Yào zěnme chī?
Zhōng yào jiù kěyǐ le.

Dialogues

 3

Buying a silk padded jacket

> **LISTEN FOR...**
> **yī jiàn sīchóu mián'ǎo** a silk padded jacket
> **wǒ chuān** (lit. I'm wearing) It's for me.
> **wǒ xǐhuan huángsè de** I like the yellow one.

Shop assistant	Nǐ hǎo, mǎi diǎnr shénme?
Zhāng Lì	Wǒ xiǎng mǎi yī jiàn sīchóu mián'ǎo.
Shop assistant	Shì nǐ zìjǐ chuān de ma?
Zhāng Lì	Wǒ chuān.
Shop assistant	Xǐhuan shénme yánsè de?
Zhāng Lì	Wǒ xǐhuan huángsè de.
Shop assistant	Shì shi zhè jiàn ba.
Zhāng Lì	Hǎo de.

sīchóu silk	**yánsè** colour
mián'ǎo padded jacket	**huáng** yellow
zìjǐ self	**shì** to try

jiàn a 'measure word', used for items of clothing. When it occurs in conjunction with the noun, there is no need to translate it, but it must be included. **Yī jiàn sīchóu mián'ǎo**, a silk padded jacket.

shì nǐ zìjǐ chuān de ma? (lit. it is you self wear) Is it for you? In full the **de** would link the preceding clause to the noun **mián'ǎo**, but here **mián'ǎo** is not spoken, since it is understood from the context.

xǐhuan shénme yánsè de? Which colour do you like?

huáng sè de the yellow one. (Sometimes people say **huáng de**, leaving out the **se**. Both are correct.) **De** is added to the colour to link it to the noun. It defines 'yellow' as functioning adjectivally. Again, **mián'ǎo** is omitted after **de**, but understood from the context.

shì shi to try. The verb is repeated to make the sentence less formal. It also indicates the action is only going to take a short while, 'to have a try.'

shì shi zhè jiàn ba. Try this one.

 4

Too big! Is there a smaller one?

LISTEN FOR...
hǎoxiàng yǒudiǎnr dà It seems a bit big.
xiǎo hào de small sized one
nà jiù yào zhè jiàn ba I want this one. (I'll take this one.)

Zhāng Lì	Hǎoxiàng yǒudiǎnr dà.
Shop assistant	Huàn yī jiàn xiǎo… xiǎo hào de.
Zhāng Lì	Xiǎo hào de kěyǐ, héshì.
Shop assistant	Yào ma?
Zhāng Lì	Nà jiù yào zhè jiàn ba.
Shop assistant	Nà nín qù fù qián qù ba.
Zhāng Lì	Hǎo de.

hǎoxiàng to seem	**hào** number, size
dà big	**héshì** suitable (fits)
xiǎo small	

hǎoxiàng yǒudiǎnr dà It seems a bit big. **Hǎoxiang yǒudiǎnr xiǎo**. It seems a bit small.

huàn yī jiàn xiǎo hào de (lit. change one small sized) Change it for a small-sized one. Again **mián'ǎo** is omitted after **de**.

xiǎo hào de kěyǐ, héshì the small-sized one is OK, it fits.

nà nín qù fù qián qù ba (lit. in that case you go pay money go). The second **qù** is not necessary but is used to emphasize that the movement is away from the speaker. In many Chinese shops, the assistant gives the customer a slip bearing the purchase price, which the customer takes to a separate cash desk, pays, and then returns to the assistant with a receipt to exchange for the goods.

Practise what you have learned

Refer to p. 109 for colours and clothes mentioned in your
pronunciation practice.

4 Rearrange the jumbled words so that each sentence makes sense and
then match each to its English translation. (Answers on page 112.)

(1) **jiàn xiǎo huàn hǎo de yī**   (a) It seems to be a bit big.
(2) **huáng de xǐhuan wǒ sè**   (b) I want to buy a pair of trousers.
(3) **xiǎng tiáo wǒ yī mǎi kùzi**   (c) The small-sized one is OK, it fits.
(4) **dà yǒudiǎnr hǎoxiàng**   (d) I like the yellow one.
(5) **hǎo de kěyǐ héshì xiǎo**   (e) I'll take this one.
(6) **jiàn nà yào ba zhè jiù**   (f) Change it for a small-sized one.

5 On the recording you will hear five questions similar to those you
might be asked when shopping in a Chinese store. Reply to each
question. There is a list of possible replies below to help you, but they
are not in the order you will need them.

Hǎoxiàng yǒudiǎnr dà.   **Wǒ chuān.**
Wǒ xǐhuan huángsè de.   **Hǎo, héshì.**
Wǒ xiǎng mǎi yī jiàn sīchóu mián'ǎo.

6 Have a go at buying a jacket and practise talking to the assistant in a store.

You will need: **lán**   blue

Dialogues

5

Changing traveller's cheques

> **LISTEN FOR...**
> **wǒ kěyǐ yòng lǚxíng zhīpiào duìhuàn...**   Can I use traveller's
> cheques to exchange for...
> **Yīngbàng**   pound sterling
> **hùzhào**   passport

Wáng Jūn   Wǒ kěyǐ yòng lǚxíng zhīpiào duìhuàn wàihuìquàn ma?
Bank assistant Kěyǐ.
Wáng Jūn   Ao.
Bank assistant Wǒ kàn nǐ nèi ge ... èr shí Yīngbàng. Nín xiān tián yī zhāng dānzi.
Wáng Jūn   Hǎo, xièxie.
Bank assistant Nín de xìngmíng.
Wáng Jūn   Xìngmíng.
Bank assistant Guójí.
Wáng Jūn   Guójí.
Bank assistant Hùzhào hàomǎ, hái yǒu fàndiàn, zhù nǎ ge fàndiàn...
Wáng Jūn   Ao, fàndiàn.
Bank assistant Duì, hǎo. Ránhòu, nín zài bǎ zhè zhīpiào shàng qiānshang míngzi.
Wáng Jūn   Qiānshang míngzi.
Bank assistant Ai, zhīpiào shàng qiānshang míngzi... hǎo, wǒ kàn yīxià nín de hùzhào.

lǚxíng zhīpiào traveller's cheque
duìhuàn to exchange (money)
Yīngbàng pound sterling
xìngmíng full name

guójí nationality
hùzhào passport
qiān/qiānshang to sign
míngzi name

> **wàihuìquàn** Foreign Exchange Certificate (FEC). There used to be a special currency for foreigners to use in China, but more recently it has been phased out.
>
> **kàn nǐ nèi ge** (lit. look your that one) let's see your ...
>
> **tián yī zhāng dānzi** fill in a form. **Zhāng** is a 'measure word' for something made of paper, previously encountered in Unit 3, Dialogue 6 (remember **yī zhāng fāpiào**, a receipt). Refer to the *Grammar* of Unit 3 for a reminder if you need to.
>
> **Hùzhào hàomǎ, hái yǒu fàndiàn, zhù nǎ ge fàndiàn?** (lit. passport number, also hotel, stay which hotel?) The bank clerk is going down the form and pointing out each category with his pen.
>
> **zhīpiào shàng** on the cheque. **Shàng** goes after the noun. **nín zài bǎ zhè zhīpiào shàng qiānshang míngzi** (lit. you again this cheque on sign briefly name) Then just sign your name on the cheque. Don't worry about the **ba**. It introduces a grammatical structure which is quite complicated, and as a beginner you can get by without it.
>
> **wǒ kàn yīxià nín de hùzhào** (lit. I look briefly your passport) I'll have a quick look at your passport. **Nín de** means 'your'. Refer back to Unit 2's *Grammar* section for a reminder if you need one.
>
> In this Dialogue Wáng is receiving information and repeats much of what he is told by the bank clerk to make sure he gets it right.

New word: **Měiyuán** US dollar

6 *Buying souvenirs in the Friendship Store*

> **LISTEN FOR...**
> **jìniànpǐn** souvenir
> **hái yǒu qítā de dōngxi?** Are there still other things?
> **Wǒ jiù tiāo...** I just choose...

Wáng Wǒ xiǎng mǎi diǎnr jìniànpǐn dài huíqù gěi péngyou. Nín kàn wǒ xuǎn diǎnr shénme hǎo ne?

Shop assistant Wǒ jiànyì nín mǎi Zhōngguó de sīchóu tóujīn, hái yǒu zhēnsī shǒupà, háiyǒu shǒuhuìshān. Shǒuhuìshān de tú'àn yǒu ... jùyǒu Zhōngguó tèsè de Chángchéng, xióngmāo, Tiāntán, háiyǒu Jīngjù liǎnpǔ děng, fēicháng shòu wàibīn huānyíng.

Wáng Háiyou qítā de dōngxi ma?

Shop assistant Hái yǒu ... jùyǒu Zhōngguó tèsè de Jǐngtàilán, háiyǒu Jǐngdézhèn ... Jǐngdézhèn cíqì děng.

Wáng Aō, nà wǒ jiù tiāo yī tào Jǐngdézhèn de cíqì ba.

Shop assistant E, nà hǎo, Jǐngdézhèn de cíqì zài shìjiè fēicháng yǒumíng, wàibīn yě fēicháng xǐhuan. Nàme wǒ jiù dài nín qù sān lóu kàn kan ba.

dài huíqù to take back
péngyou friend
xuǎn to choose
jiànyì to suggest
tóujīn scarf
zhēnsī pure silk
shǒupà handkerchief
shǒuhuìshān hand-painted T-shirt
tú'àn pattern, design

Chángchéng the Great Wall
xióngmāo panda
děng etc.
fēicháng extremely
Jǐngtàilán cloisonné enamel
cíqì porcelain
tiāo choose
tào set (crockery)
shìjiè the world
yǒumíng famous

---

dài huíqù gěi péngyou to take back for friends

nín kàn in your opinion

wǒ xuǎn diǎnr shénme hǎo ne? (lit. I choose a little what good?) What can I choose that is good?

shǒuhuìshān de tú'àn yǒu... Designs in the hand-painted T-shirt line are…

Hái yǒu qitā de dōngxi ma? Remember **ma** is usually added to the end of a sentence to indicate a question, but is not absolutely necessary.

jùyǒu Zhōngguó tèsè to have Chinese characteristics (a phrase also used in connection with the political system, as in 'socialism with Chinese characteristics'). Each of the designs which follow is linked by **de** to the preceding descriptive phrase, for example, **Zhōngguó tèsè de xióngmāo**, 'the characteristically Chinese panda'.

Jīngjù liǎnpǔ 'painted faces' from Běijīng (Peking) Opera. The T-shirts are decorated with illustrations of the highly stylized and colourful painted faces of the Běijīng Opera.

fēicháng shòu wàibīn huānyíng extremely well received by foreign guests. The construction of this phrase is rather complicated for a beginner. To understand it in this context is enough. **Fēicháng** 'extremely' is a useful word to learn.

Jǐngdézhèn a town famous for its porcelain. **Jǐngdézhèn de cíqì zài shìjiè fēicháng yǒumíng**. Jǐngdézhèn porcelain in the world extremely famous). **Zài** is used with **shìjiè** to mean in the world. Note its position in the sentence, 'where' goes before 'what'.

nàme wǒ dài nín qù sān lóu kàn kan ba (lit. in that case I'll take you go to the third floor to have a look). **Kàn kan** means 'to have a look'. Repetition of **kàn** 'to look', emphasizes it. **Kàn kan** can be translated as 'to have a look'; compare **shì shi** meaning 'to have a try' in Dialogue 3.

Shop receipts

Practise what you have learned

7

Fill in the blanks in the sentences below selecting words from the box. English translations are given to help you. (Answers on page 112.)

(1) **Wǒ kěyǐ yòng _____ duìhuàn _____ ma?**   Can I exchange traveller's cheques for foreign exchange certificates?

(2) **Nín _____ tián yī _____ dānzi.**   First fill in the form.

(3) **_____, _____, _____ hàomǎ, fàndiàn.**   Name, nationality, passport number, hotel.

(4) **Ránhòu, zài zhīpiào _____ qian yixià míngzi.**   Then, just sign your name on the cheque.

hùzhào	wàihuìquàn
xiān	lǚxíng zhīpiào
zhāng	xìngmíng
guójí	shàng

8

Indicate the correct word under the picture of each item. (Answers on page 112.)

(1) _____   (2) _____   (3) _____   (4) _____

(5) _____   (6) _____   (7) _____   (8) _____

(9) _____   (10) _____   (11) _____   (12) _____

(a) **shǒuhuìshān**	(b) **yī hé chá**	(c) **yī hé ruǎn jiāonáng**
(d) **hùzhào**	(e) **sīchóu tóujin**	(f) **èr shí Yīngbàng**
(g) **xióngmāo**	(h) **shǒupà**	(i) **Jǐngtàilán**
(j) **yī jiàn sīchóu mián'ǎo**	(k) **xìnyòngkǎ**	(l) **lǚxíng zhīpiào**

9

Listen to the recording

Match each sentence you hear with its English translation below, indicating the number of the sentence it corresponds to in the box. The Pinyin sentences are also listed as a guide, but not in the order you will hear them. (Answers on page 112.)

A   Extremely popular among foreigners. ☐

B   Foreigners also like it very much. ☐

C   I would like to buy a souvenir for a friend. ☐

D   Cloisonné with Chinese characteristics. ☐

E   Jǐngdézhèn porcelain is world famous. ☐

F   I suggest you buy a Chinese silk scarf. ☐

G   Do you have any other things? ☐

H   We also have hand painted T-shirts. ☐

Wàibīn yě fēicháng xǐhuan.
Fēicháng shòu wàibīn huānyíng.
Wǒ xiǎng mǎi diǎnr jìnìanpǐn dài huí qù gěi péngyou.
Hái yǒu qítā de dōngxi ma?
Hái yǒu shǒuhuìshān.
Jǐngdézhèn de cíqì zài shìjiè shàng fēicháng yǒumíng.
Jùyǒu Zhōngguó tèsè de Jǐngtàilán.
Wǒ jiànyì nín mǎi Zhōngguó de sīchóu tóujīn.

10

Now have a go at buying a gift for a friend. Lǐ will prompt you.

You'll need: **Hái yǒu qítā de dōngxi ma?**
Wǒ jiù tiāo...
yī tào Jǐngdézhèn de cíqì

Painting cloisonné

Key words and phrases

To learn

yào; zhì gǎnmào de yào	medicine; medicine to treat a cold
zhōng yào	Chinese medicine
xī yào	Western medicine
yào zěnme chī?	How do I take the medicine?
tóu téng	headache
wèi téng	stomach ache
sǎngzi téng	sore throat
sīchóu	silk
mián'ǎo	padded jacket
kùzi	trousers
chènyī	shirt
qúnzi	skirt
jiàn	measure word (clothes, upper body)
tiáo	measure word (clothes, lower body)
chuān	to wear
héshì	to fit
yánsè	colour
huáng(sè)	yellow
shì	to try
hǎoxiàng	to seem
xiǎo hào	small size
dà hào	big size
fù qián	to pay the money
xìnyòngkǎ	credit card
lǚxíng zhīpiào	traveller's cheque
duìhuàn	to exchange (money)
Yīngbàng	Pound Sterling
Měiyuán	US Dollar
Rénmínbì	Rénmínbì (RMB), Chinese currency (lit. People's currency)
guójí	nationality
hùzhào	passport
qiān	to sign
dài huíqù	to take back
péngyou	friend
jìnìanpǐn	souvenir
tiāo	to choose
tào	set (crockery)
fēicháng	extremely
wàibīn	foreign guests

To understand

yī tiān liǎng cì	twice a day
měi cì chī liǎng lì	every time take two tablets
Chángchéng	the Great Wall
cíqì	porcelain
shìjiè	the world
yǒumíng	famous
jùyǒu Zhōngguó tèsè	to have Chinese characteristics

Grammar

Word order

The most effective way to get to grips with word order is to listen to the authentic dialogues which form the basis of this course, and, in time, to develop a feel for the language. But learning example sentences to use as models to adapt for your own use is also worthwhile.

'Who', 'what'

The subject, 'Who' (which can in fact be person, place or time), goes first in the sentence, followed by the verb or adjective:

Wǒ shì lùshī.   I am a lawyer.
Wǒ hěn máng.   I am very busy.
Tā chī fàn.   He eats food.
Běijīng yǒu shí ge fàndiàn.   Běijīng has ten hotels.
Xiànzài shì jiǔ diǎn.   Now is 9 o'clock.

'Who', 'when', 'what'

The word relating to the time something happens goes before or after the subject, and before the verb:

Tā jīntiān qù Zhōngguó.
(lit. he today goes China.)
Today he is going to China.

Wǒ jīntiān hěn máng.
(lit. I today very busy.)
Today I am very busy.

'Who', 'where', 'what'

The place where something happens goes after the subject and before the verb:

Tā zài jiā chī fàn.
(lit. he at home eats.)
He eats food at home.

Wǒmen zài nǎr chī fàn?
(lit. we where eat?)
Where shall we eat?

In the following sentence, the place is the object and therefore goes after the verb:

Tā míngtiān qù Zhōngguó.
(lit. he tomorrow goes to China.)
Tomorrow he is going to China.

'Who', 'when', 'where', 'what'

A complete sentence follows this structure:
subject + time when + place where + verb + object.

Tāmen jīntiān zài jiā chī fàn.
(lit. they today at home eat.)
Today they eat at home.

Wǒmen míngtiān zài Tiān'ānmén Guǎngchǎng děng nǐ.
(lit. we tomorrow at Tiān'ānmén Square wait you.)
We'll wait for you tomorrow at Tiān'ānmén Square.

11 Unjumble the following sentences. (Answers on page 112.)

(a) **chī jiā míngtiān tā zài fàn**
Tomorrow he will eat at home.

(b) **yǐnliào shénme zhèr nǐmen yǒu dōu**
What drinks do you have here?

(c) **wǒ qù fàndiàn jīntiān Běijīng**
Today I am going to the Beijing Hotel.

(d) **néng tā zài dǎ nàr diànhuà ma**
Can he make a phonecall there?

(e) **jīntiān děng nǐmen Tiān'ānmén Guǎngchǎng zài wǒ**
Today I wait for you at Tiān'ānmén Square.

Some colours:			
bái	white	**hēi**	black
lán	blue	**zǐ**	purple
hóng	red	**huáng**	yellow

Some clothes:			
kùzi	trousers	**qúnzi**	skirt
	chènyī	shirt	

Anyone for a teapot?

Read and understand

Weights and measures

China mainly uses the metric system:

Metric	Chinese	Imperial
1 kilogram	1 **gōngjin**	2.2 pounds
500 grams	1 **jin**	1.1 pounds
50 grams	1 **liǎng**	
5 grams	1 **qián**	

Prices for vegetables are usually per **jin** or **liǎng**, just as we express them per kilogram or gram:

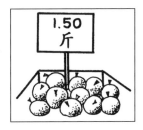   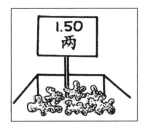

¥1.50 per **jin**   ¥1.50 per **liǎng**

You may also come across traditional Chinese measures, if not in China, then perhaps in your reading:

Metric	Chinese	Imperial
1 metre	3 **chǐ**	3.28 feet
1 kilometre	2 **lǐ**	0.62 miles
1 hectare	15 **mǔ**	2.47 acres
1 litre	1 **gōngshēng**	0.22 gallons
1 tonne (metric ton)	1 **dūn**	0.98 tons

Did you know?

Shopping

The shopping experience in China has been transformed in the recent period of economic reform. While once foreign visitors were restricted to shopping in the state-owned 'Friendship Stores' (**yǒuyì shāngdiàn**), which stocked goods imported from the West (off-limits to most Chinese people and not dealing in People's Currency (RMB)), they can now go shopping anywhere, and in the contemporary context this includes brand new luxury shopping centres. Friendship Stores – especially the larger ones, in Běijīng, Shànghǎi and Guǎngzhōu for example – often have a good range of Chinese artefacts and souvenirs, albeit more expensive than elsewhere, and are good places to buy Western cigarettes and spirits. Hotel shops too stock the latter, and sell postcards, photographic film, souvenirs and some foreign newspapers and magazines. Most hotels also sell typically Chinese items to buy as presents: scroll paintings, calligraphy, paper-cuts, silk dressing-gowns, cloisonné ware, chopsticks, tea and dinner sets, linen table-cloths, embroidery, painted kites, jade, calligraphy sets, and so on. In the international hotels the range will be greater; items will perhaps be more expensive than in local stores, but generally of a better quality.

Antiques

Many of the Friendship Stores have antique sections, and many cities have antique shops. Beware of being stopped outside a tourist site and offered 'antique' coins or other items. While you may wish to purchase these as mementoes, they are usually not worth the price being asked. Local 'folk art', embroidered bags, and hand-made toys, for example, are better souvenirs to buy from local people at these sites. Bear in mind that antiques must carry a red seal to indicate they are approved for export, and a special customs declaration form must be filled in before leaving the country.

Markets

Markets are everywhere, and a visit to one is a valuable cultural experience. Whereas in the shops prices are fixed, at markets bartering is usual, and skills learned in local markets in other countries will stand you in good stead in China. If a stall holder shows no sign of budging on price – often outrageously high compared to overall income – the secret is to walk away. He or she may not only reduce the price, but run after you to let you know it.

The range of goods on sale in markets often has to be seen to be believed. It varies according to the produce and crafts of the area. There are the usual fruit and vegetables; live chickens to take home 'fresh' strung on the back of a bicycle; swimming fish, again to ensure freshness at table; hundreds of herbs and animal organs for Chinese medicine preparations – the list is endless. Items are often simply laid out on the ground, with the seller squatting beside them. Measurements are made on old-fashioned balancing scales. The wrapping is newspaper tied with string, and the cost is calculated on an abacus.

Your turn to speak

12

You want to buy a souvenir to take home as a gift for a friend, and go looking for something typically 'Chinese' in the Friendship Store. See what you find, with the assistant's help.

You will need: **yì tiáo sīchóu qúnzi**
shǒuhuìshān

*Buying souvenirs
– 'folk crafts'*

Answers

<table>
<tr><td rowspan="8">Practise what
you have
learned</td></tr>
</table>

Practise what you have learned

Exercise **1** (1) zhì gǎnmào de (2)   zhōng yào, xī yào
(3)   ruǎn jiāonáng (4)   lì (5)   chī (6)   cì, cì
(7)   xìnyòngkǎ

Exercise **2** (1)T; (2)F; (3)T; (4)T; (5)F; (6)F

Exercise **4** (1)f Huàn yī jiàn xiǎo hào de.
(2)d Wǒ xǐhuan huáng sè de.
(3)b Wǒ xiǎng mǎi yì tiáo kùzi.
(4)a Hǎoxiàng yǒudiǎnr dà.
(5)c Xiǎo hào de kěyǐ, héshì.
(6)e Nà jiù yào zhè jiàn ba.

Exercise **7** (1)   lǚxíng zhīpiào, wàihuìquàn (2)   xiān, zhāng
(3)   xìngmíng, guójí, hùzhào (4)   shàng

Exercise **8** (1)c; (2)k; (3)j; (4)l; (5)f; (6)d; (7)e; (8)h; (9)a; (10)i;
(11)b; (12)g

Exercise **9** A 5; B 7; C 1; D 4; E 8; F 2; G 6; H 3

Grammar

Exercise **11** (a) Tā míngtiān zài jiā chī fàn.
(b) Nǐmen zhèr dōu yǒu shénme yǐnliào?
(c) Wǒ jīntiān qù Běijīng Fàndiàn.
(d) Tā néng zài nàr dǎ diànhuà ma?
(e) Wǒ jīntiān zài Tiān'ānmén Guǎngchǎng děng
nǐmen.

MAKING TRAVEL ARRANGEMENTS

What you will learn

- to buy a rail or plane ticket
- to understand the various classes of rail accommodation
- to ask from which platform your train leaves
- to find out where to get your ticket checked
- the ordinal numbers
- about train travel

Before you begin

In this Unit focusing on train travel, remember that China is a vast country, so distances between major tourist destinations are usually great. This explains the absence of such phrases as 'A day return to…' – more often than not it is impossible to return on the same day! In fact, in China you do not book a single (one-way) or a return (round trip), but a seat or sleeper on a particular train.

You will find it useful to revise dates and times covered in Unit 6. The *Key words and phrases* for booking flights in Unit 6 are also worth looking over.

On the Li River, Guilin

Dialogues

1 *Buying an underground (= subway) ticket*

> **LISTEN FOR...**
> **yī zhāng piào**   a ticket
> **cóng zhèr kěyǐ zhíjiē dào Qiánmén ma?**
> (lit. from here can directly to Qiánmén?)
> Can one get directly to Qiánmén from here?

Girl	Ai, shīfu, yào yī zhāng piào. Duōshao qián?
Ticket assistant	Wǔ jiǎo qián.
Girl	Cóng zhèr kěyǐ zhíjiē dào Qiánmén ma?
Ticket assistant	Bù kěyǐ. Nín děi chū zhàn, guò mǎlù, héng guò mǎlù, dào lù nán de kǒu, jìn zhàn shàng chē.
Girl	Ao, xièxie.
Ticket assistant	Bù yòng xiè.

cóng	from	**héng**	horizontal
chū	to exit	**jìn**	to enter

ai   used to attract the assistant's attention, comparable to 'hey!' It is not polite.

shīfu   (lit. master) nowadays used as an alternative to 'comrade', for example, to address someone in an informal position of authority.

Qiánmén   an area in Běijīng, near Tiān'ānmén

jiǎo   a unit of currency, the same as **máo**. Refer to the information on currency in Unit 3 if you need to.

cóng zhèr...   from here..., usually goes at the beginning. (The subject, I, **wǒ**, for example, might come first.) **Cóng** 'from' emphasizes the place which is the starting point, **cóng Qiánmén** 'from Qiánmén'. **Lí** 'away from' emphasizes the distance. **Lí zhèr hěn yuǎn**. It's very far from here.

nín děi chū zhàn, guò mǎlù   (lit. must go out of the station, cross the road)

héng guò mǎlù   (lit. horizontally cross the road). The station is situated at an intersection and **héng**, 'horizontal' or 'crosswise', emphasizes the orientation of the road being crossed. It is not essential to learn. **Guò mǎlù** is sufficient.

dào lù nán de kǒu   (lit. to reach street south entrance) to get to the entrance on the southern side of the road. **De** links the main noun, **kǒu** 'entrance', with the words which describe it.

jìn zhàn   enter the station

shàng chē   board the train

Useful phrase: **huàn chē**   change trains

2 *Booking a 'soft sleeper' on the 119 train to Hángzhōu.*

> **LISTEN FOR...**
> **yī zhāng dào Hángzhōu de huǒchē piào** a rail ticket to Hángzhōu
> **yìngwò** hard sleeper
> **ruǎnwò** soft sleeper

Lǐ Míng	Nǐ hǎo, wǒ xiǎng mǎi yī zhāng dào Hángzhōu de huǒchē piào.
Booking assistant	Ai, dào Hángzhōu de chē cì shì yī bǎi yī shí jiǔ cì. Xiànzài wǒmen dào Hángzhōu de yìngwò piào yǐjing shòu wán le, zhǐ yǒu ruǎnwò piào.
Lǐ Míng	Hǎo ba, nà wǒ jiù mǎi yī zhāng ruǎnwò piào ba.
Booking assistant	Hǎo ba, zhè zhāng ruǎnwò piào de piàojià shì yī bǎi jiǔ shí wǔ yuán.
Lǐ Míng	Hǎo de, zhè shì...

huǒchē	train	**zhǐ**	only
yǐjing	already	**piàojià**	ticket price
shòu	to sell		

yī zhāng dào Hángzhōu de huǒchē piào a rail ticket to Hángzhōu. Get into the habit of breaking down complex phrases into more manageable units. For example, you have learned that **yī zhāng piào** means 'a ticket', so you can assume that the phrase sandwiched between **zhāng** and **piào** is connected with the notion of ticket. Now look at that phrase: **dào Hángzhōu de huǒchē**. **Dào Hángzhōu** means 'to Hángzhōu'; **huǒchē** means 'train'; **de** makes **dào Hángzhōu** function adjectivally. The whole phrase means 'a ticket for the Hángzhōu train'.

chē cì train number. Trains are referred to by number, not time of departure. **Dào Hángzhōu de chē cì shì yī bǎi yī shí jiǔ cì** (lit. to Hángzhōu train number is 119). The number of the train to Hángzhōu is 119. Note that **cì** 'number' comes after the train number. When trying to work out the main noun, or idea, of a sentence, it is sometimes helpful to look at what comes after **de**. Here you can locate **chē cì**, and from there build up the sentence.

xiànzài wǒmen dào Hángzhōu de yìngwò piào yǐjing shòu wán le (lit. now our to Hángzhōu 'hard sleeper' tickets have already sold out). Both 'hard sleepers' and 'soft sleepers' are available to long distance travellers on Chinese trains (see *Did you know?* on page 125). To build complex sentences like this one, you need to remember word order for time and place. Refer back to the *Grammar* of Unit 8, if you need a reminder.

zhǐ yǒu ruǎnwò piào (lit. only have soft sleeper tickets)

nà wǒ jiù mǎi yī zhāng ruǎnwò piào ba In that case I'll just buy a soft sleeper ticket. You have come across this **nà...ba** structure in previous units.

Useful words: **yìngzuò** hard seat
ruǎnzuò soft seat

Practise what you have learned

1 Match each Pīnyīn sentence with its English equivalent. (Answers on page 126.)

(1) **yī zhāng piào**   (a) a soft sleeper ticket
(2) **chū zhàn**   (b) a rail ticket
(3) **jìn zhān**   (c) enter the station
(4) **shàng chē**   (d) a ticket
(5) **yī zhāng yìngwò piào** (e) from here
(6) **yī zhāng ruǎnwò piào** (f) board the train
(7) **yī zhāng huǒchē piào** (g) a hard sleeper ticket
(8) **cóng zhèr**   (h) exit the station
(9) **huàn chē**   (i) change trains

2 Listen to Xiànbīn read five sentences and write the number of the recorded sentence in the box next to its English equivalent. (Answers on page 126.)

Can one get straight to Qiánmén from here?

You must exit the station, cross the road.

You must enter the station, board the train.

A rail ticket to Hángzhōu.

Our soft sleeper tickets to Hángzhōu are already sold out.

3 Have a go at buying rail tickets. You will need:
Wǒ xiǎng mǎi...   I want to buy...

Dialogues

3 *Which platform for the train to Xī'ān?*

> **LISTEN FOR...**
> **zài dì jǐ zhàntái**   on which platform?

Zhào Xiān   Qǐng wèn, qù Xī'ān de sān shí wǔ cì lièchē zài dì jǐ zhàntái?
Attendant   Dì liù zhàntái.
Zhào Xiān   Zài nǎli jiǎn piào?
Attendant   Qǐng nín dào èr lóu dì yī hòuchēshì jiǎn piào.

zhàntái   platform
hòuchēshì   waiting room (at railway station)   **jiǎn**   to check

> **lièchē**   train. Stick to **huǒchē**, which is the more usual word in everyday speech.
>
> **qù Xī'ān de sān shí wǔ cì lièchē**   (lit. go Xī'ān 35 number train), train number 35 going to Xī'ān. **Dào Xī'ān** would also be possible here.

dì before a number, changes it into an ordinal. For example, **dì yī** 'first', **dì èr** 'second', **dì liù** 'sixth'. **Zài dì jǐ zhàntái**, on which platform. Putting **dì** before **jǐ** 'how many', to mean 'which number?', implies that the answer will contain an ordinal number.

zài nǎli (lit. at which place)

dì yī hòuchēshì (lit. first waiting room) waiting room number one. Foreigners and perhaps high officials travelling 'soft' class are usually directed to this waiting room.

jiǎn piào check the ticket. Before you board a train in China, tickets are checked by a railway clerk at the exit to the waiting room, which usually leads directly out on to the platform.

 4 *Booking a flight to Guǎngzhōu with Air China*

LISTEN FOR…
yī zhāng fēijī piào a plane ticket

Zhāng Lì	Xiǎojie, wǒ xiǎng mǎi yī zhāng èr yuè shí bā hào qù Guǎngzhōu de, xiàwǔ de fēijī piào.
Ticket assistant	Qǐng děng yīxià… Duìbuqǐ, xiàwǔ de fēijī piào yǐjīng mài guāng le. Néng bù néng huàn ge rìzi?
Zhāng Lì	Kěyǐ.
Ticket assistant	Shí jiǔ hào de kěyǐ ma?
Zhāng Lì	Kěyǐ.

rìzi date, day

Guǎngzhōu capital of Guǎngdōng province, formerly known as Canton

fēijī piào air ticket. **Yī zhāng èr yuè shí bā hào qù Guǎngzhōu de, xiàwǔ de fēijī piào** (lit. one February 18 date go Guǎngzhōu afternoon air ticket), an air ticket to Guǎngzhōu for the afternoon of the 18th February. Again, the details about the ticket go between **yī zhāng** and **piào**. Have a look at the *Grammar* section for help with breaking down this long phrase. Note that the date goes before the time of day.

mài guāng le sold out

néng bù néng (lit. can or can't?). This is a useful and easy way of asking a question and can be used with almost any verb. Simply put together the positive, here **néng**, and negative, here **bù néng**. See *Grammar* on page 122 for further examples.

huàn ge rìzi change the date. **Huàn** '(ex)change' is usually separated from the noun with a measure word. **Huàn yī jiàn xiǎo hào de**. Change for a smaller size. (Unit 8, Dialogue 4)

shí jiǔ hào de kěyǐ ma? Is the one on the 19th OK? The noun **fēijī**, which in full would come after **de,** is omitted because it is understood from the context.

Practise what you have learned

4

In this exercise you will hear four sentences. Pair each one with one from the list below to make four short conversations, writing the number of the recorded sentence in the box next to its pair. Listen to them once through before making any attempt to pair them up. (Answers on page 126.)

(a) **Qù Běijing de huǒchē zài dì jǐ zhàntái?** ☐

(b) **Zài nǎli jiǎn piào?** ☐

(c) **Wǒ xiǎng mǎi yī zhāng sì yuè shí jiǔ hào qù Xī'ān de, xiàwǔ de fēiji piào.** ☐

(d) **Bù néng.** ☐

5

Listen to the conversation and mark the following statements true, 'T', or false, 'F'. (Answers on page 126.)

(a) The customer enquires about soft sleepers. ☐

(b) Soft sleeper tickets are already sold out. ☐

(c) The customer can change the date of travel. ☐

(d) Train number 35 to Xī'ān goes from platform number six. ☐

(e) The tickets are checked in waiting room number one on the second floor (British English 'first floor'). ☐

6

Using the sentence below as a pattern, ask from which platform the listed trains leave. Each time you ask the question, change the place and train number following the list. After each question, you will hear the correct version spoken by Xiànbīn, and then a response from Xiǎoyún. Write the platform number given by Xiǎoyún in the appropriate column below. (Answers on page 126.)

Pattern:
Qù Xī'ān de sān shí wǔ cì huǒchē zài dì jǐ zhàntái?
The number 35 train to Xī'ān is on which platform?

Destination	Train number	Platform
Xī'ān	35	
Běijing	95	
Shànghǎi	20	
Hángzhōu	140	

7

Practise the phrases you have learned to buy a ticket and ask for the information you need following Lǐ's prompts.

Dialogue

5

Where are you going?

> **LISTEN FOR...**
> **dào nǎr qù?**   Where are you going? (lit. to where go?)

Jiànjí	Dào nǎr qù a?
Hènián	Wǒ yào qù Guǎngzhōu.
Jiànjí	Dào Guǎngzhōu gàn shénme ya?
Hènián	Yǒu ge péngyou yuē wǒ zài nàr zuò diǎnr shēngyi.
Jiànjí	Qù guo Guǎngzhōu ma?
Hènián	Qù guo. Nǐ shàng nàr qù a?
Jiànjí	Wǒ dào Hángzhōu

yuē	to arrange	**gàn**	to do
nàr	there	**shàng**	to go

> **dào Guǎngzhōu gàn shénme?**   (lit. To Guǎngzhōu do what?) What are you going to do in Guǎngzhōu?
>
> **yǒu ge péngyou**   a friend I have. **Yī ge** is shortened to simply **ge**.
>
> **yuē wǒ zài nàr zuò diǎnr shēngyi**   (lit. arrange me at there to do some business) arranged with me to do some business there
>
> **qù guo Guǎngzhōu ma?**   (lit. go ever Guǎngzhōu?) Have you ever been to Guǎngzhōu? Put **yǐqián** 'in the past' at the beginning to emphasize 'before'. **Yǐqián qù guo Guǎngzhōu ma?** Have you ever been to Guǎngzhōu before? (Refer to Unit 2, Dialogue 5, for a reminder of **guo**.)
>
> **qù guo.**   I have been before.
>
> **nǐ shàng nǎr qù a?**   (lit. you go where go?) A common way of asking, 'Where are you going?' Strictly speaking, **qù** is not essential as **shàng** means 'go', but it emphasizes the direction away from the speaker.
>
> **wǒ dào Hángzhōu**   (lit. I to Hángzhōu). Jiànjí, in contrast, leaves out the verb 'to go' altogether, as it is implied by the context, and by Hènián's question.

Buying a ticket

Practise what you have learned

8

Listen to three short conversations between a passenger and a booking clerk about trains to Guǎngzhōu and fill in the blanks below. (Answers on page 126.)

(1) The _____ day train is at _____ a.m. / p.m.

(2) The _____ day train is at _____ a.m. / p.m.

(3) The _____ day train is at _____ a.m. / p.m.

9

At the booking office buy tickets using the details below to construct your sentences. Speak in the pause; a correct version will follow. A list of Pinyin words and phrases is also given to help you. Begin each sentence with **Wǒ xiǎng mǎi...** 'I want to buy...'.

(1) two train tickets to Guǎngzhōu
For example: **Wǒ xiǎng mǎi liǎng zhāng dào Guǎngzhōu de huǒchē piào.**

(2) three plane tickets to Shànghǎi

(3) one soft sleeper ticket to Xī'ān

(4) two hard sleeper tickets to Tiānjīn

(5) one plane ticket for February 18th

(6) two tickets to Xī'ān on the number 35 train

èr yuè shí bā hào	**ruǎnwò**
1/2/3 zhāng dào... piào	**yìngwò**
huǒchē	**sān shí wǔ cì**
fēijī	

10

You meet a friend at the railway station and he asks you about your travel plans. You will need:
jīntiān today
zuò diǎnr shēngyi do some business
qù guo I have been before

Beijing railway station

Key words and phrases

To learn

yī zhāng piào	a ticket
yī zhāng dào...de huǒchē piào	a rail ticket to...
yìngwò	hard sleeper
ruǎnwò	soft sleeper
yìngzuò	hard seat
ruǎnzuò	soft seat
cóng zhèr kěyǐ zhíjiē dào... ma?	Can one get to...directly from here?
shàng chē	board the train
huàn chē	change trains
chē cì	train number
dì jǐ zhàntái?	which platform?
jiǎn piào	check the ticket
hòuchēshì	waiting-room
yǐjing	already
zhǐ yǒu...	There is (are) only...
néng bù néng...?	(lit. can / can't...?) Can one...?
nǐ gàn shénme?	What are you doing?
nǐ shàng nǎr qù?	Where are you going?
dào nǎr qù?	Where are you going?

To understand

huàn ge rìzi	change the date

Grammar

Building / breaking down phrases

As you learned earlier, adding **de** to a phrase and putting it before a main noun links the phrase and noun. The **de** effectively makes the preceding phrase function adjectivally. Look at the following examples:

(1) **dào Hángzhōu de huǒchē**   (lit. to Hángzhōu train) the train going to Hángzhōu
(2) **yì zhāng ruǎnwò piào de piàojià**   the ticket price of a soft sleeper ticket
(3) **qù Xī'ān de 35 cì lièchē**   train number 35 going to Xī'ān

Such phrases as (1) and (3) can be sandwiched between **yì zhāng** and **piào** to specify the type of ticket requested or stated. Look at the way in which the following phrases are built:

yì zhāng piào   a ticket
yì zhāng xiàwǔ de fēijī piào   an afternoon flight ticket
yì zhāng dào Hángzhōu de huǒchē piào   a rail ticket to Hangzhou
yì zhāng èr yuè shí bā hào qù Guǎngzhōu de piào   a ticket to Guǎngzhōu on 18 February

As suggested in the notes to Dialogue 2, it is useful when faced with a complex phrase to break it down into manageable units, and work out what each of these mean, rather than trying to understand the whole at once. For example, the following sentence,

yì zhāng èr yuè shí bā hào qù Guǎngzhōu de, xiàwǔ de huǒchē piào

can be broken down into,

yì zhāng ... piào   a ticket
èr yuè shí bā hào   February 18
qù Guǎngzhōu de   to Guǎngzhōu
xiàwù de huǒchē   the afternoon train

and then put back together,

a rail ticket to Guǎngzhōu on the afternoon of 18 February.

Asking a question

A simple way of forming a question is to put together the positive and negative forms of the verb, that is to insert **bù** between the repeated verb. For example,

néng bù néng?   Can you or can't you?
yào bù yào?   Do you want it or not?
shì bù shì?   Is it or isn't it?

Ordinal numbers

These are formed simply by prefixing **dì** to the cardinal numbers,
dì yī   first
dì èr   second
dì sān   third
dì sì   fourth and so on.

Note that **dì jǐ?** is 'which number?', the 'how many-th'?

11

Unjumble the words to make sentences. The English is given to help you. Answers on page 126.

(1) **piào zhāng yī**
a ticket

(2) **piào fēijī zhāng yī**
an air ticket

(3) **zhāng piào yī Guǎngzhōu de dào**
a ticket to Guǎngzhōu

(4) **yī piào xiàwǔ zhāng de**
an afternoon ticket

(5) **sān zhāng dào shí liù yuè piào yī Běijīng hào de**
a ticket to Běijīng on 16 March

(6) **piào huǒchē Hángzhōu yī dào zhāng de**
a rail ticket to Hángzhōu

Guangzhou

Read and understand

'Through the back door'

Guānxi

Personal 'connections' – **guānxi** – are important in China, a country where goods and services are in short supply, and bureaucracy in excess. For Chinese people, cultivating and maintaining a network of well-placed contacts outside the family circle is a way of life. Using their own **guānxi** network, people find access to goods and services, even jobs, which are otherwise not available to them. However, it is generally understood that the favour will be returned later – definitely a case of 'You scratch my back, I'll scratch yours'.

Waiting for the train – platform snacks

Did you know?

Getting around – train travel

Distances between the cities on your itinerary in China are probably great, so if time is limited the most practical way of travelling is by air. China's airline has an extensive network connecting all major destinations, and continues to improve its service to meet the needs of the ever increasing business and tourist sectors.

If time is not a major consideration, however, travelling by train is definitely worthwhile. If the prospect of viewing the Chinese countryside from the carriage window is not a sufficient attraction, consider what you have to gain in your impression of Chinese culture and society. It is also a good way to get talking to people and practise your language skills – people will be delighted if you do so.

Reservations must always be made in advance, usually three to five days beforehand, since long-distance trains fill up. Trains are referred to by number and not departure times. Tickets are for a certain seat or bunk on a particular train on a certain day, and not single or return to a particular place. Return tickets are not in fact the norm; the first thing you need to concern yourself with on arrival in a city is procuring a ticket to get out of it. This usually involves waiting in a very long queue, although you can pay a representative of the local or national travel service a small fee to organize it for you – there are travel desks in all major hotels.

There are four types of accommodation. 'Hard seat' means a place on wooden or plastic-covered benches, and 'soft seat' (not always available) the same with a cushion. 'Hard sleeper' has three tiers of berths arranged in blocks of six, stretching through an open carriage; 'soft sleeper' has four berths to a compartment, two up and two down, with a small table and lamp. If you choose 'hard sleeper', the middle bunk is best for stretching out: there is not much room between the top bunk and the ceiling, and the bottom bunk tends to be used by day by fellow passengers as a seat.

Thermos flasks of hot water are provided, and filled up regularly by the train attendant. Cups with lids and sachets of tea are provided in soft sleeper. In hard sleeper people bring out their own – Chinese people often carry a jam jar with tea leaves in the bottom, and during the journey simply keep refilling it with the hot water supplied.

There is usually a restaurant car, for which tickets are often sold in advance by a dining car attendant – you and the other occupants of your carriage will be summoned when it is your turn to eat. Snacks can also be bought from station platforms; there is often a mad dash off the train for supplies when it draws into a station, and a loud bell announces when the train is about to depart again.

A public address system keeps passengers diverted with announcements – of rules to adhere to for a pleasant journey – and broadcasts of music, news, comedy, and so on. In 'soft sleeper' there is a volume control knob to be found under the table, so turn it right down if you prefer not to wake up at about 5 a.m. ('early to bed, early to rise' is the maxim for train travel). Lights go out early, so it is worth carrying a torch (= flashlight) for late-night reading or finding your way to the toilet.

Your turn to speak

 12

Practise making travel arrangements using the *Key words and phrases* you have come across in this unit.

Answers

Practise what you have learned

Exercise 1   (1)(d); (2)(h); (3)(c); (4)(f); (5)(g); (6)(a); (7)(b); (8)(e); (9)(i)

Exercise 2   2, 1, 4, 5, 3

Exercise 4   (a)2; (b)3; (c)1; (d)4

Exercise 5   (a)F; (b)F; (c)F; (d)T; (e)T

Exercise 6   3, 8, 1, 2

Exercise 8   (1) Tuesday 4.30 p.m.; (2) Thursday 2.15 p.m.; (3) Friday 5.45 a.m.

Grammar

Exercise 11   **yì zhāng piào**
yì zhāng fēijī piào
yì zhāng dào Guǎngzhōu de piào
yì zhāng xiàwǔ de piào
yì zhāng sān yuè shí liù hào dào Běijīng de piào
yì zhāng dào Hángzhōu de huǒchē piào

First class coach

ORDERING A MEAL

What you will learn

- the words for various dishes on a Chinese menu
- to say you don't eat meat
- to order fast food/take-away
- Table manners
- about food and harmony

Before you begin

Chinese food Cantonese style is very familiar to us in the West; in the UK Chinese take-away has become part of the national culture. In this Unit you will learn something about Chinese food, and the way Chinese people put together various dishes to make a balanced meal. As reflected in Dialogue 4, take-away *Western* style has conversely become a feature of *Chinese* life, notably in the major cities, where McDonalds and Kentucky Fried Chicken have recently opened shop.

In Units 3 and 7 you learned how to order drinks and buy things in shops using the verb **lái**. For example,

gěi wǒ lái   bring me…
zài lái   in addition bring…

These phrases are also useful for ordering food and come up again in this Unit.

Street snacks

Dialogues

1

What dishes shall we order?

LISTEN FOR...
zánmen lái   let's get
wǒ bù néng chī ròu   I am a vegetarian (lit. I cannot eat meat)
nǐ kàn...zěnmeyàng?   What do you think about...?
zài lái   also bring
zài yào   also want

Jiànguó	Wǒ xiān diǎn jǐ ge cài?
Hènián	Kěyǐ a.
Jiànguó	Zánmen lái ge shuǐzhǔ ròu piànr.
Hènián	Hēi, duìbuqǐ, wǒ ... wǒ bù néng chī ròu, lái liǎng ge sùcài ba?
Jiànguó	Hǎo ba. Nà nǐ kàn qiàng yóucài zěnmeyàng?
Hènián	Kěyǐ.
Jiànguó	Zài lái yī ge jìn'gōu yùsǔn.
Hènián	Kěyǐ.
Jiànguó	Nǐ kàn, hái zài yào yī ge shénme cài?
Hènián	Zài yào yī ge tángcù báicài ba.
Jiànguó	Xíng. Nà jiù zhè yàng ma?
Hènián	Jiù zhè yàng.

diǎn	to order (meal)	**sùcài**	vegetable dishes
shuǐzhǔ	boiled	**qiàng**	stir-fried
ròu	meat, usually pork	**tángcù**	sweet-and-sour
piànr	slice	**báicài**	Chinese leaves
hēi	hey		

---

cài   (lit. vegetables) used to refer to a dish. In China you order a number of dishes to share; food does not come on an individual plate. At the beginning of a meal it is customary to decide how many dishes to order, depending on how hungry you are, or on the importance of the guest you are entertaining.

wǒ xiān diǎn jǐ ge cài?   (lit. I first order a few dishes?). **Jǐ**, usually a 'question word' meaning 'how many?', may alternatively mean 'a few'. Jiànguó is making a suggestion, so the sentence can be translated 'Shall I first order a few dishes?'

zánmen   we. **Zánmen** is used when 'we' includes both the speaker and the person addressed. **zánmen lái...**   (lit. we get...). Jiànguó is making a suggestion, 'let's get...'. **Zánmen lái ge shuǐzhǔ ròu piànr**. Let's get a boiled sliced pork. The **ge** in this sentence is short for **yī ge** 'one'.

wǒ bù néng chī ròu   (lit. I not can eat meat) I can't eat meat. Hènián means he is a vegetarian. Vegetarianism is not common in China and it is not usual to find a 'vegetarian alternative', but owing to the variety of vegetable dishes on offer in restaurants, it is possible to avoid eating meat.

yóucài   rape leaves. These look similar to Chinese leaves, but are green instead of white.

---

nà nǐ kàn qiàng yóucài zěnmeyàng? in that case what do you think about stir-fried rape? **Nǐ kàn...zěnmeyàng?** 'What do you think about?' / 'How about?' is a useful phrase to learn.

jīn'gōu yùsǔn gold hook white bamboo shoots, a fancy name for bamboo shoots. Just learn **sǔn**, bamboo shoots.

nǐ kàn in your opinion, short for **nǐ kàn...zěnmeyàng?** as above.

nǐ kàn, hái zài yào yī ge shénme cài? (lit. you see, still in addition want one what dish?) In your opinion, what further dish do we want? **Hái zài** is unnecessarily repetitive. Either **hái** or **zài** alone would have been sufficient here: **hái yào** / **zài yào**.

 2

Discussing a menu

> **LISTEN FOR...**
> **liáng cài** cold dish
> **rè cài** hot dish

Jiànguó	Hǎo, nà zánmen jiù diǎn liǎng ge liáng cài, xiān... hǎo bù hǎo?
Wáng	Hǎo.
Jiànguó	E, tā bǐjiǎo yǒu tèdiǎn de yī ge jiù shì jī kuàir, yī ge ne jiù shì niúròu. Xíng bù xíng?
Wáng	Ao, niúròu, néng bù néng huàn yī ge cài?
Jiànguó	Nà jiù huàn yī ge páigǔ.
Wáng	Nà hǎo ba.
Jiànguó	Zánmen zài lái diǎn liǎng ge rè cài. Rè cài ne tā bǐjiào yǒu tèdiǎn de yī ge ... guōbā yóuyú.
Wáng	Ao, wǒ tài xǐhuan chī le.
Jiànguó	E... ránhòu zài lái yī ge ne ... gānshāo xiānyú
Wáng	Hǎo.
Jiànguó	Nà jiù zhè yàng.
Wáng	Nà jiù zhè yàng ba.

bǐjiào	rather, quite	**páigǔ**	spare-ribs
tèdiǎn	characteristics	**yóuyú**	squid
jī	chicken	**gānshāo**	dry-roasted
kuàir	chunk	**xiānyú**	fresh fish
niúròu	beef		

zánmen jiù diǎn liǎng ge liáng cài, xiān... Let's just order two cold dishes, first.... A meal usually starts with cold dishes and moves on to hot dishes and rice, finishing with soup. Jiànguó was about to propose a dish with **xiān** 'first', but then stopped to check whether his suggestion was acceptable to Wáng.

hǎo bù hǎo? (lit. Good not good?) Is it OK or not? This sentence is the same type as **Néng bù néng?** introduced in Unit 9.

tā bǐjiào yǒu tèdiǎn de yī ge [cài] jiù shì jī kuàir, yī ge ne jiù shì niúròu. One rather characteristic dish is the chicken chunks, another is the beef. Jiànguó is referring to dishes characteristic of Sìchuān cuisine. The sentence is rather complicated. Just learn the important words, **jī kuàir** 'chicken chunks' and **niúròu** 'beef'.

huàn yī ge cài? (lit. change a dish?). **huàn yī ge páigǔ** (lit. change for a spare-ribs). As in previous Units, **huàn** is separated from the noun with a 'measure word'.

guōbā   rice crust, a light and very crispy batter coating.

yī ge guōbā yóuyú   one squid in rice crust

tài xǐhuan chī le   (lit. extremely like to eat). In Unit 4 you learned that **tài** ... **le** sandwiching a phrase or an adjective means 'extremely'.

ránhòu zài lái yī ge ne ... gānshāo xiānyú   then also get a dry-roasted fish. The **ne** has no particular meaning. Chinese people tend to insert **ne** all over the place! Compare the use of 'er' in English.

Market snacks

Practise what you have learned

1

Match the Pinyin words in the box to the foods listed here, writing the word in the space provided. (Answers on page 140.)

(1) beef   _____
(2) Chinese leaves   _____
(3) spare-ribs   _____
(4) fresh fish   _____
(5) pork   _____
(6) bamboo shoots   _____
(7) squid   _____
(8) chicken   _____

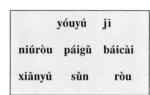

yóuyú	jī	
niúròu	páigǔ	báicài
xiānyú	sǔn	ròu

2

Match each Pinyin sentence with its English translation. (Answers on page 140.)

(a) **Wǒ xiān diǎn jǐ ge cài.**

(b) **Zánmen diǎn liǎng ge liáng cài.**

(c) **Zánmen lái yī ge jī kuàir.**

(d) **Nǐ kàn qiàng yóucài zěnmeyàng?**

(e) **Wǒ bù néng chī ròu.**

(f) **Néng bù néng huàn yī ge cài?**

(g) **Tài xǐhuan chī le.**

(1) What do you think of stir-fried rape?
(2) Let's get one chicken chunks.
(3) I like to eat it very much.
(4) Is it possible to change for another dish?
(5) First I'll order a few dishes.
(6) Let's order two cold dishes.
(7) I don't eat meat.

3

You are in a restaurant with a friend going through the menu, but it is proving difficult to choose as you have different tastes. Keep making suggestions; you will get there in the end! You will need the words for spare-ribs, fresh fish, vegetable dishes and stir-fried rape.

Fast food

Dialogues

3

The waitress suggests a soup

Xiǎojie	Zài lái yī ge tāng ba?
Jiànguó	E... hǎo, yào yī ge suānlà...
Xiǎojie	Sānxiāntāng.
Jiànguó	Suānlàtāng. Lìngwài jiù diǎn yīxiē yǐnliào.
Xiǎojie	Kěyǐ.
Jiànguó	E... píjiǔ, yī, èr, sān, sì, sì píng píjiǔ, e... liǎng ge Yēzizhīr. Hǎo, jiù zhè yàng, yǒu shénme...
Xiǎojie	Lái diǎnr xiǎochī ba, Sìchuān fēngwèir xiǎochī?
Jiànguó	E...
Xiǎojie	Dàndànmiàn a?
Jiànguó	Bù yào le. Yào mǐfàn ba, yī rén èr liǎng.
Xiǎojie	Xíng la, xiānsheng jiù zhè yàng?
Jiànguó	Hǎo, xièxie a.
Xiǎojie	Bù kèqi.

sānxiāntāng	three-kinds-of-seafood soup	**píng**	bottle
suānlàtāng	hot-and-sour soup	**Yēzizhīr**	coconut juice
lìngwài	in addition	**fēngwèir**	local flavour
yīxiē	some		

---

zài lái yī ge tāng ba? Also bring a soup?

lìngwài jiù diǎn yīxiē yǐnliào (lit. In addition just order some drinks.)

lái diǎnr xiǎochī ba? Shall I bring some snacks?

dàndànmiàn Sìchuān noodles with peppery sauce. **Miàn** is noodles.

yī rén èr liǎng two *liǎng* (of rice) per person. The rice comes in a large bowl with more than enough to go round.

xíng la, xiānsheng jiù zhè yàng? All right, sir, now that's it? **La** combines the question word **a**, and **le**, which indicates a change of situation, 'no more'. Soup and rice come at the end of a meal, so the waitress assumes they have finished their order.

Here are some more words to help you order a Chinese meal. Check their pronunciation on the recording.

jī sī shredded chicken
huángguā cucumber
tiáo stick
huángguā tiáo cucumber cut into matchsticks (julienne style)
dòufu tofu, bean curd
mápó dòufu a famous hot and spicy beancurd dish said to be named after the woman with a pock-marked face who created it.
qīngcài green vegetable
bōcài spinach
dòuyá bean sprouts

---

4 *At a fast-food restaurant*

LISTEN FOR...
sān fènr kǎo ji   three portions of roast chicken
nín zài zhèr chī háishi ná zǒu?   Eat in or take away?
(lit. you here eat, or take away?)
yī tǒng   a can

Waitress	Nín xūyào shénme ya?
Wáng	Wǒ mǎi sān fènr kǎo ji.
Waitress	Sān fènr kǎo ji. Nín zài zhèr chī háishi ná zǒu a?
Wáng	E... zài zhèr chī.
Waitress	Zài zhèr chī. Nín hái xūyào biéde ma?
Wáng	E... wǒ zài lái yī tǒng Xuěbì.
Waitress	Xuěbì.
Wáng	Kělè.
Waitress	Kělè.
Wáng	Hái yǒu yi tǒng Yēzhīr.
Waitress	Yēzhīr. Hái yào biéde ma, nín?
Wáng	Bù yào le.
Waitress	Yīgòng shì sān shí sān kuài wǔ. Zhǎo nín liù shí liù kuài wǔ.

ná zǒu   take away   **kělè**   cola
Xuěbì   Sprite   **Yēzhīr**   coconut juice

nín hái xūyào biéde ma?   (lit. You still want other?) Do you want anything else?

Bù yào le   Nothing more.

Fast food

Practise what you have learned

4   **Cài** is a useful word to know when talking about Chinese cooking. It can mean 'dish', 'cuisine', or 'vegetable'.

Choosing from the list below, write a word on each of the branches on the left which combines with **-cài** to match each of the branches on the right. (Answers on page 140.)

(a) **qīng-**
(b) **rè-**
(c) **bō-**
(d) **yóu-**
(e) **Chuān-**
(f) **liáng-**
(g) **sù-**
(h) **bái-**

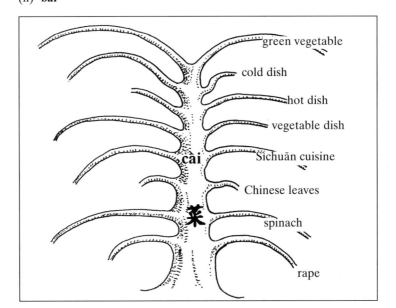

green vegetable

cold dish

hot dish

vegetable dish

Sìchuān cuisine

Chinese leaves

spinach

rape

cài

5   Many of the dishes you have come across combine the name of the food with its cooking method (for example **kǎo jī** 'roast chicken') or with the way it has been prepared for eating (for example **jī kuàir** 'chicken chunks'). Of course, the cooking / preparation words can also be combined with names for other foods – recognizing them will enable you to understand more of the dishes on a Chinese menu.

Fill in the blanks on the menu opposite with a word selected from the box below it. (Answers on page 140.)

```
┌─────────────────────────────┐
│  ┌───────────────────────┐  │
│  │        Menu           │  │
│  │   ─────── ròu ───────  │  │
│  │   boiled pork slices   │  │
│  │                        │  │
│  │   huángguā ───────     │  │
│  │   cucumber in julienne strips │
│  │                        │  │
│  │   jī ───────        •  │  │
│  │   shredded chicken     │  │
│  │                        │  │
│  │   ─────── jī           │  │
│  │   roast chicken        │  │
│  │                        │  │
│  │   ─────── ròu          │  │
│  │   sweet-and-sour pork  │  │
│  │                        │  │
│  │   ─────── dòufu        │  │
│  │   hot and spicy bean curd │
│  │                        │  │
│  │   ─────── yóuyú        │  │
│  │   squid in rice crust  │  │
│  └───────────────────────┘  │
└─────────────────────────────┘
```

```
┌────────────────────────────────┐
│               guōbā            │
│      tiáo                      │
│                     kǎo        │
│                        tángcù  │
│   shuǐzhǔ                      │
│             piànr              │
│                         sī     │
│         mápó                   │
└────────────────────────────────┘
```

 6 True or false? Listen to the recording, and then mark the statements below true or false, writing 'T' or 'F' in the relevant box. Correct those statements which are wrong. (Answers on page 140.)

The woman buys four portions of roast chicken. ☐

The woman buys three portions of roast chicken. ☐

They will eat in the shop. ☐

She buys a can of cola and two cans of Sprite. ☐

 7 Now you go to a fast-food restaurant and order a take-away. You will need the words for ordering a portion of roast chicken and a can of cola.

Key words and phrases

To learn

diǎn jǐ ge cài	order a few dishes
wǒ bù néng chī ròu	I cannot eat meat
sùcài	vegetable dishes
yóucài	rape leaves
sǔn	bamboo shoots
báicài	Chinese leaves
qīngcài	green vegetable
bōcài	spinach
huángguā	cucumber
dòuyá	bean sprouts
liáng cài	cold dishes
rè cài	hot dishes
tángcù	sweet-and-sour
jī	chicken
ròu	meat, usually pork
niúròu	beef
páigǔ	spare-ribs
yóuyú	squid
yú	fish
jī sī	shredded chicken
dòufu	tofu, bean curd
mápó dòufu	a famous hot bean curd dish
tāng	soup
suānlàtāng	hot-and-sour soup
píng	bottle
tǒng	can
xiǎochī	snack
mǐfàn	cooked rice
kǎo jī	roast chicken
zài zhèr chī háishi ná zǒu	eat in or take away
kělè	cola
kuàir	chunk
piànr	slice
tiáo	stick
guōbā	rice crust
gānshāo	dry-roasted
shuǐzhǔ	boiled
qiàng	stir-fried

To understand

Xuěbì	Sprite

Grammar

Word building

Each syllable in a Pinyin word represents a Chinese character. Pinyin words are formed by combining characters which together correspond in meaning to an English word. For example,

Tángcù ròu 'sweet-and-sour pork' is the transliteration of three characters:
táng 'sweet', **cù** 'sour' and **ròu** 'pork'

An appreciation of the transliteration system is particularly useful in understanding the names of dishes, since these are often formed from a combination of the name of the food and the word(s) for the way it is cooked (for example **tángcù ròu** 'sweet-and-sour pork') or the way it is prepared (for example **ròu piànr** 'pork slices').

In this Unit, therefore, it is useful to break down the names for dishes into syllables and learn these separately. For example, understanding **piànr** as 'slices' and **ròu** as 'pork' is probably more useful than understanding **ròu piànr** as 'pork slices', since both **ròu** and **piànr** will be found combined with other words on a Chinese menu. Some such useful syllables encountered in this Unit are:

ròu	pork	**tángcù**	sweet-and-sour
jī	chicken	**cài**	dish, cuisine, vegetable
yú	fish	**piànr**	slices
kǎo	roast	**kuàir**	chunks
chǎo	stir-fry	**tiáo**	sticks
qiàng	stir-fry	**sī**	shredded
shuǐzhǔ	boiled		

8   Match the following Pinyin words to their English translations.

(1) **tángcù ròu**   (a) chicken chunks
(2) **kǎo ròu**   (b) shredded chicken
(3) **tángcù yú**   (c) sweet-and-sour fish
(4) **jī kuàir**   (d) roast pork
(5) **jī sī**   (e) sweet-and-sour pork

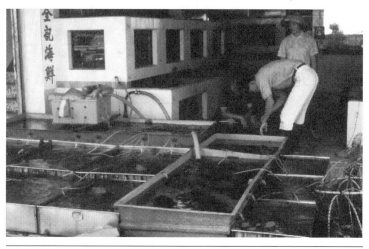

Fresh fish

Read and understand

Using chopsticks

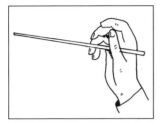 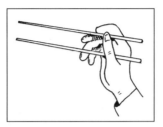 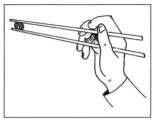

Table manners – don't insult your host!

- Don't gesture with your chopsticks, jab food with them, or leave them sticking up in your food.
- Don't begin to eat until everyone has been served. A host usually signals the time to begin eating.
- Accept the rice bowl offered to you by your host with two hands.
- Use your chopsticks to take food from the common plate to your bowl. Then raise the bowl to your mouth and push the food into your mouth with your chopsticks.
- Don't serve yourself without offering to others, at least those on either side of you. This also applies to taking tea. When served with tea, tap the table with your fingers to convey thanks.
- Don't turn over the fish; when the fish on top is finished, the skeleton will be removed to expose the meat below.
- Don't allow co-diners to know which dish is your favourite by your eating pattern!
- Don't scrape the remains of one dish into your own bowl, unless a new dish has been brought out.
- At the end of a banquet, take only a token portion of rice to express that you have been provided with a real feast. Do eat rice with the other dishes, however – otherwise you may be considered a glutton!
- Using a toothpick is acceptable provided you cover your mouth with your left hand.

Home cooking

Did you know?

Food and harmony

In Chinese gastronomy, the love of good food is intertwined with a traditional belief that a well-balanced diet is vital to the well-being of body and soul. The aim is to maintain peak health to enable the body to resist disease. Attention is paid in cooking to harmonizing the 'Five Flavours': sour, to nourish the bones; bitter, for the breath; sweet, for the flesh; pungent, for the muscles; and salty, for the blood. A balanced meal is a harmonious mix of hot and cold, sweet and sour, plain and spicy, meat and pickle, fish and greens, and care is taken to contrast taste and texture, colours and cooking methods.

But harmony is not achieved merely from the ingredients. All foods are considered to possess 'heating', **yáng**, 'cooling', **yīn**, or neutral characteristics. The correct blending of **yīn** and **yáng** is essential, as is the relationship of the eater to the food – the way it combines with his or her natural state. The season is also taken into account: more calming and cooling foods are appropriate in summer and more stimulating foods, to give the body stamina to withstand the cold, in winter. Even a person's current circumstances must be considered. For example, a person who requires a lot of energy should eat foods to provide this, as opposed to foods which will soothe and still the spirit.

The concepts of 'heating' and 'cooling' do not relate to the temperature or spiciness of foods, but to the effect the foods have on the body. Heating foods add **yáng** to the body, cooling foods add **yīn**, and how much this affects a person depends on their own natural state.

A very active, outgoing person is considered to be a **yáng** type, a quiet introvert is **yīn**. To keep in balance, a **yáng** person must eat plenty of **yīn** food – one who consumes too much heating food may become irritable. A **yīn** person, on the other hand, should avoid cooling foods. Of course, not everyone fits one of these two extremes. Many people combine elements of both types, even change according to their circumstances or environment, but this in itself suggests they may be able to modify their temperament with a carefully thought-out change of diet. Foods themselves are changed by the way in which they are cooked. Frying, roasting, grilling, smoking, and adding spices to food all make it **yáng**. **Yīn** methods are boiling, steaming and stewing.

Some heating **yáng** foods

apricots, beef, celery, chicken, coriander, garlic, ginger, grapes, oats, olives, onions, pineapple, shrimp, sugar, vinegar, walnuts, wine

Some cooling **yīn** foods:

aubergine, banana, bean curd, beer, cucumber, lettuce, marrow, mushrooms, oranges, spinach, sunflower seeds, green tea, tomatoes, wheat

Some neutral foods:

apples, cabbage, carrots, cauliflower, figs, honey, milk, peanuts, pork, rice, sweetcorn, yoghurt

Your turn to speak

9

Once you have mastered the *Key words and phrases* of this Unit,
practise going through a menu and ordering a meal in a restaurant.

Answers

**Practise what
you have
learned**

Exercise 1 (1) **niúròu**, (2) **báicài**, (3) **páigǔ**, (4) **xiānyú**, (5) **ròu**,
(6) **sǔn**, (7) **yóuyú**, (8) **jī**

Exercise 2 (a)5; (b)6; (c)2; (d)1; (e)7; (f)4; (g)3

Exercise 4 a, f, b, g, e, h, c, d

Exercise 5 **shuǐzhǔ**, **piànr**, **tiáo**, **sī**, **kǎo**, **tángcù**, **mápó**, **guōbā**

Exercise 6 All are False. The woman buys two portions of roast
chicken. They will take away. She buys a can of
Sprite and two cans of cola.

Grammar

Exercise 8 (1)(e); (2)(d); (3)(c); (4)(a); (5)(b)

Kentucky Fried Chicken

McDonald's, Beijing

What you will learn

- to say you like or dislike something
- to say something is your favourite or least favourite
- about Chinese festivals
- about some sports and games
- about the four types of Chinese cuisine

Before you begin

In Unit 7 you came across the verb **xǐhuan** 'to like', when talking about what you would like in shops. Now learn to use this verb to express your likes and dislikes.

Double happiness

Dialogues

1

Do you like...?

Neighbour	Nǐ xǐhuan guò nián ma?
Boy	Xǐhuan.
Neighbour	Wèi shénme ne?
Boy	Yīnwei guò nián kěyǐ chī hǎo dōngxi, hái kěyǐ fàng pào.

guò   to pass   **fàng pào**   to set off fireworks

> **guò nián**   (lit. passing year) the lunar New Year or Spring Festival, the most important Chinese festival. **Yīnwei guò nián** (lit. because passing year) because at New Year... **Guò** also means 'to celebrate'.
>
> **chī hǎo dōngxi**   to eat good things. This sounds rather childish – learn **chī hǎo fàn** 'to eat good food'.
>
> **hái kěyǐ fàng pào**   (lit. in addition can set off fireworks)

2

My favourite...

Boy	Wǒ zuì xǐhuan chī de shì bāozi hé chǎo gānr, háiyǒu... háiyǒu xīcān, zhōngcān. Wǒ zuì bù xǐhuan chī de shì en... xīhóngshì chǎo jīdàn, hái yǒu nà ge... hái yǒu miànbāo jiā xiāngcháng sānmíngzhì.

bāozi steamed stuffed buns		**miànbāo** bread
chǎo gānr stir-fried liver		**jiā** to sandwich
xīhóngshì tomato		**xiāngcháng** sausage
jīdàn chicken egg		**sānmíngzhì** sandwich

> **zuì**   goes before the verb or adjective to express 'most'.
>
> **Wǒ zuì xǐhuan chī de shì bāozi.**   My favourite food is *bāozi*. **De** is used here in the same way as explained in the *Grammar* of Unit 6; '*the one* I most like to eat is *bāozi*'.
>
> **Wǒ zuì bù xǐhuan chī de shì...**   My least favourite food is.... Simply put **bù** before **xǐhuan** to form the negative.
>
> **xīhóngshì chǎo jīdàn**   (lit. tomato stir-fried egg) stir-fried egg and tomato.
>
> **miànbāo jiā xiāngcháng sānmíngzhì**   (lit. bread sandwiching sausage sandwiches) sausage sandwiches. Note **jiā** 'to sandwich' is a verb.

Useful phrase: **wǒ gèng xǐhuan**   I prefer

Practise what you have learned

1

Refer to the *Grammar* section, for ways in which to use **xǐhuan** to express varying degrees of 'liking' something, then fill in the blanks in the following sentences with words from the box below. (Answers on page 152.)

(1) **Nǐ** _____ **Zhōngcān ma?**
Do you like Chinese food?

(2) _____.
Yes I do.

(3) _____.
No I don't.

(4) **Wǒ** _____ **xǐhuan Xīcān.**
I prefer Western cuisine.

(5) **Wǒ** _____ **xǐhuan Zhōngguó.**
I like China very much.

(6) **Wǒ** _____ **xǐhuan chī de shì tángcù ròu.**
The food I most like to eat is sweet-and-sour pork.

(7) **Wǒ** _____ **de yǐnliào shì píjiǔ.**
My least favourite drink is beer.

(a) **zuì bù xǐhuan**	(b) **zuì**	(c) **xǐhuan**
(d) **bù xǐhuan**	(e) **gèng**	(f) **xǐhuan**
	(g) **hěn**	

2

Two friends are talking about the foods they like. Listen to their conversation and then mark off the sentences below as true 'T', or false 'F'. (Answers on page 152.)

New words:
má hot (food)
Lǔcài Shāndōng cuisine (see *Did you know?*, page 151)
bùguò however
qīngdàn bland

(1) Lǐ likes Chinese food better than Western cuisine.
(2) Lǐ's favourite is Shāndōng cuisine.
(3) Her least favourite is spicy food.
(4) Lǐ's favourite food is hot and spicy bean curd.

3

Practise stating your likes and dislikes. Refer to the phrases you constructed in Exercise 1 to help you.

Dialogues

3

Favourite festivals

> **LISTEN FOR...**
> **Wǔyījié**   May Day
> **Chūnjié**   Spring Festival

Zhāng Lì	Yī nián zhī zhōng nǐ zuì xǐhuan nǎ ge jiérì?
Lǐ Qiáng	Dāngrán shì xǐhuan Wǔyījié le.
Zhāng Lì	Wèi shénme?
Lǐ Qiáng	Yīnwei Wǔyījié zhèng shì chūn nuǎn huā kāi, wǒmen kěyǐ chūqu jiāoyóu. Nǐ xǐhuan nǎ ge jiérì a?
Zhāng Lì	Wǒ zuì xǐhuan Chūnjié.
Lǐ Qiáng	Wèi shénme?
Zhāng Lì	Yīnwei Chūnjié hěn rènao.
Lǐ Qiáng	Dàjiā dōu kěyǐ zài yìqǐ wánr.
Zhāng Lì	Duì.

jiérì	festival	**rènao**	lively
zhèng	just, just then	**dàjiā**	everyone
chūqu	to go out	**yìqǐ**	together
jiāoyóu	outing, excursion	**wánr**	have fun, e.g. on an outing

> **yī nián zhī zhōng**   during the year
>
> **nǐ zuì xǐhuan nǎ ge jiérì?**   (lit. you most like which festival?)
>
> **dāngrán shì Wǔyījié le**   of course it is May Day. **Le** indicates a positive exclamation.
>
> **yīnwei Wǔyījié zhèng shì chūn nuǎn huā kāi**   (lit. because May Day just is [the time when] spring warms flowers bloom). Lǐ Qiáng is talking poetically and not using everyday language – there is no need to learn this phrase.
>
> **wǒmen kěyǐ chūqu jiāoyóu**   we can go out on excursions. **Jiāoyóu** has connotations of a trip outside the city, to the country.
>
> **zài yìqǐ**   be together. **Dàjiā dōu kěyǐ zài yìqǐ wánr**   (lit. everyone all can together have fun). **Dōu** (all) in this case emphasizes **dàjiā** 'everyone'. Refer to the note on **dōu** in Unit 7, Dialogue 2.

4

At Spring Festival time...

> **LISTEN FOR...**
> **zài Chūnjié qījiān**   at Spring Festival time
> **wǒ kěyǐ huí jiā**   I can return home

Zhāng Lì	Wǒ xǐhuan guò Chūnjié. Yīnwei zài Chūnjié qījiān, wǒ yǒu hěn cháng de jiàrì. Wǒ kěyǐ huí... jiā hé qīnrén tuánjù, kàn wǒ... de háizi.

qījiān	period, time	**hé**	with
hěn	very	**qīnrén**	relatives
cháng	long	**tuánjù**	reunite

zài … qíjiān   during

jiàrì   holiday, usually referring to time off work, rather than a holiday away.

wǒ yǒu hěn cháng de jiàrì.   I have a very long holiday.

wǒ kěyǐ huí jiā hé qīnrén tuánjù…   (lit. I can return home with relatives reunite…). Note that in Chinese you always say 'return home', not 'go home'. **Jiā**, often meaning 'family', can also mean 'home'.

kàn wǒ de háizi   see my child. Zhāng Lì's son lives with her parents in a different city.

Practise what you have learned

4

Fill in the blanks with a word or phrase chosen from the box. (Answers on page 152.)

(1) _____ **nǐ zuì xǐhuan nǎ ge jiérì?**
Which festival in the year do you most like?

(2) _____ **shì Chūnjié.**
Of course it is the Spring Festival.

(3) _____ **zài Chūnjié qíjiān, wǒmen kěyǐ** _____.
Because during Spring Festival we can eat good food.

(4) **Wǒ xǐhuan** _____.
I like new year.

(5) _____ **, wǒmen kěyǐ fàng pào.**
At Spring Festival time, we can set off fireworks.

(6) _____ **dōu kěyǐ zài yìqǐ wánr.**
Everyone can be together to have fun.

(7) **Wǒmen kěyǐ** _____.
We can go on outings.

(a) **zài Chūnjié qíjiān**
(b) **guò nián**
(c) **dāngrán**
(d) **yī nián zhī zhōng**
(e) **dàjiā**
(f) **chī hǎo fàn**
(g) **yīnwei**
(h) **chūqu jiāoyóu**

5

On the recording you will hear Xiànbīn talking about what he likes and dislikes. Listen to what he says and then tick (✓) the appropriate boxes below. (Answers on page 152.)

New word: **jiǎozi**   type of dumpling

	likes	dislikes		likes	dislikes
Spring Festival			fish and vegetables		
set off fireworks			beer		
jiǎozi			Qīngdǎo		
meat					

6

On a visit to China you may wish to tell Chinese friends about Christmas. Practise now, following the prompts. Some words and phrases are listed below to help you.

New word: **Shèngdànjié**   Christmas

yī nián zhī zhōng   during the year / **jiérì**   festival / **zài Shèngdànjié qījiān**   at Christmas time / **dàjiā dōu**   everyone all / **zài yīqǐ**   be together / **chī hǎo fàn**   eat good food / **rènao**   lively / **jiàrì**   holiday / **huí jiā**   return home / **hé qīnrén tuánjù**   reunite with relatives

Dialogues

5

Sports...

> **LISTEN FOR...**
> **dǎ lánqiú**   to play basketball
> **tī zúqiú**   to play football (= soccer) (lit. to kick football)
> **pǎopao bù**   to jog
> **dǎda pīngpāngqiú**   to play table tennis
> **róudào**   judo

Teacher	Nǐ kèyú shíjiān xǐhuan shénme ya?
Pupil	En ... dǎ lánqiú, tī zúqiú, en... pǎopao bù, dǎda pīngpāngqiú, róudào.
Teacher	Nǐ zuì xǐhuan shénme ne?
Pupil	Róudào.

kèyú   out of class   **pǎo bù**   to jog
tī   to kick   **róudào**   judo

> **nǐ kèyú shíjiān xǐhuan shénme ya?**   (lit. you out of class time like what?) What do you like to do in your spare time?
>
> **dǎ lánqiú**   play basketball; **dǎ** 'hit' is used to mean 'play' for all ball games in which the hands are used.

> **pǎopao bù, dǎda pīngpāngqiú**   do some jogging and play a bit of table tennis. The repetition of verbs, for example **dǎ**, **tī**, **pǎo**, adds the sense of 'a bit of'. It sounds less formal.

6

...and hobbies

LISTEN FOR...
zài gōngzuò zhī hòu   after work
yǒushí   sometimes
yī kāishǐ   in the beginning
kūzào   dull
yǒu yìsi   interesting

Zhāng Lì	Nǐ zài gōngzuò zhī hòu dōu zuò xiē shénme ne?
Lǐ Qiáng	Ao, wǒ yǒushí dǎda pái, yǒushí xiàxia wéiqí. E..., bùguò, wǒ zuìjìn zài liànxí shūfǎ.
Zhāng Lì	Liàn shūfǎ hěn yǒuqù ba?
Lǐ Qiáng	Ao, e... yī kāishǐ juéde bǐjiào kūzào, dànshì hòulái ne juéde hěn yǒu yìsi.

gōngzuò	to work, work	**yǒuqù**	fascinating, interesting
bùguò	however	**juéde**	to feel
zuìjìn	recently	**dànshì**	but
liàn	to practise, to exercise	**hòulái**	later on

nǐ zài gōngzuò zhī hòu dōu zuò xiē shénme?   This first sentence is rather long. You can break it down into shorter phrases: **Nǐ** 'you', **zài gōngzuò zhī hòu** 'after work', **zuò** 'to do', **xiē shénme?** 'some what?': 'What do you do after work (in your spare time)?' **Dōu** is used here in the same way as in Unit 7, Dialogue 2; it indicates that the reply is expected to contain a list. It is not absolutely necessary, and you can learn the sentence construction without it.

xià   to play, used when talking about board games.

dǎ pái   play cards. The Chinese are enthusiastic card players, and tend to throw the cards down on the table; hence **dǎ** 'hit' is used to express 'play'.

wǒ yǒushí dǎda pái, yǒushí xiàxia wéiqí   I sometimes play cards, sometimes play go. Go is a Chinese board game.

liànxí shūfǎ   practise calligraphy. **Bùguò, wǒ zuìjìn zài liànxí shūfǎ** However, I have recently been practising calligraphy. **Zài** used in this way indicates continuous action, 'I have been (and still am)'. **Tā zài dǎ diànhuà**. He is in the process of making a phone call.

liàn shūfǎ hěn yǒuqù ba?   (lit. to practise calligraphy very interesting?)

hòulái ne juéde hěn yǒu yìsi   (lit. later on feels very interesting)

Note: to make **yǒu yìsi** negative, use **méi**: **méiyǒu yìsi**, 'no interest', 'not interesting'.

Practise what you have learned

7 Write the correct Pinyin word(s) underneath each of the following pictures of hobbies and sports, choosing from those given in the box below. (Answers on page 152.)

1

2

3

4

5

6

> (a) **róudào**   (b) **lánqiú**   (c) **zúqiú**   (d) **pīngpāngqíu**
> (e) **pǎo bù**   (f) **liàn shūfǎ**   (g) **pái**

8 Which is the odd one out? (Answers on page 152.)

dǎ / tī   **lánqiú**
         pái
         zúqiú
         pīngpāngqiú

9 What do you like doing in your spare time? Tell Xiànbīn, following Lǐ's prompts, to practise some of the words and phrases below.

zài gōngzuò zhī hòu   after work
yī kāishǐ   in the beginning
hòulái   later on
yǒushí..., yǒushí...   sometimes..., sometimes...
yǒu yìsi   interesting
kūzào   dull
yóuyǒngchí   swimming pool

Key words and phrases

To learn

dǎ lánqiú	to play basketball
tī zúqiú	to play football
dǎ pái	to play cards
pǎo bù	to jog
dǎ pīngpāngqiú	to play table tennis
róudào	judo
guò nián	passing (lunar New) Year; celebrate New Year
yī nián zhī zhōng	during the year
jiérì	festival
Wǔyījié	May Day
Chūnjié	Spring Festival
wèi shénme	why
yīnwei	because
yǒushí…, yǒushí…	sometimes…, sometimes…
jiāoyóu	outing
zài yīqǐ	to be together
zài gōngzuò zhī hòu	after work
wánr	to have fun
bùguò	however
yǒuqù	fascinating, interesting
yī kāishǐ	in the beginning
juéde	to feel
kūzào	dull
dànshì	but
hòulái	later on
yǒu yìsi	interesting
bāozi	steamed stuffed buns
xīhóngshì	tomato
jīdàn	chicken egg
miànbāo	bread
xiāngcháng	sausage
sānmíngzhì	sandwich

To understand

xià wéiqí	to play go
liànxí shūfǎ	to practise calligraphy

Grammar

I like, I most like, I most dislike

zuì 'most' is used with adjectives or verbs to express the highest degree of comparison. For example,

(a) **Wǒ zuì xǐhuan chī xīhóngshì chǎo jīdàn**. I most like stir-fried egg and tomato.
(b) **Wǒ zuì bù xǐhuan chǎo gānr**. I most dislike stir fried liver.
(c) **Wǒ zuì xǐhuan chī de shì bāozi**. What I most like to eat is *baozi* (steamed stuffed buns).

I prefer

Gèng 'prefer' goes before **xǐhuan**. For example,

(a) **Wǒ gèng xǐhuan chī tángcù ròu**. I prefer to eat sweet-and-sour pork.
(b) **Wǒ gèng xǐhuan kān háizi**. I prefer to look after the child(ren).

Good, better, best

Gèng and **zuì** can also be used with adjectives. For example,

(a) **Zhè ge fàn hěn hǎo**. This food is very good.
(b) **Nà ge fàn gèng hǎo**. That food is better.
(c) **Zhè ge yú gèng dà**. This fish is bigger.
(d) **Zhè ge yú shì zuì hǎo de**. This fish is best.
(e) **Zhè ge yú shì zuì dà de**. This fish is biggest.

10 Unscramble the Pīnyīn sentences to match the English ones. (Answers on page 152.)

(1) I like Spring Festival very much.
hěn wǒ Chūnjié xǐhuan

(2) I prefer to drink jasmine tea.
xǐhuan gèng hē wǒ huāchá

(3) I most like Beijing.
xǐhuan Běijīng zuì wǒ

(4) The festival I like most is Spring Festival.
Chūnjié jiérì zuì wǒ shì xǐhuan de

(5) The vegetable I like least is Chinese leaves.
cài báicài shì bù wǒ zuì xǐhuan de

Read and understand

The character below means 'happiness'. Two written side by side form 'double happiness', which always features at weddings pasted on walls and windows as you can see from the photographs below and on p. 141.

Did you know?

China's cuisine

There is not one Chinese cuisine but four:

Běijīng and Shāndōng **Lǔcài**	In this, one of the coldest parts of China, dishes are cooked with ingredients to warm the body, for example, bean curd with pepper sauce. The speciality is Peking (Běijīng) Duck, eaten with pancakes, spring onions and plum sauce. Others are 'Beggar's Chicken', Bird's nest soup and Mongolian hotpot.
Shànghǎi **Huáiyángcài**	Shànghǎi's position on the coast ensures a rich variety of seafood for the surrounding area. Favoured ways of preparing dishes in the region are the well-known sweet-and-sour method, and the 'red-cook' method, where chunks of meat are cooked for a long time in sugar, soy, ginger and mixed spices.
Sìchuān **Chuāncài**	Spices are considered necessary in hotter, damper climates, to stimulate the appetite; Sìchuān cooking is the hottest of the four categories. Hot bean curd and peppery noodles are staples of this region's diet.
Cantonese **Yuècài**	The majority of restaurants outside China serve this style. Steam and water are used more than frying in the preparation of dishes, and vegetables are cooked for the shortest time possible to maintain crispness. Typical is dim sum (Mandarin **diǎnxin**), a variety of little dumplings and meats, chosen from carts wheeled round restaurant tables.
Staples	Rice is the staple in southern and central China; north of the Yángzi it is wheat, usually in the form of noodles and steamed buns. Tea has long been the national drink, and tours to southern China will often include a trip to a tea plantation.

Your turn to speak

11

People in China are usually very friendly, and if you travel on a train someone will often strike up a conversation with you. In this exercise, you practise the phrases you have learned, to express likes and dislikes to a man who has started talking to you on a train.

Some phrases are listed below to help you, but not in the order you need them.

zhù zài nàr   lives there
yīnwei   because
zài Shèngdànjié qījiān   at
   Christmas time
yóu yǒng   to have a swim

jiàn shēn   to keep fit
wǒ péngyou   my friend
qù guo   I have been before
wǒ qù   I am going

Answers

Exercise **1**   (1) (c)/(f); (2) (c)/(f); (3)(d); (4)(e); (5)(g); (6)(b);
   (7)(a)

Exercise **2**   (1) T; (2) F; (3) F; (4) T

Exercise **4**   (1)(d); (2)(c); (3)(g),(f); (4)(b); (5)(a); (6)(e); (7)(h)

Exercise **5**   Likes Spring Festival, fish and vegetables, beer,
   Qingdǎo. Dislikes the rest.

Exercise **7**   (1)(b); (2)(c); (3)(e); (4)(d); (5)(g); (6)(f)

Exercise **8**   **Zúqiú** is the odd one out since it goes with **tī** and not
   dǎ.

Grammar

Exercise **10**   (1) **Wǒ hěn xǐhuan Chūnjié.**
   (2) **Wǒ gèng xǐhuan hē huāchá.**
   (3) **Wǒ zuì xǐhuan Běijīng.**
   (4) **Wǒ zuì xǐhuan de jiérì shì Chūnjié.**
   (5) **Wǒ zuì bù xǐhuan de cài shì báicài.**

12

TALKING ABOUT YOUR TOWN AND THE WEATHER

What you will learn

- to understand the weather forecast
- to talk about the weather and seasons

- to describe places
- to plan a trip
- the titles of books for further reading on China

Before you begin

When you meet people in China, they inevitably ask you which cities you have visited and what you think of them. In this Unit you will learn the language you need to reply, and also to talk about your own home town.

Weather words and phrases are also introduced. While the weather itself is not a conversation piece in China, it is useful to be able to express if you are hot or cold, or to understand a weather forecast.

The Great Wall

Dialogues

1

What does the weather forecast say?

LISTEN FOR...
jīntiān zánmen shàng Xiāngshān wánr?
Today we go to Xiāngshān to have fun?
tiānqì yùbào shuō the weather forecast says
qíng fine, clear
yǒu fēng there is wind, it's windy
xià yǔ to rain, it's raining
bù zhīdao don't know

Wife	Jīntiān zánmen shàng Xiāngshān wánr?
Husband	Hǎo a.
Wife	Nǐ tīng dao tiānqì yùbàogào zěnme shuō de?
Husband	En... tiānqì yùbào shuō shàngwǔ shì qíng, xiàwǔ hǎoxiàng yǒu fēng.
Wife	En... bù zhīdào jīntiān xià bù xià yǔ a?
Husband	Hǎoxiàng shì méi yǒu.
Wife	Ai, nà xíng a, zánmen qù a.
Husband	Hǎo ba.

shàng to go to, to ascend
tīng to hear, to listen to
tiānqì weather

---

shàng to go, an alternative to **qù**

Xiāngshān (lit. Fragrant Mountain) mountain in the west of Běijīng.

nǐ tīng dao tiānqì yùbàogào [shì] zěnme shuō de? Did you get to hear what the weather report said? **Dao**, with fourth tone **dào** meaning 'to reach', here indicates attainment of the action, in this case **tīng** 'to hear'. The *Grammar* section on page 162 explains this point more fully with further examples. **Yùbàogào** (forecast) is less common than **yùbào**. To be grammatically correct the sentence needs a **shì** as indicated in square brackets. Learn the sentence with **shì**.

shàngwǔ shì qíng, xiàwǔ hǎoxiàng yǒu fēng the morning is fine, in the afternoon it seems there is wind

zhīdao to know, used for facts. **Nǐ zhīdao ma?** Do you know? **Bù zhīdao.** I don't know. 'To know' in the sense of knowing a person is **rènshi**. **Nǐ rènshi tā ma?** Do you know him?

bù zhīdao jīntiān xià bù xià yǔ a? (lit. not know today rain or not?) Do you know whether it will rain today or not? Note that **xià yǔ** means 'it is raining', and that to express, for example, 'tomorrow there is rain', you would say, **míngtiān yǒu yǔ**. Similarly, **xià xuě** is 'it is snowing', and **yǒu xuě** means 'there is snow'.

hǎoxiàng shì méi yǒu it seems there is none. Seemingly not.

nà xíng a, zánmen qù a So all right, let's go.

2

What's the climate like in China?

Lǐ: Zhōngguó de qìhòu ne yǒu yī ge tèdiǎn, jiùshì zài dà bùfen dìqū, dōng, xià, chūn, qiū – zhè sìjì ne dōu bǐjiào fēnmíng, xī bù dìqū ne... e... bǐjiào gānzào, dōng bù dìqū, xiāngduì láishuō ne, bǐjiào shīrùn, érqiě ne, běifāng bǐjiào hánlěng, érqiě ne, yě bǐjiào gānzào. Nánfāng dìqū ne, bǐjiào wēnnuǎn yīxiē, yě bǐjiào shīrùn.

qìhòu	climate	**sìjì**	four seasons
tèdiǎn	characteristic	**fēnmíng**	distinct
jiùshì	precisely, i.e.	**shīrùn**	humid
dìqū	region	**érqiě**	moreover

bùfen   part, section, shortened later on to **bù**. **Dà bùfen**, majority. **Zài dà bùfen dìqū** in the majority of the country. **Dà bùfen de rén**, the majority of people.

zhè sìjì ne dōu bǐjiào fēnmíng   these four seasons are all rather distinct. **Bǐjiào** is used when making a comparison.

dōng, xià, chūn, qiū   winter, summer, spring, autumn. These are short forms. In the longer versions the words are suffixed by the word **tiān** 'weather'. **Dōngtiān** is 'winter', **xiàtiān** 'summer', **chūntiān** 'spring', **qiūtiān** 'autumn'.

xiāngduì láishuō   comparatively speaking. You don't need to learn this.

bǐjiào wēnnuǎn yīxiē   (lit. comparatively warm a little) rather warmer.

Note that in the dialogue you hear **xī bù** 'western part' and **dōng bù** 'eastern part'; **běi bù** 'northern part' and **nán bù** 'southern part' are also possible.

New words: **nuǎnhuo**   warm (weather)
lěng   cold (weather)

Practise what you have learned

1

1_____ 2_____ 3_____

4_____ 5_____ 6_____

From the list below, choose the appropriate Pīnyīn word to describe the weather in each picture. (Answers on page 166.)

(a) **xià xuě**   (d) **lěng**
(b) **nuǎnhuo**   (e) **qíng**
(c) **yǒu fēng**   (f) **xià yǔ**

2

Choosing words from the box below, complete the Pīnyīn sentences to match their English translations. Check your answers on the recording.

(1) _____ **yùbào zěnme shuō de?**
What does the weather report say?

(2) **Shàngwǔ yǒu** _____, **xiàwǔ** _____ _____.
Wind in the morning, rain in the afternoon.

(3) **Běijīng de** _____ **bǐjiào** _____.
Běijīng's climate is rather dry.

(4) **Guǎngzhōu de** _____ **bǐjiào shīrùn.**
Guǎngzhōu's climate is rather humid.

(5) **Běijīng de** _____ **hánlěng.**
Běijīng's winter is freezing cold.

(6) _____, _____, _____, _____ **zhè sìjì dōu hěn fēnmíng.**
The four seasons – spring, summer, autumn, winter – are all distinct.

dōngtiān	sìjì	chūn	qìhòu
xià	tiānqì	dōng	fēng
gānzào	yǒu yǔ	qiū	qìhòu

3

You will hear a weather forecast on the recording relating to the map below. Listen to it as many times as necessary, then complete the following statements by ticking (✓) in the appropriate boxes. (Answers on page 166.)

New phrase: **qìwēn hěn gāo** very high temperature

(1) In the east, it is…
    warm ☐   hot ☐   cold ☐

(2) In Shànghǎi, the temperature is…
    low ☐   high ☐

(3) In the west, it is…
    hot and dry ☐   hot and humid ☐

(4) In the south, it is…
    hot and dry ☐   hot and humid ☐

(5) In the morning in Guǎngzhōu, there will be…
    snow ☐   rain ☐

(6) In the north, it is…
    cold ☐   a little cold ☐   very cold ☐

(7) In Běijīng in the afternoon there will be…
    snow ☐   rain ☐   wind ☐

(8) Tomorrow will be…
    hot ☐   windy ☐   fine ☐

Dialogues

3

What is Hángzhōu like?

> **LISTEN FOR...**
> **nàr fēngjǐng zěnmeyàng?** (lit. how is the scenery there?)
> What is the scenery like?
> **hěn měi** very beautiful
> **shénme shíhou** when, at what time

Man	Nǐ qù guo Hángzhōu ma?
Woman	Qù guo.
Man	Nàr hǎo wánr ma?
Woman	En... Hěn hǎo wánr.
Man	En... nàr de fēngjǐng zěnmeyàng?
Woman	Hěn měi.
Man	Shénme shíhou zánmen yīqǐ zài qù wánr yi wánr, hǎo ma?
Woman	Hǎo a.

> **Hángzhōu** a city in southern China known for its 'typical' Chinese scenery. **Nǐ qù guo Hángzhōu ma?** Have you ever been to Hángzhōu?
>
> **shénme shíhou zánmen yiqǐ zài qù** (lit. at what time we together again go?). **Shénme shíhou** is literally 'when', but in the context of this sentence can be translated as 'sometime'.
>
> **wánr yi wánr?** to have a good time, to enjoy oneself a bit. As in previous dialogues, the speaker repeats the verb to emphasize it, and to make the sentence less formal. **Yi** is not necessary, but it is common to separate the repeated verb with **yi**. **Wánrwanr** is also possible.

4

A family day out in Běijīng

> **LISTEN FOR...**
> **Běijīng shì de quánmào** a panoramic view of Běijīng city
> (lit. Běijīng city's panoramic view)
> **Tiān'ānmén zhuàn wán le** Having finished wandering around Tiān'ānmén
> **zhè ge zhǔyì bù cuò** this idea is not bad

Hènián	Jīntiān wǒmen dài Zhòuzhou shàng nǎr qù ne?
Zhāng	Wǒ xiǎng xiān dào Jǐngshān kàn yi kàn, yīnwei zài nàli wǒmen kěyǐ kàn dao Běijīng shì de quánmào.
Hènián	Xíng a, ránhòu, wǒmen kěyǐ zhíjiē dài tā qù Gùgōng la.
Zhāng	Duì. Kàn wán Gùgōng, wǒmen kěyǐ zhíjiē dào Tiān'ānmén.
Hènián	Tiān'ānmén zhuàn wán le, wǒmen kěyǐ chī dùn zhōngwǔ fàn, ránhòu, zài dài tā qù shāngyè dàshà kàn yi kàn.
Zhāng	Hǎo, zhè ge zhǔyì bù cuò.

nàli that place
quánmào panoramic view
Gùgōng the Forbidden City
zhuàn to wander around

wán finish
shāngyè dàshà department store
zhǔyì idea
bù cuò not bad

---

dài to take, lead (someone to somewhere).

Jīntiān wǒmen dài Zhòuzhou shàng nǎr qù ne? (lit. Today we take Zhòuzhou to where go?). Zhòuzhou is the name of the couple's child.

Jǐngshān Coal Hill in Běijīng. **Shān** means 'mountain'.

kàn yī kàn to have a little look. As in Dialogue 3 the repeated verb is separated with **yī**. **Kànkan** is also possible.

yīnwei zài nàli because at that place

kàn dao get to see. **Dao** has the same meaning here as it does in Dialogue 1, **tīng dao**. Have a look at the *Grammar* section on page 162 for more details.

kàn wán Gùgōng (lit. finish looking at the Forbidden City). **Wán** complements **kàn** indicating completion. It is being used in the same way as **dao**. Again see the *Grammar* section.

dùn a 'measure word' for **fàn** 'meal'. It is needed here because the meaning is 'some lunch'. The speaker could also have suggested, **wǒmen kěyǐ chī fàn**, we can eat.

zhōngwǔ fàn lunch

Tiān'ānmén zhuàn wán le having finished wandering around Tiān'ānmén. **Le** makes the sentence past tense.

zài dài tā qù... also take him go.... **Dài** on its own is not enough. For the meaning to be clear, **qù** must also appear.

Overlooking The Forbidden City

Practise what you have learned

Before you begin the exercises, turn to the *Grammar* section to check out the way to use phrases which came up in Dialogue 4: **kàn dao**, **kàn wán**, and **zhuàn wán**.

4

Match each Pīnyīn sentence with its English equivalent. (Answers on page 166.)

(1) **Wǒmen dài tā shàng nǎr qù?**
(2) **Nàr fēngjǐng zěnmeyàng?**
(3) **Zài nàli wǒmen kěyǐ kàn dao Běijīng shì de quánmào.**
(4) **Zhè ge zhǔyì bù cuò.**
(5) **Zánmen qù Gùgōng kàn yi kàn.**
(6) **Gùgōng zhuàn wán le, wǒmen kěyǐ chī dùn zhōngwǔ fàn.**

(a) This idea is not bad.
(b) At that place we can get to see Beijing's panoramic view.
(c) What's the scenery like there?
(d) Having finished wandering around the Forbidden City we can eat lunch.
(e) Let's go to the Forbidden City and have a look.
(f) Where shall we take him?

5

Wáng is visiting friends in Běijīng. Listen to him saying in Mandarin what he has been up to, and then answer the following questions. (Answers on page 166.)

1 What is Wáng doing in Běijīng?
  (a) He is on business.
  (b) He is a tourist.

2 Has he ever been before?
  (a) Yes.
  (b) No.

3 Where does he go first?
  (a) By bus to Tiāntán.
  (b) Directly to Jǐngshān.

4 Why does he go to Jǐngshān?
  (a) To have a look at the panoramic view of the city of Běijīng.
  (b) To have lunch.

5 What is the plan for tomorrow?
  (a) Visiting friends.
  (b) Shopping for souvenirs.

6

A Chinese friend, Xiǎo Chén, is visiting you in London and you discuss the day's plan with another friend. You may find it useful to look again at the phrases you used in Exercise 4 before starting this exercise.

Key words and phrases

To learn

tīng dao	to have heard
kàn dao	to get a look
kàn wán	to finish seeing
zhuàn wán	to finish wandering
tiānqì yùbào shì zěnme shuō de?	What did the weather report say?
tiānqì yùbào	weather forecast
shàngwǔ shì qíng	fine in the morning
yǒu fēng	windy
xià yǔ	to rain
rè	hot
nuǎnhuo	warm
lěng	cold
quánmào	panoramic view
nàr fēngjǐng zěnmeyàng?	How's the scenery there?
shénme shíhou?	when? at what time?
dài… shàng nǎr qù?	to take…to where?
dài tā qù…	take him / her to…
zhè ge zhǔyì bù cuò	this idea's not bad
qìhòu	climate
gānzào	dry
shīrùn	humid
hánlěng	freezing cold (climate)
wēnnuǎn	warm (climate)
nánfāng	southern part, in the south
běifāng	northern part, in the north
bùfen / bù	part, section
sìjì	four seasons
dōngtiān	winter
xiàtiān	summer
chūntiān	spring
qiūtiān	autumn
shāngyè dàshà	department store
hǎoxiàng	it seems
bù zhīdào	don't know

To understand

érqiě	moreover
fēnmíng	distinct
dìqū	region

A Beijing street

Grammar

Verb 'complements'

The words **wán** and **dao** can modify the meaning of a verb. Thus **kàn** on its own means 'to see'. By following it with **wán**, it suggests the completion of the action is suggested. For example,

kàn wán Gùgōng   finish seeing Gùgōng

Following **kàn** with **dao** suggests attainment of the action.
kàn dao   get to see

These words are known as verb 'complements'.

To put such phrases in the past, add **le**:

Tiān'ānmén zhuàn wán le   having finished wandering around Tiān'ānmén
mài wán le   sold out
kàn dao le Běijīng shì de quánmào   having got to see the panoramic view of Beijing city
or, **Wǒmen kàn dao Běijīng shì de quánmào le**   We got to see the panoramic view of Běijīng city

The following sentences exemplify ways of negating with verb complements.
Wǒmen méi kàn wán Gùgōng.   We have not finished looking at the Forbidden City
Zài nàli kàn bù dao Běijīng shì de quánmào.   At that place it is not possible to get a look at the panoramic view of the city of Běijīng.

Note that **bù** indicates that attainment or completion of the action is impossible, while **méi** makes the whole sentence negative.

7 Fill in the blanks with **wán, dao, bù** or **méi**. (Answers on page 166.)

(1) **Nǐ kàn ＿＿ tā le ma?**
Did you get to see him?

(2) **Qīngdǎo píjiǔ mài ＿＿ le.**
The Qīngdǎo beer is sold out.

(3) **Nǐ tīng ＿＿ tiānqì yùbào shì zěnme shuō de?**
Did you get to hear what the weather forecast said?

(4) **Tiāntán zhuàn ＿＿ le, wǒmen kěyǐ chī dùn zhōngwǔ fàn.**
Having finished wandering around the Temple of Heaven, we can eat lunch.

(5) **Nǐmen kàn ＿＿ shāngyè dàshà le ma?**
Did you get to see the department store?

(6) **Wǒmen méi kàn ＿＿.**
We didn't get to see it.

(7) **Wǒmen kàn ＿＿ dao shāngyè dàshà.**
We cannot possibly see the department store.

Read and understand

Brand names

Names are important in Chinese, so when the names of foreign companies and brand names are translated, care is taken to choose appropriate characters. Often these not only sound like the English, but incorporate a particular meaning in Chinese. For example,

English	*Chinese*	*meaning*
Avon	**Yǎfāng**	elegant fragrance
Coca Cola	**Kěkǒukělè**	nice to taste and happy
Marlboro	**Wànbǎolù**	10,000 treasure road
Dunhill	**Dēng Xǐ Lù**	set foot on happy road
Sprite	**Xuěbì**	green snow
7 Up	**Qī Xǐ**	seven happinesses
Nestlé	**Què Cháo**	birds nest
Pizza Hut	**Bì Shèng Kè**	must win customers
BMW	**Bǎo Mǎ**	precious horse
Peugeot	**Biāo Zhì**	beautiful handsome

Sometimes, however, names are simply transliterated, and have no special meaning in Chinese. For example,

Siemens	**Xīménzi**
Kodak	**Kēdá**
Sharp	**Xiàpǔ**
Philips	**Fēilìpǔ**
Pierre Cardin	**Pí'ěr Kǎdān**
Ferrari	**Fǎlálì**
Nike	**Nàikè**

East meets West at the airport

Did you know?

Book list

China is a vast subject on which there are literally hundreds of books available. In perusing this selection remember Confucius said that if he showed someone one corner of a thing, then that person should be able to discover the other corners independently!

History and politics

Red Star Over China, Edgar Snow
Snow spent over a decade (1928–41) in China. His reports to Western newspapers included accounts by Long March participants, and Máo's life story as he himself told it to Snow. First published in 1937.

100 Years of Revolution, Harrison Salisbury
A history of the evolution of modern China under Western influence, from a former *New York Times* correspondent. Stunning photographs and illustrations.

The Chinese People Stand Up, Elizabeth Wright
Traces the history of the People's Republic up to the tumultous events on Tiān'ānmén Square in 1989.

Cultural Revolution

Wild Swans, Jung Chang
Probably the most famous book on China of the last few years, it traces the history of Jung Chang's own family living through this traumatic period.

Chen Village, Anita Chan, Richard Madsen, Jonathan Unger
An enthralling account of a South China farming village in the throes of the Maoist Revolution.

Foreigners in China

Alive in the Bitter Sea, Fox Butterfield
Another best-seller, by a *New York Times* correspondent, one of the first through the 'Open Door'. Worth a read, but controversial, owing to Butterfield's cynical and critical examination of everything he sees.

Discos and Democracy, Orville Schell
Another American journalist's personal observations, this time focusing on the 1980s and the impact of the economic reforms on lifestyles.

Behind the Wall, Colin Thubron
A travelogue with much insight into Chinese society. A good one to read before you go.

The Reform period

Riding the Tiger, Gordon White
Assesses the political dynamics of the reforms and their impact, concluding with an analysis of the options for China's political future.

Fiction

The Good Earth, Pearl Buck
Illuminates life in the countryside in traditional, pre-revolutionary China, many features of which prevail even today.

Half of Man is Woman, Zhang Xianliang
The main character is imprisoned in a labour camp for political crime. A moving story of hope against all odds.

Travel guides   There are so many, and the choice is a personal one. The Collins
Guides are worth a mention for their beautiful photographs. For
people travelling on business, *The Economist Guide to China* is useful.

Shopping for books

Your turn to speak

8   Chat to Xiǎoyún about a trip she is taking to Běijīng tomorrow. Some of the words and phrases you will need are listed below, but not in the same order.

tiānqì yùbào   wǒ jiànyì
hěn měi   yǒuyìsi
Gùgōng zhuàn wán le   míngtiān xiàwǔ
nǐ xiǎng shàng nǎr qù?   méi qù guo

Answers

On Tian'anmen Square

What you will learn

- to say what you do for a living (and the words for various occupations)
- to describe where you live
- to talk about the members of your family
- to discuss retirement
- about religions in China

Before you begin

When talking about yourself in China, you will have to adapt the language you know to fit your individual circumstances. For example, you may not know the word for company director, but you have learned how to say 'I do business', **Wǒ zuò shēngyi**. For this reason, a selection of useful phrases to be modified for your own purpose are given in the *Grammar* section of this Unit.

Folk religion

Dialogues

1

What do you do?

> **LISTEN FOR...**
> **nǐ zài Zhōngguó zuò shénme?** What do you do in China?
> **wǒ zài... gōngzuò.** I work at ...
> **Hànyǔ** Chinese language

Zhāng Lì	Nǐ zài Zhōngguó zuò shénme?
Friend	Wǒ zài Zhōngguó Rìbào gōngzuò.
Zhāng Lì	Nǐ de Hànyǔ jiǎng de bù cuò.
Friend	Hái kěyǐ ba, bù tài hǎo.

jiǎng to speak

> **nǐ zài Zhōngguó zuò shénme?** (lit. you in China do what?) The place comes before the verb; remember the order 'who', 'where', 'what'. **Gàn** is the more usual word for 'to do' (see Unit 9, Dialogue 5).
>
> **Zhōngguó Rìbào** China Daily, a national newspaper in English.
>
> **Wǒ zài Zhōngguó Rìbào gōngzuò.** I work at the China Daily. In Chinese you don't say 'work *for* a company', but 'work *at* a company'. **Wǒ zài Běijīng Fàndiàn gōngzuò.** I work at the Běijīng Hotel. **Wǒ zài bówùguǎn gōngzuò.** I work at the museum.
>
> **Hànyǔ** (lit. Hàn language) Chinese language. Most Chinese are Hans. Some other languages are **Yīngyǔ** 'English', **Fǎyǔ** 'French', and **Déyǔ** 'German'. **Wàiyǔ** means 'foreign language'.
>
> **nǐ de Hànyǔ jiǎng de bù cuò.** (lit. Your Chinese is spoken not bad.) You speak good Chinese. Learn this sentence as a model and practise modifying it for your own use. **Nǐ de Yīngyǔ jiǎng de hěn hǎo.** (lit. Your English is spoken very good.) You speak very good English. **Tā de fàn zuò de hěn hǎo.** (lit. His meal is cooked very good.) He cooks well.

2

My profession is...

> **LISTEN FOR...**
> **wǒ shì...** I am...
> **wǒ de zhíyè shì...** My profession is...

Lǐ	Wǒ shì chūzū qìchē sījī.
Chén	Wǒ shì hùshi.
Zhāng	Wǒ de zhíyè shì xīnwén jìzhě.
Dèng	Wǒ de zhíyè shì lǜshī.

chūzū qìchē	taxi	**xīnwén jìzhě**	journalist
sījī	driver	**lǜshī**	lawyer
hùshi	nurse		

> The four people were responding to the question,
> **Nǐ gàn shénme gōngzuò?** (lit. You do what work?)

Practise what you have learned

1

Fill in the blanks with the appropriate word selected from the list below. (Answers on page 180.)

(1) **Nǐ** .... **shénme gōngzuò?**
What do you do?

(2) **Wǒ** .... **Zhōngguó Rìbào**

....
I work at the China Daily.

(3) **Wǒ shì** ....
I am a journalist.

(4) **Wǒ shì** ....
I am a taxi driver.

(5) **Wǒ de zhíyè shì** ....
My profession is nurse.

(6) **Wǒ de** .... **shì**

....
My profession is lawyer.

(a) **hùshi**
(b) **zhíyè**
(c) **gōngzuò**
(d) **zuò / gàn**
(e) **chūzū qìchē sìji**
(f) **lǜshī**
(g) **xīnwén jìzhě**
(h) **zài**

2

Listen to Xiǎoyún read the sentences in Exercise 1 and write down in order the number corresponding to each one. Which sentence is missing? (Answers on page 180.)

....

3

Using the words for occupations you have come across so far, practise saying what you do, and asking others about their jobs. You will need some of the following phrases, but not in the same order.

Nǐ zài…gōngzuò?	**chūzū qìchē sìji**
Nǐ gàn shénme gōngzuò?	**lǜshī**
Wǒ shì…	**hùshi**
Wǒ de zhíyè shì…	**Zhōngguó Rìbào**
xīnwén jìzhě	

Dialogues

3

Where do you live?

> **LISTEN FOR...**
> **nǐ jiā zhù zài shénme dìfang?** (lit. Your family lives at what place?)
> **lí shì zhōngxīn hěn yuǎn?** (lit. Away from the city centre very far?)

Zhāng Lì	Nǐ jiā zhù zài shénme dìfang?
Colleague	Wǒ jiā zhù zài Shíjǐngshān qū... en... Bājiǎo Zhōnglǐ shí èr lóu.
Zhāng Lì	Nà lí shì zhōngxīn hěn yuǎn a?
Colleague	En... bùguò, fùjìn yǒu dìtiě, hái kěyǐ.

dìfang place, region   **Bājiǎo Zhōnglǐ** name of a
Shíjǐngshān name of a place   housing complex
qù district   **lóu** building

> **nǐ jiā zhù zài shénme dìfang?** Where do you live? In response to
> this question, you would usually expect the name of a city, district /
> area and street; these elements would occur in that order, i.e.
> moving from general to specific.
>
> **wǒ jiā zhù zài Shíjǐngshān qū...** (lit. My family lives at
> Shíjǐngshān district...)
>
> **Bājiǎo Zhōnglǐ shí èr lóu** Number 12 building, Bājiǎo Zhōnglǐ.
> Again, note the order from general to specific.
>
> **shì zhōngxīn** city centre. **Nà lí shì zhōngxīn hěn yuǎn a?** (lit.
> So away from city centre very far?) Is it very far away from the city
> centre? Remember **lí** 'away from' goes at the beginning of the
> sentence; it came up in Unit 5, Dialogue 3: **Lí zhèr bù yuǎn**. Not
> far away from here.
>
> **bùguò, fùjìn yǒu dìtiě** (lit. However, the vicinity has an
> underground.) There is an underground station nearby.

4

I'm retired

> **LISTEN FOR...**
> **nín xiànzài hái gōngzuò ma?** (lit. You now still work?)
> **tuìxiū le** retired
> **nín píngcháng zài jiā zuò diǎnr shénme?** (lit. You usually at
> home do some what?)
> **bāngzhe jiā li** helping in the family
> **kānkan háizi** look after the children

Hènián	Dàye, nín xiànzài hái gōngzuò ma?
Old man	Wǒ yǐjing tuìxiū le.
Hènián	Tuìxiū jǐ nián le?
Old man	Bā nián le.
Hènián	Nín píngcháng zài jiā zuò diǎnr shénme ya?
Old man	Bāngzhe jiā li liàolǐ diǎnr jiāwù, huòzhě kānkan háizi.
Hènián	A...

yǐjing already
tuìxiū to retire
píngcháng / píngshí usually
bāng help
kān to look after
háizi child(ren)

> **dàye, nín xiànzài hái gōngzuò ma?** (lit. Grandpa, you now still work?) **Tā xiànzài hái xiě shū ma?** (lit. He now still writes a book?)
>
> **tuìxiū jǐ nián le?** (lit. retired how many years?). **Le** here indicates the past tense (this usage is explained in Unit 15). **Gōngzuò jǐ nián le?** (lit. Have worked how many years?) The man could have replied, **Wǒ bù gōngzuò le**. I no longer work. (In this case, the **le** would indicate a change of situation: 'I used to work but I don't any more'.)
>
> **nín píngcháng zài jiā zuò diǎnr shénme ya?** (lit. You usually at home do some what?). Another word for 'often' is **píngshí**. This is the word that you will be using. **Nín píngshí zài Lúndūn zuò diǎnr shénme?** (lit. You usually in London do some what?)
>
> **bāngzhe** **-zhe** added to a verb, here **bāng** 'help', indicates a continuous or prolonged action, 'helping'. **Zuòzhe**, sitting. **Dǎzhe diànhuà**, making a phone call.
>
> **liàolǐ diǎnr jiāwù** do some housework
>
> **huòzhě** or. As explained in Unit 5, Dialogue 5, **huòzhě** is used in a statement, whereas in a question, which poses a choice, **háishi** is used: **Nǐ xiǎng chī zhōngcān háishi xīcān?** Would you like to eat Chinese or Western food?
>
> **kānkan háizi** looking after the child(ren). Remember nouns scarcely ever take the plural form.
>
> Most Chinese families in cities have only one child as a result of the one-child policy introduced to control China's vast population.

Advocating 'one child policy'

Practise what you have learned

4 Fill in the blanks with the correct words selected from the box.
(Answers on page 180.)

(1) **Nǐ jiā ____ shénme dìfang?**
Where does your family live?

(2) **Nǐ xiànzài hái ____ ma?**
Do you still work now?

(3) **Wǒ yǐjing ____ le.**
I am already retired.

(4) **Nín ____ zài jiā ____ diǎnr shénme?**
What do you usually do at home?

(5) **Bāng zhe jiā li ____ ____.**
Helping in the family to do housework, and look after the child.

zuò	kānkan háizi	gōngzuò	liàolǐ jiāwù
	píngshí	zhù zài	tuìxiū	

5 Lǎo Lǐ meets former colleague Ms Chén in the street. Listen to their conversation, then answer the following questions in English. A few Pīnyīn phrases are given to help you, but not in the order in which they occur. (Answers on page 180.)

New word: **huó** work carried out at home

(1) What does Lǎo Lǐ do? ....

(2) What does he usually do at home?...

(3) Where is he going? ....

(4) What is he doing today? ....

(5) Does he live around here? ....

(6) Why is Ms Chén around here? ....

lí zhèr bù yuǎn	**liàolǐ jiāwù**
mǎi diǎnr cài	**zuò zhōngwǔ fàn**
zuò shēngyi	**tuìxiū le**
kānkan háizi	

6 Practise saying where you live following Lǐ's prompts. You will need:

Lúndūn London
lù road
běifāng the Northern part of the country

Dialogue

5

About my family

> **LISTEN FOR...**
> **fùqin** father
> **mǔqin** mother
> **dìdi** younger brother
> **mèimei** younger sister
> **fùmǔqin** parents
> **tāmen niánjì dà le** They are old.

Chén   Wǒ de jiā zài Zhōngguó de Hénán shěng Kāifēng shì. Wǒ jiā li yǒu fùqin,
mǔqin, yǒu yī ge dìdi, háiyǒu liǎng ge mèimei. Wǒ de fùmǔqin dōu shì
tuìxiū de gànbù. Tāmen niánjì dà le. Xiànzài yǐjing tuìxiū zài jiā. Wǒ de
dìdi zài tiělù, shì tiělù jǐngchá. Wǒ de yī ge mèimei ne zài shāngdiàn
gōngzuò. Lìng yī ge mèimei zài yī ge xíngzhèng bùmén gōngzuò.

shěng	province	**tiělù**	railway
gànbù	cadre (government official)	**jǐngchá**	policeman
niánjì	age	**shāngdiàn**	shop

> **wǒ de jiā zài Zhōngguó de Hénán shěng Kāifēng shì** (lit. My family
> in China's Hénán province Kāifēng city). Note that the speaker
> moves from the general, 'China', to the specific, 'Kāifēng city'. **Wǒ de
> jiā zài Yīngguó de Lúndūn shì**. My family is in London, in the UK.
> **Wǒ de jiā zài Měiguó de Jiālìfúnìyà zhōu Jiùjinshān shì**. My family
> is in San Francisco, California state, in the USA.
>
> **wǒ jiā li yǒu fùqin, mǔqin, yǒu yī ge dìdi, háiyǒu liǎng ge mèimei**. (lit.
> My family in there are father, mother, there is one younger brother,
> in addition two younger sisters). Chinese words for family
> relationships are very specific. This originates from Confucian times
> when every one knew his or her place within the family hierarchy.
> For example, words for 'aunt' identify whether the aunt is 'first' or
> 'second' (the oldest being 'first'), and whether she is on the mother's
> or father's side of the family. Have a look at *Read and understand*.
>
> **wǒ de fùmǔqin dōu shì tuìxiū de gànbù** My parents are both (lit.
> all) retired cadres (officials). **Tuìxiū** 'retire' is used as an adjective.
> **Wǒ de péngyou shì tuìxiū de lǜshī**. My friend is a retired lawyer.
>
> **niánjì dà** (old-aged). **Shàng niánjì de rén** (lit. getting on in age
> people). **Lǎo nián rén**, old people. **Zhōng nián rén**, middle-aged
> people. **Niánqīng rén**, young people.
>
> **xiànzài yǐjing tuìxiū zài jiā** (lit. Now already retired at home).
> There is no need for a **le** to indicate the past tense (as in the
> example in Dialogue 4) because **yǐjing** indicates that it has already
> happened (see Unit 15).
>
> **wǒ de dìdi zài tiělù, shì tiělù jǐngchá** (lit. My younger brother at
> railway is railway policeman).
>
> **wǒ de yī ge... lìng yī ge...** the one... the other.... **Wǒ de yīge
> mèimei ne zài shāngdiàn gōngzuò.** (lit. My one younger sister in a
> shop works) One of my younger sisters works in a shop. **Lìng yī ge
> mèimei zài yī ge xíngzhèng bùmén gōngzuò**. The other younger
> sister works in an administration department.

Practise what you have learned

7 Wáng, who is ten years old, introduces his family. Match each picture with the Pinyin label which seems to describe the person's family relationship to Wáng. (Answers on page 180.)

 (a)
 (d)

fùqin
dìdi
mèimei
yéye
mǔqin

 (b)
 (e)

 (c)

8 On the recording you will hear four people describing their families. First listen then identify the picture which fits each person's description, writing the number on the recording in the appropriate space. (Note that the person talking does not appear in the picture.) (Answers on page 180.)

New words:

àiren spouse **nǎinai** grandmother (on father's side)
gēge older brother **nǚháir** girl
jiějie older sister **nánháir** boy

a)_____ b)_____

c)_____ d)_____

9

On the recording you will hear Xiànbīn say the words for various jobs and activities.

(a) Write the number of the word which corresponds to each picture in the appropriate space. The words appear in the box below. (Answers on page 180.)

(b) Go back and repeat each word or phrase after Xiànbīn in the pause to practise your pronunciation.

---

lùshī	chūzhū qìchē sījī	jǐngchá
zuò shēngyi	liàolǐ jiāwù	kān háizi
zài shāngdiàn gōngzuò	hùshi	xīnwén jìzhě

Key words and phrases

To learn

Hànyǔ (Zhōngwén)	Chinese language
Yīngyǔ	English
Fǎyǔ	French
Déyǔ	German
nǐ de Hànyǔ jiǎng de bù cuò	Your Chinese is not bad.
nǐ xiànzài hái gōngzuò ma?	Do you still work now?
nín píngshí zài jiā zuò diǎnr shénme?	What do you usually do at home?
chūzū qìchē	taxi
sījī	driver
hùshi	nurse
zhíyè	profession
xīnwén jìzhě	journalist
lǜshī	lawyer
tiělù	railway
jǐngchá	policeman
shāngdiàn	shop
nǐ zhù zài shénme dìfang?	Where do you live?
shì zhōngxīn	city centre
yǐjing	already
tuìxiū (le)	retire(d)
píngshí/píngcháng	usually
bāng	help
liàolǐ jiāwù	to do housework
huòzhě	or (statement)
kān	to look after
háizi	child(ren)
shěng	province
qū	district
fùqin	father
mǔqin	mother
dìdi	younger brother
mèimei	younger sister
fùmǔqin	parents
jiějie	older sister
gēge	older brother
nǎinai	grandmother (on father's side)
yéye	grandfather (on father's side)
lǎolao	grandmother (on mother's side)
lǎo ye	grandfather (on mother's side)
àiren	spouse
nánháir	boy
nǚháir	girl
lǎo nián rén	old people
niánqīng rén	young people
zhōng nián rén	middle-aged people
yī ge... lìng yī ge...	the one... the other...

To understand

xíngzhèng bùmén	administration department
Zhōngguó Rìbào	China Daily
gànbù	cadre

Grammar

-zhe '-ing'

-zhe '-ing' is attached to a verb to show that an action is ongoing:

bāngzhe jiā li helping in the family
kānzhe háizi looking after the child/ren
or prolonged:
tā zuòzhe He is / was sitting.

Sentence patterns

It is often easier to learn phrases than to build up sentences from scratch, and the following eight sentences, which have occurred in this Unit, are useful to learn and use as models. The words underlined are those which may be changed. Practise modifying the sentences to suit your own circumstances.

Nǐ zài <u>Zhōngguó</u> gàn shénme? What are you doing in China?
Wǒ zài <u>Zhōngguó Rìbào</u> gōngzuò. I work at the China Daily.
Nǐ de <u>Hànyǔ jiǎng</u> de <u>bù cuò</u>. Your Chinese is not bad.
Wǒ de zhíyè shì <u>lùshī</u>. My profession is lawyer.
Nǐ <u>jiā</u> zhù zài shénme dìfang? You live at what place?
Wǒ jiā zài <u>Yīngguó de Sussex shěng Brighton shì</u>. My family lives in the English county of Sussex, in the city of Brighton.
Nín xiànzài hái <u>gōngzuò</u> ma? Are you now still working?
Nín píngshí <u>zài shāngdiàn</u> gàn diǎnr shénme? What do you usually do at the shop?

10 Select the correct word from the box below to fill each gap. Write the letter of the word you have chosen in the space. (Two of the words will not be needed.) Check your answers on page 180.

(1) **Nǐ zài ____ gàn shénme?**
What are you doing in America?

(2) **Wǒ zài ____ gōngzuò.**
I work at the post office.

(3) **Nǐ de ____ ____ de ____.**
You play table tennis very well.

(4) **Wǒ de ____ shì ____.**
My profession is lawyer.

(5) **Nǐ ____ zhù zài shénme dìfang?**
Your friend lives at what place?

(6) **Wo jiā zài Zhōngguó de Shāndōng ____ Qīngdǎo ____.**
My family lives in the Chinese province of Shāndōng, in the city of Qīngdǎo.

(7) **Nín xiànzài hái ____ ma?**
Are you now still listening?

(a) **péngyou**	(b) **zhíyè**	(c) **pīngpāngqiú**
(d) **gōngzuò**	(e) **shěng**	(f) **hěn hǎo**
(g) **Měiguó**	(h) **tīng**	(i) **gōngzuò**
(j) **shì**	(k) **lùshī**	(l) **dǎ**	(m) **yóujú**

Read and understand

Family relations

Chinese has very specific names for family relations. You use different words depending on whether family members are on your mother's or father's side, and their rank in terms of age relative to their siblings.

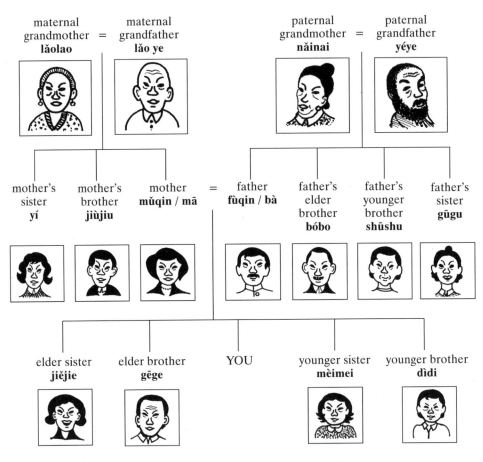

Sometimes a number is used with the names of relatives which expresses whether they are first born, second born, etc. For example you might call your mother's sister who is the second born child in that family **èr yí**, 'second aunt'. If her brother is the eldest child, he will often be referred to as **dà jiù**, 'big (i.e. eldest) uncle'.

Did you know?

Religions

Confucianism

Confucius (Kǒng Zi) lived from 551 to 479 BC in modern-day Shāndōng Province, where, in Qǔfǔ, it is possible to visit his birthplace. Strictly, Confucianism is more a system of thought and moral philosophy than a religion. Confucius' aim was to produce an ordered society by fostering obedience to authority and respect for superiors, including ancestors, within a family context. He held that if everyone carried out their duties according to their social position, the world and heaven would remain in harmony. There is now no Confucian cult, but the Confucian approach to government and society remains observable.

Daoism

The teachings of Daoism are ascribed to Lǎo Zi who reputedly wrote the *Dào Dé Jīng* 'The Way and Its Power' in the fifth century BC. Daoism complemented Confucian regulation of public and family life with reflections on the place of the self in the cosmos. Contemplation of the **Dào** 'way' was to bring inner peace and attunement with all being. Traditionally, the Daoist was concerned to achieve immortality, through gymnastics and herbal medicines, and harmony, through balance of **yīn** and **yáng** – male and female forces. Daoism developed as a religion with a number of deities, to whom temples are dedicated.

Buddhism

Buddhism entered China in the first century AD. Mahayana ('Great Vehicle') Buddhism was adopted, and after a long process of adaptation, various Chinese schools emerged, including Chán, meditative Buddhism, eventually transmitted to Japan, where it is known as Zen. Buddhism still has a following in China, although the extent of its influence is difficult to ascertain, since many of its rituals have been incorporated into Chinese popular religion.

Islam

Islam came to China in the seventh century AD. China has more than 20 million Muslims, most of them belonging to the minority nationalities of the north-west and elsewhere (Uygurs, Kazaks, Uzbeks, Huí).

Christianity

Christianity had a limited impact in the seventh century through Nestorians, and in the sixteenth century through the Jesuits. During the Opium Wars in the mid-nineteenth century missionaries came in force to China. Christianity had some impact, but was rejected as 'foreign' by many. Today there are around 10 million Christians in China, and Christianity is increasingly accepted as a Chinese religion.

Popular folk religion

Integral to Chinese folk religion is a preoccupation with death, the afterlife and the worship of ancestors. Traditionally, it is thought the deceased must be kept happy because of their powers to inflict punishments or grant favours. Possessions are buried with the dead for use in the next world.

Household gods and goddesses, bad spirits and 'sleeping dragons' must all be appeased to keep luck on one's side.

Communism sought to break these ancient traditions, but folk religion, rather than being wiped out, has adapted, and even incorporates elements of Marxism and modernization. Representations of Máo, for example, appear in homes alongside New Year pictures of the Kitchen God.

11

Your turn to speak

On a trip to China, you are introduced to your travel guide who has never been out of China and is very interested in life in the West. Practise what you would say to her. You will need:

Wǒ jiào... I am called
Wǒ jiā zhù zài... My family lives in...
Wǒ jiéhūn le. I am married.

Answers

Practise what you have learned

Exercise 1	(1)(d); (2)(h),(c); (3)(g); (4)(e); (5)(a); (6)(b),(f)
Exercise 2	3, 1, 5, 2, 4; number 6 does not occur
Exercise 4	(1) **zhù zài** (2) **gōngzuò** (3) **tuìxiū** (4) **píngshí, zuò** (5) **liàolǐ jiāwù, kānkan háizi**
Exercise 5	(1) Lǎo Lǐ is retired. (2) Housework and looks after child. (3) Buying vegetables. (4) Cooking lunch. (5) Yes, not far from here. (6) She is on business.
Exercise 7	(a) **fùqin** (b) **mǔqin** (c) **yéye** (d) **dìdi** (e) **mèimei**
Exercise 8	(a) 4; (b) 1; (c) 3; (d) 2
Exercise 9	2, 8, 1, 9, 6, 5, 3, 4, 7

Grammar

Exercise 10	(1)(g); (2)(m); (3)(c),(l),(f); (4)(b),(k); (5)(a); (6)(e),(j); (7)(h)

Thousand Buddha Mountain

What you will learn

- to talk about future plans
- to invite someone to (do) something
- about consumerism in China

Before you begin

Whereas in other languages verbs take different forms according to number, gender and tense, in Chinese they are always the same in form. This means that verbs are simple to learn, but that you need to be aware of other words which give a clue as to the time of the action or event described.

A verb essential to know when talking about the future is one you have already met:

wǒ xiǎng   I would like.

This and other ways of discussing the future are the focus of this Unit.

The new consumerism

Dialogues

1

What is your next move?

> **LISTEN FOR...**
> **xià yi bù**   next move
> **nǐ xià yi bù yǒu shénme dǎsuàn?**   (lit. you next move have what
> plan?) What are you planning for your next move?
> **wǒ xiǎng**   I would like
> **zěnme xiǎng qǐ**   (lit. how come to mind)
> How come you are thinking of...?

Jiànjí	Yánchéng, nǐ xià yi bù yǒu shénme dǎsuàn a?
Yánchéng	En... xià yi bù wǒ xiǎng zìjǐ zuò xiē shēngyi.
Jiànjí	Ao, zěnme... xiǎng qǐ zìjǐ zuò shēngyi?
Yánchéng	E... zìjǐ zuò shēngyi ne, zhè yàng shōurù bǐjiào duō yīxiē.

dǎsuàn   plan(s), to plan
zìjǐ   self
xiǎng qǐ   to call to mind, occur
shōurù   income

> **nǐ xià yi bù yǒu shénme dǎsuàn?**   What are you planning for your
> next move? **Nǐ yǒu shénme dǎsuàn?** 'What plans do you have?' is
> simpler to learn.
>
> **zìjǐ zuò xiē shēngyi**   (lit. self do some business). **Zìjǐ** 'self' here
> has the sense of 'on my own'; in other words Yánchéng would like
> to be self-employed.
>
> **zěnme**   how / how come
>
> **zěnme... xiǎng qǐ zìjǐ zuò shēngyi?**   (lit. How come... it occurs to
> you self do business?) How come you are thinking of doing
> business on your own?
>
> **zhè yàng shōurù bǐjiào duō yīxiē**   (lit. this way income rather
> more somewhat) I can make a bit more money this way.

2

I am about to...

> **LISTEN FOR...**
> **wǒ mǎshàng yào jiéhūn le**   I am about to get married very soon.
> **zhùhè nǐ**   (lit. congratulate you)
> **wǒ zhǔnbèi...**   I intend...
> **wǒ zài Shànghǎi zhǎngdà de**   I grew up in Shanghai.

Wáng Wěi	Wǒ mǎshàng yào jiéhūn le.
Zhāng Lì	Ao, zhùhè nǐ, nǐ yǒu shénme dǎ... jìhuà ma?
Wáng Wěi	Ao, shì zhè yàng de. Wǒ zhǔnbèi wǔ yuèfèn qù Shànghǎi lǚxíng.
Zhāng Lì	Nǐ yǐqián qù guo Shànghǎi ma?
Wáng Wěi	Wǒ zài Shànghǎi zhǎngdà de.
Zhāng Lì	Zhè zhǔyì bù cuò.

mǎshàng	immediately, very soon	**lǚxíng**	to travel
zhùhè	to congratulate	**yuèfèn**	month, the same as yuè
jìhuà	plan	**zhǎngdà**	to grow up
zhǔnbèi	to prepare, to intend, to plan	**yǐqián**	before, ago

---

yào... le Yào and **le** sandwiching the verb indicate that something is about to happen, in this case getting married. **Fēijī yào qǐfēi le.** The plane is about to take off.

nǐ yǒu shénme dǎ... jìhuà ma? (lit. you have what plans?) Zhāng Lì was going to say **dǎsuàn** 'plans', the word used in Dialogue 1, but changed her mind and said **jìhuà** instead. The words are more or less the same in meaning, although **jìhuà** may indicate a firm plan, and **dǎsuàn** less definite intention. Note that **shénme** is a question word, so Zhāng Lì could have omitted **ma**.

shì zhè yàng de it is like this

wǒ zhǔnbèi wǔ yuèfèn qù Shànghǎi lǚxíng I intend in May to go to Shànghǎi to travel. Remember that the time always goes before the verb.

wǒ zài Shànghǎi zhǎngdà de I grew up in Shànghǎi. Learn this phrase, inserting the name of the city or country of your own childhood. **Wǒ zài Lúndūn zhǎngdà de.** I grew up in London. **Wǒ zài Niǔ Yuē zhǎngdà de.** I grew up in New York.

Practise what you have learned

1

Match the Pīnyīn phrases to their English translations. (Answers on page 192.)

(1) **Nǐ yǒu shénme jìhuà?**
(2) **Nǐ xià yī bù yǒu shénme dǎsuàn?**
(3) **Wǒ xiǎng qù Zhōngguó.**
(4) **Wǒ zhǔnbèi qù Zhōngguó.**
(5) **Wǒ yào qù Zhōngguó le.**

(a) I'd like to go to China.
(b) I intend to go to China.
(c) What plans do you have?
(d) I am about to go to China.
(e) What are you planning for your next move?

2

Fill in the gaps with words from the box below. The English translations of each sentence are given to help you. (Answers on page 192.)

(1) **Wǒ _____ huí jiā guò Chūnjié _____.**
I am about to go home to celebrate Spring Festival.

(2) **Nǐ yǒu shénme ____?**
What plans do you have?

(3) **Wǒ ____ zuò dìtiě.**
I intend to travel by underground.

(4) **Xià yī bù wǒ ____ qù Měiguó lǚxíng.**
My next move is to go to America to travel.

(5) **Wǒ ____ mǎi jìnìanpǐn.**
I'd like to buy souvenirs.

zhǔnbèi	xiǎng	dǎsuàn
yào	le	yào

3

Have a chat with Xiànbīn about your planned trip to China.
You will need:

Tiāntán The Temple of Heaven
Gùgōng The Forbidden City
Tiān'ānmén Tiān'ānmén (lit. the Gate of Heavenly Peace)

Dialogue

3

What shall we do tonight?

> **LISTEN FOR...**
> **jīntiān wǎnshang** tonight
> **kàn diànyǐng** see a film
> **kàn huàjù** see a play
> **tīng Jīngjù** listen to Běijīng (Peking) Opera
> **tīng bù dà dǒng** can't understand much
> **dǎ májiàng** play mah-jong

Jiànjí	Yánchéng, zánmen jīntiān wǎnshang gàn diǎnr shénme?
Yánchéng	Jīnr wǎnshang?
Jiànjí	Ao.
Yánchéng	Jīnr wǎnshang kàn diànyǐng zěnmeyàng?
Jiànjí	Kàn diànyǐng a, zánmen... kàn huàjù qù ba?
Yánchéng	Kàn huàjù..., huàjù, āiyō, huàjù hǎoxiàng yìsi yě bù tài dà. Xiànzài méi yǒu duōshao hǎo jù.
Jiànjí	Nà, tīng Jīngjù a?
Yánchéng	Tīng Jīngjù, Jīngjù, Jīngjù...
Jiànjí	Tīng bù dà dǒng.
Yánchéng	Tīng bù dà dǒng. Zánmen niánqīng rén zhè wányìr hǎoxiàng hǎo duō shì tīng bù tài dǒng de.
Jiànjí	Nà zánmen dǎ pūkè ba?
Yánchéng	Dǎ pūkè?

Jiànjí	En.
Yánchéng	Dǎ pūkè? Xíng. Yàobùrán, zánmen gāncuì dǎ májiàng, zěnmeyàng?
Jiànjí	En, nà yě kěyǐ.
Yánchéng	Xíng, nà hǎo lei. Jīnr wǎnshang dǎ májiàng la.
Jiànjí	Hǎo lei.

dǒng to understand
pūkè playing cards
yàobùrán otherwise

---

jīnr wǎnshang tonight, the same as **jīntiān wǎnshang**. **Jīnr** is a short form, often used by Běijingers. Stick with **jīntiān**.

kàn diànyǐng zěnmeyàng? How about seeing a film? You encountered this way of using **zěnmeyàng** in Unit 10, Dialogue 1, **Qiàng yóucài zěnmeyàng?** How about stir-fried rape?

zánmen kàn huàjù qù ba? Shall we go and see a play?

huàjù hǎoxiàng yìsi yě bù tài dà (lit. play seems interest also not too big) A play does not seem very interesting either.

duōshao in earlier units appeared as a question word meaning 'how many'. When used in a statement, as here, it means 'many'.

xiànzài méi yǒu duōshao hǎo jù. Now there are not many good plays. **Huàjù** is shortened to **jù**. Learn this useful sentence structure, and modify it to different contexts by changing the noun: **Xiànzài méi yǒu duōshao hǎo diànyǐng.** Now there are not many good films.

tīng bù dà dǒng (lit. can't understand much). This is a useful phrase to learn. If someone says something to you, and you don't quite understand, you can say, **Tīng bù dǒng.** I don't understand, or **Tīng bù dà dǒng.** I can't understand much. People may ask you, **Tīng dǒng le ma?** Have you understood?, in which case, hopefully yours will be the confident reply, **Tīng dǒng le.** I have understood.

wányìr (lit. toy) in this context meaning 'thing'.

zánmen niánqīng rén zhè wányìr hǎoxiàng hǎo duō shì tīng bù tài dǒng de. This is a long sentence; to translate it, break it down into phrases: **zánmen niánqīng rén** 'we young people', **zhè wányìr** 'this thing', **hǎoxiàng hǎo duō** 'it seems a good many', **shì tīng bù tài dǒng de** 'are not too understood / understandable'. The complete sentence means: 'Young people cannot understand a good many of these plays'.

dǎ pūkè to play cards, the same as **dǎ pái**

gāncuì just, simply. **Yàobùrán, zánmen gāncuì dǎ májiàng?** Otherwise let's just play mah-jong? **Nǐ gāncuì shuō xíng háishi bù xíng.** (lit. You simply say all right or not all right) Just say yes or no.

Practise what you have learned

4 Here are some things you might like to do on a night off. Match up each Pinyīn phrase with the correct English translation. (Answers on page 192.)

(1) play cards   (a) **kàn diànyǐng**
(2) listen to Běijīng Opera   (b) **kàn huàjù**
(3) see a film   (c) **tīng Jīngjù**
(4) see a play   (d) **dǎ pūkè**
(5) play mah-jong   (e) **dǎ májiàng**

5 Your turn to speak. You are in Běijīng. You bump into an acquaintance who wishes to invite you out for the evening. Respond to his enquiries and make an arrangement following Lǐ's prompts. You will need:

kàn diànyǐng yìsi bù tài dà   to see a film is not much fun
liáo tiānr   to chat
dǎ diànhuà   make a phone call

Dialogues

4

Let's go on an outing tomorrow

> **LISTEN FOR...**
> **yuē ge shíjiān ba?**   Let's / shall we arrange a time?

Táng	Míngtiān wǒmen qù jiāoyóu, hǎo ma?
Chén	Hǎo a, yuē ge shíjiān ba?
Táng	Míngtiān shàngwǔ jiǔ diǎn yī kè.
Chén	Zài shénme dìfang?
Táng	Tiān'ānmén Guǎngchǎng.
Chén	Hǎo de, bù jiàn bù sàn.

yuē   to arrange
shíjiān   time

> **míngtiān wǒmen qù jiāoyóu, hǎo ma?**   (lit. tomorrow we go on an outing, OK?)
>
> **Tiān'ānmén Guǎngchǎng**   Tiān'ānmén Square
>
> **bù jiàn bù sàn**   until we meet

Entry ticket

5 *Are you doing anything?*

> **LISTEN FOR...**
> **yǒu shì ma?**   (lit. Do you have something?)
> Are you doing anything?
> **méi shénme shì**   I'm not doing anything.
> **zhǎo**   to call for, for example, **wǒ zhǎo nǐ**, I'll call for you
> **dǎ diànhuà gěi Xiǎo Wáng**   make a phone call to Xiǎo Wáng
> **kàn tā qù bù qù**   see if he wants to go or not

Liú	Ai, jīntiān wǎnshang yǒu shì ma?
Shāng	Méi shénme shì.
Liú	Jīntiān wǎnshang wǒmen qù kàn diànyǐng hǎo ma?
Shāng	Hǎo ba.
Liú	En... jīntiān wǎnshang qī diǎn duō yǒu yī ge diànyǐng.
Shāng	Kěyǐ.
Liú	Nà wǒ liù diǎn bàn qù zhǎo nǐ. Zánmen yīqǐ qù, hǎo ma?
Shāng	Hǎo ba, wǒ děng nǐ.
Shāng	Wǒmen zài dǎ diànhuà gěi Xiǎo Wáng, kàn tā qù bù qù?
Liú	Yě xíng.

> **yǒu shì ma?**   (lit. do you have something?) Are you doing
> anything? The dialogue was recorded in Běijīng, where **shì** is often
> pronounced **shìr**. Learn **shì**.
>
> **méi shénme shì**   I'm not doing anything
>
> **qī diǎn duō**   just after seven o'clock
>
> **nà wǒ liù diǎn bàn qù zhǎo nǐ**   (lit. so I 6.30 go look for you).
>
> **zánmen yīqǐ qù**   (lit. let's together go)

Practise what you have learned

6 Listen to the conversation between Xiànbīn and Xiǎoyún and decide
whether the following are true or false. (Answers on page 192.)

(1) Xiǎoyún is free on Wednesday.
(2) Xiànbīn wants to go shopping with Xiǎoyún.
(3) Xiànbīn would like to go to the city centre but not to the
department store.
(4) Xiànbīn will call for Xiǎoyún tomorrow evening.
(5) They arrange to meet in the city centre at 9.30.

7 Xiànbīn wants to know what Xiǎoyún is doing tonight. Listen to their
conversation and answer the following questions by ticking (✓) the
correct answer. (Answers on page 192.)

(1) Tonight Xiǎoyún is going to see a play...   (a) on her own ☐
(b) with Xiànbīn ☐   (c) with someone else ☐
(2) Xiǎoyún has...   (a) two tickets ☐   (b) a ticket for herself ☐
(c) three tickets ☐

---

(3) Xiǎoyūn will...   (a) change her plan ☐   (b) go out with
Xiànbīn and have some fun ☐   (c) go and see the play ☐
(4) Xiànbīn will...   (a) go and see the play ☐   (b) go out with
Xiǎoyūn and have some fun ☐   (c) ring Lǐ Méi ☐

8 Your turn to speak. Xiànbīn is getting married. Congratulate him and then ask him about his plans. You will need some of the following phrases / sentences, but not necessarily in the same order:

Nǐ xiǎng gàn diǎnr shénme? / zài wǒ jiā / Nà wǒmen yuē ge shíjiān ba. / Nǐ yǒu shénme jìhuà? / míngtiān wǎnshang / Wǎnshang qī diǎn xíng ba?

Key words and phrases

To learn

xià yī bù	next step, next move
jìhuà	plan(s), to plan
dǎsuàn	plan(s), to plan
zhǔnbèi	to prepare, to intend, to plan
xià yī bù yǒu shénme dǎsuàn?	What's your next move?
xiǎng qǐ	to come to mind, to occur
lǚxíng	to travel
zhǎo	to call for
shōurù	income
mǎshàng	immediately, very soon
zhùhè nǐ	congratulations
wǒ zài ... zhǎngdà de	I grew up in...
huàjù	play
yìsi	interest, fun
Jīngjù	Běijīng (Peking) Opera
diànyǐng	film
dǎ pūkè	to play cards
dǎ májiàng	to play mah-jong
tīng dǒng le ma?	Have you understood?
tīng bù (dà) dǒng	can't understand (much)
tīng dǒng le	I have understood
yuē ge shíjiān	to arrange a time
bù jiàn bù sàn	until we meet
yǒu shì	(lit. to have something) to be doing something
méi shénme shì	not to be doing anything
yào...le	to be about to ...

Grammar

Talking about the future

(i) Use **yào** to talk about something you are going to do (or you want to do: see (v) below). For example,

Wǒ yào qù Zhōngguó. I am going to go to China (I want to go to China).

(ii) Such words as **míngtiān**, tomorrow, **jīntiān wǎnshang**, tonight, **míngnián**, next year, **wǔ yuè**, 'in May', denoting exactly when the action will take place, identify the action as in the future.

Wǒ wǔ yuè qù Shànghǎi. I am going to Shànghǎi in May.
Jīntiān wǎnshang tā yào qù kàn huàjù. Tonight (s)he is going to see a play.

(iii) **Zhǔnbèi** 'intend' / 'prepare', **dǎsuàn** 'plan', **jìhuà** 'plan' and **xià yī bù** 'next move' are also words which set the scene as in the future.

Wǒ zhǔnbèi qù Guǎngzhōu. I intend to go to Guǎngzhōu.
Wǒ xià yī bù xiǎng zìjǐ zuò xiē shēngyì. For my next move I would like to do some business on my own.
Nǐ dǎsuàn chī xīcān ma? Are you planning to eat Western food?
Wǒmen jìhuà qù Měiguó. We are planning to go to America.

(iv) **Wǒ xiǎng** means 'I would like'. For example,

Wǒ xiǎng dǎ májiàng. I would like to play mah-jong.
Wǒ xiǎng mǎi sān hé lǜchá. I would like to buy three boxes of green tea.

(v) **Yào** can also be used; it is more definite than **xiǎng**.

Wǒ xiǎng mǎi zhè jiàn sīchóu mián'ǎo. I would like to buy this padded silk jacket.
Wǒ yào mǎi zhè jiàn sīchóu mián'ǎo. I want to buy this padded silk jacket.

The first sentence expresses a wish, and the second a firm intention.

Note that, when a question using **yào** has been posed, a response in the negative uses **xiǎng**. For example,

Nǐ yào chī xīcān ma? Are you going to eat Western food?
Wǒ bù xiǎng chī. I would not like to.

Nǐ yào qù kàn diànyǐng ma? Are you going to see a film?
Wǒ bù xiǎng qù. I would not like to.

(vi) **Yào** before the verb and **le** at the end of the sentence means 'be about to'.

Wǒ yào jiéhūn le. I am about to get married.
Wǒ yào chī fàn le. I am about to eat.

9

Fill in the blanks with the words given below by selecting (a) or (b). (Answers on page 192.)

(1) **Nǐ ___ chī ròu háishi chī qīngcài?** (a) **yào** (b) **xiǎng**
Would you like meat or vegetables?

(2) **Wǒ bù ___ chī ròu. Wǒ ___ chī qīngcài.** (a) yào, xiǎng
(b) xiǎng, yào
I don't want meat, I would like vegetables.

(3) **Nǐ xià yi bù ___ gàn shénme?** (a) jìhuà (b) yào
What is your next move?

(4) **Nǐ jinnián yǒu shénme ___?** (a) zhǔnbèi (b) jìhuà
What are your plans for this year?

(5) **Wǒ ___ qù Yīngguó xué Yīngyǔ.** (a) zhǔnbèi (b) yào
I intend to go to England to study English.

(6) **Wǒ ___ jiéhūn le.** (a) xiǎng (b) yào
I am about to get married.

(7) **Nǐ yào qù mài dōngxi ma? Wǒ bù ___ qù.** (a) yào (b) xiǎng
Are you going to buy some things? I don't want to go.

Read and understand

Consumer language

As in any language, new words are being created all the time to cope with new technology. How has Mandarin coped with the influx of foreign consumer items imported into China through the 'open door'?

Sometimes words reflect a Chinese outlook:

computer	**diàn nǎo**	electronic brain
Walkman	**suí shēn tīng**	next to body listen
CD	**jī guāng chàng piàn**	laser singing plate
hamburger	**hànbǎo bāo**	Hamburg dumpling
shampoo	**xiāng bō**	fragrant wave
polaroid	**bǎo lì lái**	precious beauty come

Other words are simply transliterated and have no particular meaning in Chinese:

T-shirt **tìxùshān**; chocolate **qiǎokèlì**; karaoke **kǎlā OK**; McDonalds **Màidāngláo**; Kentucky **Kěndéjī**

The following names for foods that have entered China are particularly interesting cross-cultural hybrids. Each combines a Chinese word that has an appropriate meaning with one that has no meaning but sounds like the original foreign word!

milk shake **nǎi xī** (**nǎi** is 'milk'); apple pie **píngguǒ pài** (**píngguǒ** is 'apple'); pizza **bǐ sà bǐng** (**bǐng** is a kind of pancake)

Did you know?

Contemporary China: consumerism

Consumption habits have changed dramatically in recent years, particularly in urban China, following the economic reforms introduced by Dèng Xiǎopíng in the early 1980s under the banner 'Socialism with Chinese Characteristics'. The accompanying playing down of 'Marxism–Leninism–Máo Zédóng Thought' has allowed people to become indifferent to politics; to fill the ideological vacuum, they have turned to material things.

The emphasis has shifted from quantity to quality with regard to food, and sales of ready-made clothes have soared. In the 1980s, colour televisions, washing machines and refrigerators replaced bicycles, wristwatches and sewing machines as the most popular consumer goods. In the 1990s, video recorders, air conditioners and audio products became the top products. Sales of private housing, cars and telephones, and the demand for home services and interior decoration have also increased. Concern for improving personal appearance, no longer categorized as a 'bourgeois deviation', is seen as an appropriate response to improved living standards. It is estimated that purchasing power will become more diversified: expenditure on investment, house purchase, and such non-commodity items as medical treatment, education, tourism and recreation are anticipated.

Luxury spending is on private cars, international designer fashion, and the use of such leisure facilities as the Oriental Recreation Park in the eastern suburbs of Běijīng or the North China International Shooting Range. Beauty parlours, cosmetic surgery salons, keep-fit centres, dance halls and karaoke bars have all become part of the contemporary urban scene. Children's goods and tourism have also become huge growth areas.

The contemporary emphasis on style and beauty contrasts with that of the Maoist period, when practicality was of primary importance. The blue 'uniform' of that era, worn by both sexes, reflected the aim of achieving an egalitarian, socialist society; anyone who tried to express individuality was condemned as 'bourgeois', and accused of trying to subvert the ideals of the revolutionary cause. In the 1990s, the construction of a personalized image in accordance with contemporary trends, especially Western ones, serves the Party in its attempt to convince the world of its changed outlook and improved standards. The old saying that trousers should be worn for three years as new, for three years as old, and then another three patched up, is certainly out of date. A proliferation of books, magazines, films, television programmes and advertisements leave no doubt as to the 'look' in vogue.

In recent years, shopping has become a leisure activity with greater significance than simply the buying of essentials. This is reflected in plans for new shopping centres. The Běijīng Municipal Government intends to renovate existing stores and to construct new luxury shopping centres (each over 10,000 square metres), to total 100 by the year 2000 – there are currently about 15. Shopping is not limited to shops: door-to-door sales, and television and radio shopping are recent phenomena.

Your turn to speak

Xiànbīn is trying to find out what you are doing at the weekend, **zhōumò**. He would like to see you, but you have a lot on. See if you can find a time to get together. You will need:

bówùguǎn   museum.

Answers

Street café

What you will learn

- to talk about what you have done
- to talk about your daily routine
- some key dates in Chinese history

Before you begin

As you learned in Unit 14, the tense of a sentence is often established by a word which gives a clue to the time of the action. This is as true for the past as it is for the future: for the past **le** is added to indicate completion of an action.

Before listening to the recording, have a look at the *Grammar* section on page 202, which explains with examples the way to use **le** to indicate events which happened in the past. This will help you understand new examples which come up in the following Dialogues.

Dr Sun Yat Sen, Guangzhou

Dialogues

1

What gifts did she buy?

> **LISTEN FOR...**
> **mǎi le** bought

Teacher	Nǐ xǐhuan hé nǐ de xiǎo péngyoumen wánr ma?
Boy	Xǐhuan.
Teacher	Jīnnián guò nián, māma gěi nǐ mǎi le shénme lǐwù a?
Boy	Yǒu wánjù hái yǒu xiézi.

lǐwù presents
wánjù toys

> **péngyoumen** friends. The suffix **-men** added to a noun which refers to people, for example **péngyou**, makes the noun plural. You came across this in Unit 2, Dialogue 3.
>
> **jīnnián** this year. 'Next year' is **míngnián**. 'Last year' is **qùnián**.
>
> **māma gěi nǐ mǎi le shénme lǐwù a** (lit. mum for you bought what presents). **Le** goes directly after the verb because the question is about a specific object, **shénme lǐwù** 'what presents' (see point **B**(iii) in the *Grammar* section). It is Chinese tradition to buy new clothes to wear on New Year's Day.
>
> **xiézi** shoes. This is a childish word, so learn **xié**.

2

Why hasn't he gone?

> **LISTEN FOR...**
> **méi shàng xué** not gone to school

Hènián	Jīntiān wèi shénme méi shàng xué a?
Boy	Wǒmen xiànzài fàng jià le.

shàng xué go to school

> **Jīntiān wèi shénme méi shàng xué a?** (lit. Today why didn't go to school?) The negative form of the past tense always uses **méi**, and never **bù**. No **le** is needed in the negative.
>
> **fàng jià** (lit. release holiday) be on holiday from school.
>
> **Wǒmen xiànzài fàng jià le** (lit. we now release holiday). The **le** in this sentence is not to be confused with the past-tense **le**. It indicates a change in situation. We were in school but now we are on holiday. (It functions the same way as the **le** in **bù yào le** 'don't want any more', in Unit 3, Dialogue 2.)

Practise what you have learned

1

(a) Refer to the *Grammar* section for help with where to put **le**, then put the following sentences into the past tense. (Answers on page 206.)

    (1) **Wǒ péngyou gěi wǒ mǎi lǐwù.**
    (2) **Zuótiān wǎnshang qù kàn huàjù.**
    (3) **Wǒmen kàn yī ge hěn yǒu yìsi de huàjù.**
    (4) **Wǒ zài Běijīng Fàndiàn de kāfēitīng děng nǐ.**

(b) Make the following sentences negative. (Answers on page 206.)

    (1) **Wǒmen shàng xué le.**
    (2) **Lǎo Wáng kàn diànyǐng le.**
    (3) **Wǒ chī fàn le.**
    (4) **Xiǎo Lǐ xué Fǎyǔ le.**

2

Xiànbīn tells you something about events in his family yesterday and today. Listen to what he has to say, and then rearrange the sentences below to reconstruct the story. (Note that although the same events are described, the mode of expression is different.)

(a) The child's mother did not return home at midday.
    Háizi de māma zhōngwǔ méi huí jiā.

(b) He bought some medicine.
    Mǎi le diǎnr yào.

(c) Yesterday his child did not go to school.
    Tā háizi zuótiān méi shàng xué.

(d) The child and his friends went to play football.
    Háizi hé tā de péngyoumen tī zúqiú qù le.

(e) His father looked after the child for him.
    Tā bàba gěi tā kān le kān háizi.

(f) He caught a cold.
    Tā gǎnmào le.

(g) In the morning he went to the shop.
    Shàngwǔ tā qù le shāngdiàn.

(h) He is retired.
    Tā tuìxiū le.

(i) She ate at the hotel.
    Tā shì zài fàndiàn chī fàn de.

3

Ring Xiànbīn and tell him what you did on your day off yesterday.

New words: **wèi?** used when answering the telephone, followed by
nǐ shì shuí? Who are you?

Dialogues

3

During Spring Festival I...

> **LISTEN FOR...**
> **wǒ hé jǐ ge lǎo péngyou jiàn le miàn**   I with a few old friends met.
> **fēicháng gāoxìng**   extremely happy
> **yǐjing duō nián méi yǒu jiàn miàn le**   (lit. already many years not met) It's already many years since we saw one another.

Zhāng Lì

Zài Chūnjié qíjiān, wǒ hé jǐ ge lǎo péngyou jiàn le miàn. Wǒmen bǐcǐ dōu fēicháng gāoxìng, yīnwei yǐjing duō nián méi yǒu jiàn miàn le. Wǒmen zài yīqǐ liáo tiānr, wánr pái, hái zuò yīxiē qítā shìqing.

lǎo péngyou old friends
bǐcǐ   each other
duō nián   many years
shìqing   matter, thing

> **wǒ hé jǐ ge lǎo péngyou jiàn le miàn**   (lit. I with few old friends met) I met a few old friends. While the two words **jiàn miàn** together mean 'to meet', **jiàn** is the verb. In this sentence, the speaker begins listing a sequence of events, so **le** splits **jiàn miàn** to come immediately after the verb. **Fàng jià** 'to be on holiday', which appeared in Dialogue 2, similarly may be split: **Wǒmen fàng le jià.** We were on holiday. (See point **B**(iv) in the *Grammar* section.) Note that it is obvious from the context that there is more than one friend, so **péngyou** (as opposed to **péngyoumen**) is sufficient.
>
> **bǐcǐ**   each other. **Wǒmen bǐcǐ dōu fēicháng gāoxìng** (lit. We each other all extremely happy). **Bǐcǐ** goes after **wǒmen**. **Wǒmen bǐcǐ shuō zàijiàn** (lit. We each other say goodbye). **Wǒmen bǐcǐ bù rènshi**. We don't know each other.
>
> **yīnwei yǐjing duō nián méi yǒu jiàn miàn le**   (lit. because already many years not met) because for many years we have not met. Here the verb is negative, using **méiyǒu** (**méi** would have been sufficient), so **le** is not necessary to indicate past tense. However, a sentence containing **yǐjing** 'already' often ends with **le**. It makes the sentence sound more finished.
>
> **wánr pái**   play cards. A colloquial alternative to **dǎ pái**
>
> **hái zuò yīxiē qítā shìqing**   also did some other things. **Le** is not used because it is clear from the context that Zhāng Lì is talking about the past.

4

Sorry to have disturbed you

> **LISTEN FOR...**
> **qǐng jìn**   please enter
> **duìbuqǐ, dǎrǎo nín le**   Sorry to have disturbed you.
> **nín néng bāng wǒ...?**   Can you help me...?

Hènián	Qǐng jìn
Neighbour	Duìbuqǐ, dǎrǎo nín le.
Hènián	Méi guānxi.
Neighbour	Wǒ mǎi le yì tái xǐyiji. Nín néng bāng wǒ tái yìxià ma?
Hènián	Zài nǎr ne?
Neighbour	Fàng zài lóuxià le.
Hènián	Nà wǒmen xiànzài qù ba?
Neighbour	Hǎo ba, xièxie.

fàng to put, to place   **lóuxià** downstairs
xǐyiji washing machine

---

qǐng jìn please enter. Most families live in apartment blocks (= apartment houses), and Hènián's door was not locked.

Wǒ mǎi le... Le goes after the verb because the noun is preceded by a quantity (see point **B**(i) in the *Grammar* section).

yì tái xǐyiji a washing machine. **Tái** is the 'measure word' used for machines.

tái to carry, used for heavy things which require more than one person to lift them, for example furniture. (**Ná** 'carry' is used for luggage.) Don't confuse this **tái** with the **tái** in the previous sentence. Remember that in Chinese writing the two characters are different, and therefore there is no confusion.

fàng zài lóuxià le placed downstairs. This is a passive sentence. The **le** indicates the action is completed. 'Upstairs' is **lóushàng**. **Fàng zài lóushàng le**, placed upstairs. Note the use of **zài** 'at' before the word for 'upstairs' / 'downstairs'.

A courtyard

Practise what you have learned

4 Fill in the gaps in the following sentences with a phrase selected from those in the list below. (Answers on page 206.)

(1) **Duìbuqǐ, _____.**
Sorry to have disturbed you.

(2) **_____, wǒ huí jiā le.**
During Spring Festival I returned home.

(3) **_____ yīxià ma?**
Can you help me briefly?

(4) **Wǒmen _____ méi yǒu jiàn miàn le.**
It's already many years since we got together.

(5) **Xǐyìjī fàng _____ le.**
The washing machine has been put downstairs.

(a) **zài Chūnjié qījiān**
(b) **yǐjing duō nián**
(c) **dǎrǎo nín le**
(d) **nín néng bāng wǒ**
(e) **zài lóuxià**

5 Listen to Xiǎoyūn read out a postcard she has received, then answer the questions below. (Answers on page 206.)

(1) What time of year is it?
(a) summer (b) Spring Festival

(2) When did Xiǎoyūn's friend arrive in Guǎngzhōu?
(a) yesterday (b) last night

(3) How long is it since she saw family and relatives?
(a) years (b) months

(4) What did she do last night?
(a) chatted with family (b) went out to eat

(5) What is the weather like in Guǎngzhōu?
(a) warm (b) cold

6 At the airport you politely enlist help with your heavy luggage.

New words: **zhòng** heavy
xíngli luggage

Dialogue

5

Yesterday, I...

> **LISTEN FOR...**
> **qǐ chuáng**   to get up (out of bed)
> **wǒmen Zhōngguórén yǒu ... de xíguàn**   We Chinese
> people have the habit of taking a lunchtime nap.
> **qǐ lái**   to get up
> **zhǔnbèi wǎnfàn**   prepare the evening meal

Wáng   En, zuótiān zǎochén ne, wǒ shì liù diǎn bàn, dàyuē liù diǎn bàn zhèng
ne, qǐ chuáng yǐhòu ne, shūxǐ wán le ne, jiāo wǒ de xuéshēng, xué le
wàiyǔ, shàngwǔ. Zhōngwǔ, chī guo wǔfàn ne, wǒmen Zhōngguórén
yǒu wǔshuì de xíguàn, shuì le yíhuìr wǔjiào. Xiàwǔ qǐ lái ne, chū qu
sànbù, mǎi dōngxi, dàyuē wǔ diǎn zhōng, huí lái ne, zhǔnbèi wǎnfàn.
Wǎnfàn zhīhòu, kànkan diànshì a, zuò yìxiē qítā de huódòng a, jiù
zhǔnbèi shuì... wǎnshang shuì jiào le.

zǎochén morning	**xué** to learn, to study
shū to comb	**wǔfàn** lunch
xǐ to wash	**shuì wǔjiào** to have a lunchtime nap
jiāo to teach	**sànbù** to stroll
xuéshēng pupil, student	**huódòng** activity

> **zhèng**   exactly, short for **zhènghǎo**.
>
> **yǐhòu**   after or later, goes after the verb or time. **Qǐ chuáng
> yǐhòu**, after getting up; **chī fàn yǐhòu**, after eating the meal; **sān
> nián yǐhòu**, three years later.
>
> **shūxǐ**   comb the hair and wash. A combination of **shū tóu** 'to
> comb the hair' and **xǐ liǎn** 'to wash the face'.
>
> **shūxǐ wán le...**   having finished combing the hair and having a
> wash.... This is a further example of use of the verb complement',
> as encountered in Unit 12.
>
> **yǒu...de xíguàn**   to be in the habit of..., to be used / accustomed
> to.... **Wǒ yǒu zuò qìchē de xíguàn**. I am accustomed to travelling
> by car. **Wǔshuì** (lit. noon sleep) = **shuì wǔjiào**.
>
> **shuì le yíhuìr wǔjiào**. Le goes after **shuì** because **yíhuìr** represents
> a quantity of time.
>
> **qǐ lái**   to get up, implies 'stand up'. For example, you could say to
> someone sitting on a chair: **Qǐ lái, wǒmen yìqǐ qù chī fàn**. Stand
> up, we are going together to eat.
>
> **wǎnfàn zhīhòu**   after dinner. **Wǎnfàn yǐhòu** is also possible.
>
> **zuò yìxiē qítā de huódòng**   do some other activities
>
> **shuì jiào**   to sleep, the same type of verb as **jiàn miàn**. **Shuì jiào
> le**, went to sleep. But if not the end of a list of events, **shuì le jiào**.

Practise what you have learned

7

Xiǎoyún describes what she did before leaving the house this morning. Mark off the phrases in the box as you hear them. Which ones does she not use? The pictures give you clues to the phrases you hear. (Answers on page 206.)

New word: **zǎofàn**   breakfast

shū tóu	zǎofàn	xǐ liǎn
shuìjiào	shūxǐ	
qǐ chuáng		kàn diànshì
qǐ lái	shuì wǔjiào	

8

Match each Pinyin sentence with its English equivalent. (Answers on page 206.)

New words: **yòng**   to use
kuàizi   chopsticks

(1) **Zhōngguórén yǒu shuì wǔjiào de xíguàn.**
(2) **Wǒ yǒu yòng kuàizi de xíguàn.**
(3) **Tā yǒu zuò qìchē de xíguàn.**
(4) **Tā yǒu wǎnshang kàn diànshì de xíguàn.**
(5) **Tā yǒu zài jiā chī zhōngwǔ fàn de xíguàn.**
(6) **Yéye yǒu kān háizi de xíguàn.**

(a) He is in the habit of watching TV in the evenings.
(b) He is accustomed to eating his midday meal at home.
(c) Grandfather is used to looking after the child.
(d) I am accustomed to using chopsticks.
(e) Chinese people are in the habit of taking a nap.
(f) He is used to travelling by car.

9

Practise talking about the past. Yesterday, after a busy tour, you spent a relaxing day in the hotel to recuperate. Tell an accompanying traveller about it. Before you begin, you may find it useful to remind yourself of the vocabulary for hotel facilities you came across in Unit 4:

kāfēitīng   coffee shop
jiànshēnfáng   gym
shāngwù zhōngxīn   business centre

Key words and phrases

To learn

jīnnián	this year
míngnián	next year
qùnián	last year
lǐwù	presents
wánjù	toys
xié	shoes
péngyou(men)	friend(s)
shàng xué	to go to school
fàng jià	to have a holiday / day off
jiàn miàn	to meet, to get together
bǐcǐ	each other
duō nián	many years
jìn	to enter
dǎrǎo	to disturb
duìbuqǐ dǎrǎo nín le	sorry to have disturbed you
fàng	to put
lóuxià	downstairs
lóushàng	upstairs
qǐng jìn	please enter
yī tái xǐyījī	a washing machine
tái	to carry (for example, furniture)
ná	to carry (for example, luggage)
nín néng bāng wǒ...	Can you help me...
zuótiān zǎochén	yesterday morning
qǐ chuáng	to get up
shūxǐ	to comb and wash
chī wǔfàn	to eat lunch
yǒu ... de xíguàn	to be in the habit of...
shuì wǔjiào	to have a lunchtime nap
sànbù	to have a stroll

Grammar

Talking about the past

A Chinese people commonly talk about the past as if in the present tense, as in Dialogue 5:

'Xiàwǔ qǐ lái ne, chū qu sànbù, mǎi dōngxi, dàyuē wǔ diǎn zhōng, huí lái ne, zhǔnbèi wǎnfàn.'
'In the afternoon I get / got up, go / went out for a stroll, buy / bought things, around 5 o'clock return / returned, prepare / prepared evening meal.'

In this sentence, Wáng could be talking about her daily routine, i.e. what she generally does, because in Chinese verbs do not change for tense. We only know she is describing the past because at the very beginning of her description she said, **zuótiān zǎochén** 'yesterday morning'.

Words which indicate when something happened are therefore important.
Wǒmen kàn diànshì.   We are watching TV.
Wǒmen zuótiān kàn diànshì le.   Yesterday we watched TV.
Nǐ zuótiān zài jiā chī fàn le ma?   Did you eat at home yesterday?

B If an accomplished fact or completed action is described, **le** is used. **Le** goes directly after the verb when:

(i)   a number, or words indicating an amount, describe the noun:

   Tāmen chī le <u>hěn</u> <u>duō</u> fàn.   They ate lots of food.
   Tā mǎi le <u>yī</u> <u>hé</u> chá.   S/he bought a box of tea.

(ii)   an adjective precedes the noun:

   Tā chī le fēicháng hǎo de dōngxi.   S/he ate some extremely nice things.

(iii)   a specific item is referred to:

   Māma gěi nǐ mǎi le <u>shénme</u> <u>lǐwù</u>?   Mum for you bought what presents?

(iv)   events are listed or a sequence of actions described:

   Wǒmen mǎi le dōngxi, chī le fàn, kàn le diànshì, ránhòu jiù shuì jiào le.
   We bought things, ate, watched TV, then went to bed.

   Tāmen qù kàn le diànyǐng, mǎi le dōngxi, jiù huí jiā le.
   They went to see a film, bought things, and then returned home.

Note: In the final phrase of a list, **le** goes at the end of the phrase, as above.

C When none of the conditions in B above apply, **le** goes at the end:

Wǒmen kàn diànshì le.   We watched TV.
Nǐ chī fàn le ma?   Have you eaten?
Wǒmen jiànmiàn le.   We got together.
Tā qǐ chuáng le.   He got up.

D To make a sentence about something which happened in the past negative, use **méi yǒu** (shortened to **méi**) before the verb, and drop **le**:

Tā méi qǐ chuáng. He didn't get up.
Tāmen zuótiān méi zǒu. They didn't leave yesterday.
Wèi shénme méi shàng xué? Why haven't you gone to school?

To ask whether or not,

Nǐmen kàn diànshì le méi yǒu?
or, **Nǐmen kàn méi kàn diànshì?**
Did you watch TV or not?

Tāmen chī fàn le méi yǒu?
or, **Tāmen chī méi chī fàn?**
Did they eat or not?

E Where verbs are duplicated, **le** goes between the two:

Wǒmen kàn le kàn diànshì. We watched a bit of TV.
Wǒ jīntiān qù tā jiā wánr le wánr. Today I went to his home and had fun.
Wǒmen dǎ le dǎ pái. We played cards.

10 Put the following sentences into the past. (Answers on page 206.)

(1) **Zuótiān qù shì zhōngxīn mǎi dōngxi.**

(2) **Wǒmen dǎ pái.**

(3) **Tā chī fàn.**

(4) **Tāmen mǎi hěn duō jìnìanpǐn.**

(5) **Wǒ péngyou mǎi sān hé lǜchá.**

(6) **Tā bù xiǎng qù.**

(7) **Nǐmen bù qù ma?**

(8) **Wǒmen kànkan diànshì.**

(9) **Wǒ bāng tā tái yīxià xǐyījī.**

Playing cards at Temple of Heaven, Beijing

Read and understand

The pictures below are all of items you have come across in this
course. How many can you remember?

a cup of tea

----

a glass of beer

2 Yuan

----

toilet

a ticket

hotel

Did you know?

Key dates in history

China has a long history! When travelling in China you will come across many ancient relics, temples and monuments, and tour guides will bombard you with information about them. The history date line below is a quick reference for you to place whatever it is you are looking at in its historical context.

500,000 BC	Prehistoric Peking Man
551–479 BC	Life of Confucius
221–206 BC	Qín dynasty, first Great Wall
206 BC–AD 220	Hàn dynasty
581–618	Suí dynasty
618–907	Táng dynasty
970–1127	Sòng dynasty
1280–92	Marco Polo in China
1260–1368	Yuán (Mongol) dynasty
1368–1644	Míng dynasty
1644–1912	Qīng (Manchu) dynasty
1839	Beginning of Opium Wars with Britain
1842	Hong Kong Island ceded to Britain
1850–64	Tàipíng Rebellion
1898	New Territories leased to Britain for 100 years
1899–1901	Boxer Rebellion
1912	Declaration of Republic by Sun Yat-sen
1919	May Fourth Movement
1921	Chinese Communist Party Founded
1923–27	Nationalist–Communist collaboration
1927	Nationalist White Terror against Communists
1928	Soviet established in Jiāngxī and Nationalist government in Nánjīng
1930–34	Nationalist Bandit Suppression campaign against Communists
1934–35	Long March
1937	United Front against Japan
1938	Nationalist capital moved to Chóngqìng
1945	Nationalist–Communist Civil War begins
1949	Foundation of People's Republic of China (PRC)
1950	Friendship pact with Soviet Union, China enters Korean War
1956	Hundred Flowers period of free expression
1957	Anti-rightist campaign ends Hundred Flowers
1958–59	Great Leap Forward and formation of communes
1960	Split with Soviet Union begins
1966–76	Cultural Revolution
1971	Rapprochement with USA, PRC takes China seat at UN
1976	Death of Máo
1978	Democracy Wall and beginning of economic reform
1982	Communes abolished
1984	Fourteen coastal cities look for foreign investment, Sino-British agreement on return of Hong Kong to Chinese sovereignty
1989	Tiān'ānmén Square demonstration
1997	British government departs Hong Kong when it reverts to Chinese sovereignty

Your turn to speak

11　You return from a short trip and tell your Chinese friends and colleagues about what you did. Follow the prompts as usual.

And finally...

Congratulations on completing the course! Good luck with your Chinese, and have a good trip, or as they say in China, 'sail with the wind all the way', **Yī lù shùn fēng!**

Answers

Practise what you have learned

Exercise 1　(a)　(1) **Wǒ péngyou gěi wǒ mǎi lǐwù le.** (2) **Zuótiān wǎnshang qù kàn huàjù le.** (3) **Wǒmen kàn le yī ge hěn yǒu yìsi de huàjù.** (4) **Wǒ zài Běijīng Fàndiàn de kāfēitīng děng nǐ le.**

　　　　　　　(b)　(1) **Wǒmen méi shàng xué.** (2) **Lǎo Wáng méi kàn diànyǐng.** (3) **Wǒ méi chī fàn.** (4) **Xiǎo Lǐ méi xué Fǎyǔ.**

Exercise 2　c, f, g, b, e, h, a, i, d

Exercise 4　(1)(c); (2)(a); (3)(d); (4)(b); (5)(e)

Exercise 5　(1)(b); (2)(a); (3)(b); (4)(a); (5)(a)

Exercise 7　**shūxǐ, shuì wǔjiào, qǐ lái**

Exercise 8　(1)(e); (2)(d); (3)(f); (4)(a); (5)(b); (6)(c)

Grammar

Exercise 10　(1) **Zuótiān qù shì zhōngxīn mǎi dōngxi le.**
　　　　　　(2) **Wǒmen dǎ pái le.**
　　　　　　(3) **Tā chī fàn le.**
　　　　　　(4) **Tāmen mǎi le hěn duō jìniànpǐn.**
　　　　　　(5) **Wǒ péngyou mǎi le sān hé lǜchá.**
　　　　　　(6) **Tā méi xiǎng qù.**
　　　　　　(7) **Nǐmen méi qù ma?**
　　　　　　(8) **Wǒmen kàn le kàn diànshì.**
　　　　　　(9) **Wǒ bāng tā tái le yīxià xǐyījī.**

Grammar summary

Below you will find a brief summary of the main grammar points covered in this course.

WORD ECONOMY	Link verbs are not needed with adjectives as they are in English. For example, **Wǒ hěn máng.** I am very busy. Personal pronouns are often left out if it is obvious from the context to whom the question or statement refers. For example, **Shēntǐ hǎo ma?** (rather than **Nǐ shēntǐ hǎo ma?**) How is your health?
VERBS	Verbs do not conjugate: **wǒ yào, tā yào, tāmen yào** I (s)he, they want
PERSONAL PRONOUNS	**wǒ** I **wǒ de** my **nǐ/nín** you **nǐ/nín de** your **tā** he/she/it **tā de** his/her/its **wǒmen** we **wǒmen de** our **nǐmen** you (plural) **nǐmen de** your (plural) **tāmen** they **tāmen de** their
QUESTIONS AND ANSWERS	The easiest way to form a question is to add **ma** to the end of a statement. For example, **Nǐ qù guo Qīngdǎo.** You have been to Qīngdǎo. **Nǐ qù guo Qīngdǎo ma?** Have you ever been to Qīngdǎo? Another simple way of forming a question is to put together the positive and negative forms of the verb, that is to repeat the verb and insert **bù**: **Néng bù néng?** Can you or can't you? In response to questions where there is no question word, an easy way to answer 'yes' is to repeat the verb/adjective, or if answering 'no', to say **bù** plus the verb/adjective ('yes' and 'no' do not translate directly into Mandarin). For example, **Nǐ chī ma?** Are you eating? **Chī.** I am eating. **Bù chī.** I am not eating. The exception is when the verb is **yǒu** 'to have'. Yǒu is negated with **méi**, not **bù**. For example, **Nǐ yǒu nǚ'ér ma?** Do you have a daughter? **Yǒu.** Yes. **Méi yǒu.** No. When a question contains a question word, the answer can follow the structure of the question: **Jǐ wèi? Liù wèi.** How many people? Six people.

Sentences containing the following question words do not require **ma**, since these words themselves imply a question is being asked:

shénme? what?
jǐ? how many?
zěnmeyàng? how?
nǎr? where?

For example,

Nǐ jiào shénme? What are you called?
Nǐ zěnmeyàng? How are you?

'MEASURE WORDS'/ CLASSIFIERS	There must be a word separating a number and a noun for a sentence to make grammatical sense. For example, **yī bēi píjiǔ** a glass of beer **yī zhāng fāpiào** a receipt **sān kǒu rén** three people (members of the family) **yī jiàn mián'ǎo** a jacket **yī tiáo qúnzi** a skirt (It is not correct to say **yī píjiǔ, yī fāpiào**, etc.)
DE	**De** after a verb and before a noun, makes the verb function as an adjective. For example, **nǐ dìng de fángjiān** your 'booked' room **nǐ wèn de cāntīng** your 'asked about' restaurant Similarly, **de** links a noun with a preceding phrase that describes it: **Shàngwǔ qī diǎn yī kè de fēijī?** The flight at 7.15 a.m.? **Wǒ jiù zuò xīngqī èr de (fēijī).** I'll just take the Tuesday flight. **yī zhāng dào Hángzhōu de huǒchē piào** a rail ticket to Hángzhōu
LE	**Le** is used: (i) to indicate a change of situation: 　　**Bù yào le.** I don't want it any more (I did before). (ii) in exclamations: 　　**Tài hǎo le!** Very good. (iii) to form the past tense (see below)
WORD ORDER	'Who', 'when', 'where', 'what' A sentence generally follows the following structure: subject + time when + place where + verb + object **Tāmen jīntiān zài jiā chī fàn.** (lit. They today at home eat.) **Wǒmen míngtiān zài Tiān'ānmén Guǎngchǎng děng nǐ.** (lit. We tomorrow at Tiān'ānmén Square wait for you.)
Emphasis	For emphasis, the object may be stated before the comment or question relating to it. **Yào [wǒ] zěnme chī?** (lit. Medicine how eat?)

	Similarly, phrases containing the main information may come at the start for emphasis:
	Fā chuánzhēn, [nǐ] kéyǐ qù shāngwù zhōngxīn. (lit. Send a fax, can go business centre.)
Directions	**wǎng/xiàng** 'towards' comes first, then the word indicating the direction, then the verb:
	Wǎng dōng zǒu. (lit. Towards the east go.)
Lí	**Lí** '(distance) away from' comes at the beginning:
	Lí zhèr bù yuǎn jiù yǒu. (lit. away from here not far there is [one].)
Lǐ, shàng	**Lǐ** 'inside' and **shàng** 'on' always go immediately *after* the word to which they refer. This is the reverse of English:
	Nǐ yào zài kāfēi lǐ jiā nǎi ma? (lit. You want coffee inside add milk?)
	Qǐng nǐ zài zhīpiào shàng qiān yíxià míngzi. (lit. Please you cheque on sign briefly name.)
Gěi, gēn	**Gěi** 'for' and **gēn** 'with' go immediately after the subject:
	Nà [nǐ] gěi wǒ lái yì bēi báilándì ba. (lit. In that case for me bring a brandy.)
	Wǒ gěi nín chá. (lit. I for you check.)
	Qǐng [nǐ] gēn wǒ dào zhè biānr lái. Please come with me to this side
Qǐng/qǐng wèn	**Qǐng** 'please' and **qǐng wèn** 'may I ask' always come at the beginning:
	Qǐng wèn, nín yào shénme yǐnliào? (lit. May I ask, you want what drinks?)
	Qǐng shāo děng. (lit. Please a moment wait.)
Dates	Dates are always written in the order 'year', 'month', then 'date'.
	Yī jiǔ bā sān nián, wǔ yuè wǔ hào. (lit. 1983, May 5th)
	Wǒ de shēngrì shì sān yuè shí qī hào. My birthday is March 17th.
Question words	These go before the words to which they relate:
	Wǒmen jǐ diǎn chī fàn? (lit. We what time eat?)
	Tā wèi shénme qù Zhōngguó? (lit. He why goes China?)
VERB 'COMPLEMENTS'	The words **wán** and **dao** can modify the meaning of a verb. **Wán** following a verb adds the sense of completion of the action:
	kàn wán Gùgōng (lit. finish seeing Gùgōng)
	Tiān'ānmén zhuàn wán le having finished wandering around Tiān'ānmén
	When a verb is followed by **dao** attainment of the action is suggested:
	Kàn dao get to see
	kàn dao le Běijīng shì de quánmào having got to see the panoramic view of Beijing city

FUTURE	(i) When talking about something you are going to do, use **yào**:
	Wǒ yào qù Zhōnguó. I am going to go to China. (I want to go to China.)
	(ii) Words such as **míngtiān** 'tomorrow', **jīntiān wǎnshang** 'tonight', **míngnián** 'next year' and **wǔ yuè** 'in May', denoting exactly when the action will take place, indicate the future.
	Wǒ wǔ yuè qù Shànghǎi. I am going to Shànghǎi in May.
	(iii) **Zhǔnbèi** 'intend'/'prepare', **dǎsuàn** 'plan', **jìhuà** 'plan' and **xià yī bù** 'next move' also all set the scene as in the future:
	Wǒ zhǔnbèi qù Guǎngzhōu. I intend to go to Guǎngzhōu. **Wǒ xià yī bù xiǎng zìjǐ zuò xiē shēngyì.** For my next move, I would like to do some business on my own. **Nǐ dǎsuàn chī xīcān ma?** Are you planning to eat Western food? **Wǒmen jìhuà qù Měiguó.** We are planning to go to America.
xiǎng/yào	(iv) **Wǒ xiǎng** means 'I would like.' **Yào** is more definite than **xiǎng**:
	Wǒ xiǎng mǎi zhè jiàn sīchóu mián'ǎo. I would like to buy this padded silk jacket. **Wǒ yào mǎi zhē jiàn sīchóu mián'ǎo.** I want to buy this padded silk jacket. The first sentence expresses a wish, and the second a firm intention.
	When a question uses **yào**, if the response is negative, it uses **xiǎng**. For example:
	Nǐ yào chī xīcān ma? Are you going to eat Western food? **Wǒ bù xiǎng chī.** I would not like to.
	(vi) Putting **yào** before the verb and **le** at the end of the sentence indicates something is about to happen.
	Wǒ yào jiéhūn le. I am about to get married.
PAST	● Words which indicate when something happened are important: **Wǒmen kàn diànshì.** We watch TV. **Wǒmen zuótiān kàn diànshì le.** Yesterday we watched TV.
Le	● If an accomplished fact or completed action is described, **le** is used. **Le** goes directly after the verb when:
	(i) a number, or words indicating an amount, describe the noun: **Tāmen chī le hěn duō fàn.** They ate lots of food.
	(ii) an adjective precedes the noun: **Tā chī le fēicháng hǎo de dōngxi.** S/he ate some extremely nice things.
	(iii) a specific item is referred to: **Māma gěi nǐ mǎi le shénme lǐwù?** Mum for you bought what presents?
	(iv) events are listed or a sequence of actions described: **Wǒmen mǎi le dōngxi, chī le fàn, kàn le diànshì, ránhòu jiù shuì jiào le.** We bought things, ate, watched TV, then went to bed. Note: In the final phrase of a list, **le** goes at the end, as above.

	● When none of the above conditions apply, **le** goes at the end: **Wǒmen kàn diànshì le.** We watched TV.
méi / méi yǒu	● To make a sentence about something which happened in the past negative, use **méi yǒu** (shortened to **méi**) before the verb, and drop **le**:

Tā méi qǐ chuáng. He didn't get up.
Tāmen zúotiān méi zǒu. They didn't leave yesterday.
Wèi shénme méi shàng xué? Why haven't you gone to school?

To ask whether or not,
Nǐmen kàn diànshì le méi yǒu?
or, **Nǐmen kàn méi kàn diànshì?**   Did you watch TV or not?

● Where verbs are duplicated, **le** goes between the two:
Wǒmen kàn le kàn diànshì.   We watched a bit of TV.

Vocabulary

àirén spouse
ba indicates suggestion
bā eight
bā shí eighty
bā yuè August
báicài Chinese leaves
báilándì brandy
bàn half
bāng to help
bāozi steamed stuffed buns
bēi glass, cup
běi north
běifāng northern part, in the north
béng kè not at all
bǐcǐ each other
bōcài spinach
bówùguǎn museum
bù not
bù...le not...any more
bù cuò not bad
bù jiàn bù sàn until we meet
bù kèqi not at all
bù xiè not at all
bùfen / bù part, section
bùguò however
cài vegetable, dish
cāntīng restaurant
chá to check
chá tea
chà yī kè quarter to
cháguǎn teahouse
Chángchéng the Great Wall
cháyè tea leaves
chē train, vehicle
chènyī shirt
chī eat
chuān to wear
Chuāncài Sichuan cuisine
chuánzhēn fax
Chūnjié Spring Festival
chūntiān spring
chūzū qìchē taxi
cì time, 'measure word'
cíqì porcelain ware
cōng spring onion, scallion
cóng from
dà big
dǎ guójì chángtú to make an international call
dǎ lánqiú to play basketball

dǎ májiàng to play mahjong
dǎ pái to play cards
dǎ pīngpāngqiú to play table tennis
dǎ pūkè to play cards
dài huíqù to take back
dài tā qù... to take him / her to...
dàir bag
dānrénfáng single room
dànshì but
dào to arrive, to reach, to go to
dǎrǎo to disturb
dǎsuàn to plan, plan(s)
dàyuē approximately
Déguó Germany
děi to have to, must
děng to wait
Déyǔ German
diǎn o'clock
diǎn to order
diànhuà telephone
diǎnr some
diànshì TV
diànyǐng film
dìdi younger brother
dìfang place
dìng to book, reserve
dìqū region
dōng east
dǒng to understand
dōngtiān winter
dōu all
dòufu tofu, beancurd
dòuyá bean sprouts
duìbuqǐ sorry, excuse me
duìhuàn to exchange (money)
duō more
duōcháng how long
duōdà how old (people over 10)
duōshao how much
duōshao qián? how much (money)?
èr two
èr shí twenty
èr yuè February
érqiě moreover
érzi son
fā chuánzhēn to send a fax
Fǎguó France

fàn meal, rice
fàndiàn restaurant, hotel
fàng to put
fàng jià to have a holiday / day off
fángjiān room
fāpiào receipt
Fǎyǔ French
fēicháng extremely
fēn minute
fēn unit of currency
fēng wind
fēngjǐng scenery
fēnmíng distinct
fēnzhōng minute (length of time)
fù qián to pay
fùjìn nearby, vicinity
fùmǔqin parents
fùqin father
fūren wife
fùyìn to photocopy
gàn to do
gànbù cadre
gǎnmào to catch a cold
gānshāo dry roasted
gānzào dry
gāo high (temperature)
gāoshòu? How old are you? (to an old person)
gàosù to tell
ge measure word
gēge older brother
gěi for, to
gěi wo lái bring me
gēn with
gōngzuò to work
guàhào xìn registered mail
guǎi turn
guì expensive
guìxìng What is your (sur)name? (polite)
guo ever
guò to cross, to pass
guōbā rice crust
guójí nationality
hái in addition, still, also
hái xíng ba (lit. still OK) all right
háishi or (questions)
háizi child(ren)
hángbān scheduled flight
hángchéng journey (flight / boat)
hángkōng xìn air mail

hánlěng freezing cold (climate)
Hànyǔ Chinese language
hǎo good, fine, well
hào date
hào size
hǎoxiàng it seems
hē drink
hé and
hé box, packet
hěn very
héshì to fit
hóng chá black tea
hónglùdēng traffic lights
hòuchēshì waiting-room
hòulái later on
huā chá Jasmine tea
Huáiyángcài Jiāngsū cuisine
huàjù (theatrical) play
huàn to change
huáng(sè) yellow
huángguā cucumber
huí jiā to return home
húluóbo carrot
huǒchái matches
huǒchē piào rail ticket
huòzhě or (statement)
hùshi nurse
hùzhào passport
jī chicken
jǐ? how many?
jǐ diǎn le? What time is it?
jì xìn to send, mail
jiā to add
jiā family, home
jiàn measure word for clothing (upper body)
jiàn miàn to meet, to get together
jiǎn piào to check a ticket
jiǎng to speak
jiào call, to be called
jiāoyóu outing
jīdàn chicken egg
jié yīxià zhàng to pay the bill
jiéhūn le married
jiějie older sister
jiérì festival
jìhuà plan(s), to plan
jìn enter
jǐngchá policeman
Jīngjù Běijīng (Peking) Opera
Jǐngtàilán cloisonné enamel
jìniànpǐn souvenir
jīnnián this year

jīntiān today
jīsī shredded chicken
jiǔ alcohol
jiǔ nine
jiù just
jiù dào le it's just there
jiǔ shí ninety
jiǔ yuè September
jiù zhè yàng ba so be it
juéde to feel
jùyǒu Zhōngguó tèsè with Chinese characteristics
júzi orange
kāfēi coffee
kān to look after
kàn to see
kàn dao to get to see
kàn wán to finish seeing
kǎo roast
kè quarter
Kělè cola
kěyǐ can (permission)
kōng empty
kǒu entrance / exit
kǒu mouth, measure word
kuàir chunk
kuàizi chopsticks
kūzào dull
kùzi trousers
là spicy
lái to come
lán blue
lǎo old
lǎo nián rén old people
lǎolao grandmother (on mother's side)
lǎoye grandfather (on mother's side)
lěng cold
lí distance away from
lí pear
lǐ in
lì tablet
liǎng two
liáng cài cold dishes
liànxí shūfǎ to practise calligraphy
liáo tiānr to chat
liàolǐ jiāwù to do housework
líng zero
liù six
liù shí sixty
liù yuè June
lǐwù presents
lóu floor
lóushàng upstairs
lóuxià downstairs
lù road, route

Lǔcài Shandong cuisine
lùchéng journey
lǜ chá green tea
lǜshī lawyer
lǚxíng to travel
lǚxíng zhīpiào traveller's cheque
lǚyóu to tour, tourism
ma question indicator
má numb, hot
mǎi to buy
mài to sell
mǎlù road
máng busy
máo unit of currency
mápó dòufu a famous hot beancurd (tofu) dish
mǎshàng immediately
méi (used with **yǒu**) not
méi guānxi it doesn't matter, not at all
méi shénme shì don't have something on
méi shìr it doesn't matter, not at all
Měiguó America, the USA
mèimei younger sister
Měiyuán US dollar
mí lù le lost
mián'ǎo padded jacket
miànbāo bread
mǐfàn cooked rice
míngnián next year
míngtiān tomorrow
míngxìnpiànr (yì zhāng) a postcard
mǔqin mother
ná to carry (for example, luggage)
nà...ba in that case
ná zǒu to take away
nǎi milk
nǎinai grandmother (on father's side)
nán south
nánfāng southern part, in the south
nánháir boy
nǎr? where?
nàr there
ne question indicator
néng can (to be able)
nǐ(men) you (plural)
nǐ/nín hǎo hello
nián year
niánjì dà de rén old people
niánqīng rén young people

niúròu beef
nuǎnhuo warm
nǚ'ér daughter
nǚháir girl
páigǔ spare ribs
pǎo bù to jog
péngyou(men) friend(s)
piànr slice
piányi cheap
piào (yī zhāng) ticket
piàoliang beautiful
píjiǔ beer
píng bottle
píng xìn ordinary mail
píngguǒ apple
píngshí usually
pútáo grapes
pútaojiǔ wine
qī seven
qǐ chuáng to get up
qī shí seventy
qī yuè July
qiān to sign
qián money
qǐfēi take off
qìhòu climate
qǐng please
qīngcài green vegetable
qīngjiāo green pepper
qīnrén relatives
qítā other
qiūtiān autumn
qìwēn temperature
qū district
qù go
quánmào panoramic view
qùnián last year
qúnzi skirt
ránhòu then
rè hot
rè cài hot dishes
rén person
rènao lively
Rénmínbì RMB 'People's currency'
rènshi to know (person)
rì date, sun
rìzi date
ròu meat, usually pork
róudào judo
ruǎnwò soft sleeper
ruǎnzuò soft seat
sān three
sān shí thirty
sān yuè March
sànbù to have a stroll
sǎngzi téng sore throat
sānmíngzhì sandwich
shàng up

shàng chē to board the train or bus
shàng xué to go to school
shāngdiàn shop
shàngwǔ morning
shāngwù zhōngxīn business centre
shāngyè dàshà shopping centre
shāo a bit (moment)
shěng province
Shèngdànjié Christmas
shēngjiāng fresh ginger
shēngri birthday
shēngyi business
shénme? what?
shénme shíhou? when? at what time?
shēntǐ health, body
shí ten
shì matter, thing
shì to be (is, are)
shì to try
shí bā eighteen
shí èr twelve
shí èr yuè December
shí jiǔ nineteen
shí liù sixteen
shì ma? really?
shí qī seventeen
shí sān thirteen
shí sì fourteen
shí wǔ fifteen
shí yī eleven
shí yī yuè November
shí yuè October
shì zhōngxīn city centre
shíjiān time
shìjiè the world
shīrùn humid
shǒuhuìshān hand painted T-shirt
shōurù income
shǔ to be born in (horoscope year)
shuāngrénfáng double room
shuì jiào to sleep
shuì wǔjiào to have a lunchtime nap
shuǐzhǔ boiled
shuō to speak, to say
shūxǐ to comb and wash
sì four
sì shí forty
sì yuè April
sīchóu silk
sījī driver
sìjì four seasons

suānlàtāng hot-and-sour soup
sùcài vegetable dishes
suì year (of age)
sǔn bamboo shoots
tā he, she, it
tái measure word
tái to carry (for example furniture)
tài too, extremely
tāmen they
tāng soup
tángcù sweet-and-sour
táo peach
tào set (crockery)
tèsè characteristics
tī zúqiú to play football
tiān day, heaven
tián fill in
tiānqì weather
tiānqì yùbào weather forecast
tiāo choose
tiáo measure word for clothing (lower body)
tiáo stick
tiělù railway
tīng to listen
tǐng rather, very
tīng dao to have heard
tīng dǒng le to have understood
tǒng can
tóu téng headache
tǔdòu potato
tuīchí to postpone
tuìxiū [le] retire[d]
wàibīn foreign guests
wàihuì duìhuànchù bureau de change
wǎndiǎn to be delayed
wánjù toys
wǎnshang evening
wèi measure word
wèi shénme? why?
wèi téng stomach ache
wèizhi seat
wèn to ask
wēnnuǎn warm (climate)
wǒ I, me
wǒmen we
wǔ five
wǔ shí fifty
wǔ yuè May
wǔfàn lunch
Wǔyījié May Day
xī west
xī yào Western medicine
xià chē to get off the bus

xià wéiqí to play go
xià xuě to snow / it's snowing
xià yī bù next step, next move
xià yǔ to rain
xiān first
xiàng / wǎng towards
xiǎng qǐ to think, to come to mind, to occur to (someone)
xiāngcháng sausage
xiāngjiāo banana
xiānsheng sir, mister
xiànzài now
xiǎo small
xiǎochī snack
xiǎojie miss
xiǎoshí hour
xiàtiān summer
xiàwǔ afternoon
xié shoes
xièxie thank you
xiguā water melon
xíguàn habit
xǐhóngshì tomato
xǐhuan to like
xīn new
xìn mail
xìng name (surname)
xíngli luggage
xīngqī week
xīngqī èr Tuesday
xīngqī liù Saturday
xīngqī sān Wednesday
xīngqī sì Thursday
xīngqī tiān Sunday
xīngqī wǔ Friday
xīngqī yī Monday
xíngzhèng bùmén administration department
xīnwén jìzhě journalist
xìnyòngkǎ credit card
xǐyījī (yī tái) washing machine
Xuěbì Sprite
xūyào need
yān cigarettes
yángcōng onion
yánsè colour
yào medicine
yào want
yào...le to be about to...
yéye grandfather (on

father's side)
yī one
yī bǎi one hundred
yī ge..., lìng yī ge the one..., the other
yī kāishǐ in the beginning
yī nián zhī zhōng during the year
yī tiān every day, one day
yī yuè January
yīdiǎnr a little (nouns)
yīgòng altogether
yǐhòu afterwards
yīhuìr a while, in a while
yǐjing already
Yīngbàng pound sterling
yīnggāi ought, should
Yīngguó the UK
yìngwò hard sleeper
Yīngyǔ English
yìngzuò hard seat
yǐnliào drinks
yīnwei because
yìqǐ together
yìsi interest, fun
yíxià briefly
yìxiē some, somewhat
yíyàng the same
yòng to use
yǒu to have, there is / are
yòu right
yǒu fēng windy
yǒu shì to be busy (lit. to have something)
yǒu yìsi interesting
yóucài rape
yǒudiǎnr a little (verbs and adjectives)
yǒumíng famous
yóupiào (yī zhāng) a stamp
yǒuqù fascinating, interesting
yǒushí sometimes
yóuyú squid
yú fish
yuán unit of currency
yuǎn far
yuē to arrange
yuè month, moon
Yuècài Cantonese cuisine
zài in, on, at
zànshí for the time being
zǎochén morning
zǎofàn breakfast

zǎoshàng hǎo good morning
zěnme? how?
zěnmeyàng? how? / How are you?
zhāng measure word
zhǎngdà (zài... zhǎngdà de) to grow up (to grow up in...)
zhàntái platform
zhǎo to call for
zhè this
zhènghǎo exactly
zhèr here
zhǐ only
zhì to treat
zhīdao to know
zhīhòu after
zhíjiē directly
zhíyè profession
zhōng middle
zhǒng type
zhōng / xī cāntīng Chinese / Western restaurant
zhōng nián rén middle-aged people
zhōng yào Chinese medicine
Zhōngguó China
Zhōngguó Rìbào China Daily
Zhōngwén Chinese language
zhōngwǔ midday
zhōumò weekend
zhū pig
zhù to stay, to live
zhuàn wander
zhùhè nǐ congratulations, congratulate you
zhǔnbèi to prepare, intend, plan
zhǔyào mainly
zhǔyì idea
zìjǐ oneself
zǒu to go, to walk, to leave
zuìjìn recently
zuǒ left
zuò do
zuò sit
zuò 22 lù to take the number 22 (bus)
zuótiān yesterday

Index

OTHER TITLES IN THE BREAKTHROUGH

LANGUAGE SERIES FROM MACMILLAN

FRENCH FOR BEGINNERS ▼▼

Breakthrough French
Breakthrough French Activity Book – Practice for beginners
Breakthrough French Interactive CD-ROM
Breakthrough French Teacher's Guide
Breakthrough French Teacher's Cassettes
Breakthrough Video French – A classroom resource

OTHER FRENCH COURSES ▼▼

Breakthrough French 2
Breakthrough French 3 – Further French
Breakthrough Business French

GERMAN FOR BEGINNERS ▼▼

Breakthrough German
Breakthrough German Activity Book – Practice for beginners
Breakthrough German Teacher's Guide
Breakthrough German Teacher's Cassettes
Breakthrough Video German – A classroom resource

OTHER GERMAN COURSES ▼▼

Breakthrough German 2
Breakthrough Business German

SPANISH FOR BEGINNERS ▼▼

Breakthrough Spanish
Breakthrough Spanish Activity Book – Practice for beginners
Breakthrough Spanish Interactive CD-ROM
Breakthrough Spanish Teacher's Guide
Breakthrough Spanish Teacher's Cassettes
Breakthrough Video Spanish – A classroom resource

OTHER SPANISH COURSES ▼▼

Breakthrough Spanish 2
Breakthrough Business Spanish

OTHER LANGUAGES FOR BEGINNERS ▼▼

Breakthrough Italian
Breakthrough Russian
Breakthrough Japanese
Breakthrough Greek
Breakthrough Arabic

Titles are available in most larger bookshops. Your bookshop will be pleased to order for you any title not in stock.

In case of difficulty please call 01256 329242 and ask for Macmillan Direct.